War In Peace

Volume 1

War In Peace

The Marshall Cavendish Illustrated Encyclopedia of Postwar Conflict.

Editor-in-Chief
Ashley Brown

Editorial Board
Brig-Gen. James Collins Jr (USA Retd.)
Vice-Admiral Sir Louis Le Bailly KBE CB
Ian V Hogg; David Floyd
Professor Laurence Martin
Air-Vice Marshal SWB Menaul CB CBE DFC AFC

MARSHALL CAVENDISH
NEW YORK, LONDON, TORONTO

Reference Edition Published 1985

Published by Marshall Cavendish Corporation
147 West Merrick Road
Freeport, Long Island
N.Y. 11520

Printed and Bound in Italy by L.E.G.O. S.p.a. Vicenza.

British Library Cataloguing in Publication Data

Brown, Ashley
    War in peace : the Marshall Cavendish
    illustrated encyclopaedia of post-war conflict.
    1. History, Modern—1945-   2. War—History
    —20th century
    I. Title   II. Dartford, Mark
    909.82   D842

    ISBN 0-86307-293-3 (set)
           0 86307 294 1 vol. 1

Library of Congress Cataloging in Publication Data

Main entry under title:

War in peace.

  Includes bibliographies and index.
    1. Military history, Modern—20th century.   2. Military
art and science—History—20th century.   3. World politics—1945-
I. Marshall Cavendish Corporation.
U42.W373 1984   355'.009'04   84-19386
ISBN 0-86307-293-3 (set)
         0 86307 294 1 vol. 1

Editorial Staff

Editor	Ashley Brown
Editorial Director	Brian Innes
Editorial Manager	Clare Byatt
Editorial Editors	Sam Elder
	Adrian Gilbert
Sub Editors	Sue Leonard
	Simon Innes
Artwork Editor	Jonathan Reed
Artwork Buyer	Jean Morley
Picture Editor	Carina Dvorak
Picture Consultant	Robert Hunt
Design	EDC

Reference Edition Staff

Editor	Mark Dartford
Designer	Graham Beehag
Consultant	Robert Paulley
Indexers	F & K Gill
Creation	DPM Services

Foreword

Throughout recorded history the world has seldom been without war, greater or lesser, declared or undeclared. From the time Joshua toppled the walls of Jericho to the Falklands conflict in the South Atlantic, major international disturbances, small wars or actions 'less than wars' have circled the globe from East to West and North to South. Only the continent of the Antarctic has remained so far relatively untouched. While implements of war have advanced somewhat from Joshua's trumpet and sword to missiles which home in on electromagnetic radiation, the basic ingredient — man — has remained largely the same.

Caught up in his emotions, his hopes and his fears, his need to eat, to love, to sleep and to be protected from the elements, modern man is not too different from the gatherers and hunters of prehistory. And nowhere is this brought out more clearly and more strikingly than in the lethal conflicts that have raged throughout the world since 1945.

These fights may vary in appearance — indeed their levels of violence and terror tend to be proportional to the sophistication of the societies involved — yet part of their fascinating variety lies in the new and imaginative use of old weapons coupled with modern technology, and the way that men have employed these weapons in extremes of danger and at the limits of endurance.

War in Peace covers all of the more famous as well as the lesser post-World War II conflicts, from guerrilla struggles to clashes between states. During this period these wars have taken place under the towering shadow of nuclear holocaust. In some cases they have occurred as wars of proxy, fought in the way they were precisely because the vital interests of the nuclear powers were only marginally involved and the violence of the atom could not be invoked without triggering Armageddon; thus, it can be said, the nuclear stalemate has in some cases spawned lesser conflicts.

Now you can be the judge yourself as to the nature of the seemingly endless conflicts that have embroiled the world from the 1940s to the 1980s. The equipment used by each side is described and illustrated in great completeness here; battle action and the political leanings of the leaders, both military and civilian, are depicted by rare photographs and in personality profiles, while the tactics and techniques are conveyed in vivid detail. And, I warn you, the conclusions drawn are sometimes controversial — but always take account of the latest research.

Your enjoyment of *War in Peace* will be enhanced if you keep at the back of your mind the larger questions. Why was this war fought? Who were the behind-the-scenes instigators? Whose power position was changed as a result of the war?

I am confident that you will find each volume full of interest — and difficult to put down. You will find a wealth of detail about the men, the weapons and the tactics, about heroism, skill and military expertise. You will find yourself referring back to earlier chapters as you peruse the most recent one to compare, to seek similarities and differences and to see how man has progressed or regressed in recent times. May you discover, in reading *War in Peace*, as much fascination and revelation as I have found in its planning.

By James L. Collins, Jr.
Brigadier General (Retired), Former Chief of Military History, US Department of the Army

Reader's Guide

Purpose
The purpose behind *War in Peace* is to provide an objective work of reference on war and warfare from 1945 to the present day. While much has been written in various publications on the many conflicts that the world has seen since World War 2, until now there has not been a detailed reference source available on this much sought-after area of study.

This introduction to War in Peace is designed to provide the user with a full description of what is to be found in this set, where it is, and how to find it.

Structure and content
War in Peace is planned as a 13 volume set. Volumes 1−6 are available from the beginning of 1985, with the remaining volumes being published over a period of 9 months and the final 2 volumes plus the index volume (13) being delivered in the spring of 1986.

Indexing
Each volume contains a quick reference index, and there is a separate, amalgamated index available with volumes 1−6 to make reference easier over the 1st half of the set. Volume 13 will contain a fully-comprehensive, cross-referenced A−Z Index plus a Classified Index section subdivided into various categories.

Bibliography
There is an extensive English Language bibliography of currently available publications relating to post-World War 2 conflicts also in the index volume.

Authority
Volume 1 contains the Foreword by Brigadier James Collins USA Rtd, Chief consultant to the Editorial Panel, plus this Readers Guide. There are short career biographies of the noted military historians who make up the Editorial Panel on page vii and brief details of some of the major contributors to the set follow on page ix. A complete alphabetical list of all contributors appears in the index volume Acknowledgements section.

Front Matter
All volumes carry basic front matter, including staff credits, CIP data, ISBNs and copyright details. Each volume also contains a volume contents list.

Entries
There are about 600 entries altogether in the set, falling into 3 main types; chronological narratives, which usually follow the course of a particular conflict; general articles, which examine an aspect of war rather than any specific one and accompany the narratives; and special 'boxed' feature entries on individuals or armaments. Besides these are regular Key Weapons entries throughout the set, examining in detail specific weapons and weapon systems.

Illustration
There are over 4000 photos and more than 800 diagrams in War in Peace, at least half of them in color. A full list of source acknowledgements appears in the index volume.

Chronologies
There are brief summary chronologies appearing at intervals throughout the set (see individual volume contents) which list under geographical headings major military and political events of the period covered in that part of the set. A complete overall chronology will be included in the index volume.

It is hoped that a working knowledge of the components of War in Peace will enable the reader to make fullest use of the set, thereby enhancing its value as a research tool, educational reference source and general interest work.

Editorial Board

Dr John Pimlott was educated at Leicester University, studying History and the British Army. Since 1973 he has been a civilian lecturer in the Department of War Studies and International Affairs at the Royal Military Academy, Sandhurst, where his teaching specialisations include the Middle East and post-1945 British Defence Policy. he has written a number of books, including *B-29 Superfortress* (1980), *The Battle of the Bulge* (1981), *World War II in photographs* (1984), *The Middle East Conflicts* (1983) and *Vietnam: The History and the Tactics* (1982).

Contributors

David Blue served with the CIA in various countries of Southeast Asia, including Laos, and is a writer on and a student of small wars.

Gordon Brook-Shepherd spent 15 years in Vienna, first as lieutenant-colonel on the staff of the British High Commission and then as a foreign correspondent for the *Daily Telegraph*. A graduate in history from Cambridge, he is currently Chief Assistant Editor of the *Sunday Telegraph*.

Jeffrey J. Clarke is an expert on recent military history, particularly the Vietnam War, and has written for the American Center of Military History.

Major-General Richard Clutterbuck OBE has been Senior Lecturer in politics at Exeter University since his retirement from the army in 1972. His works include *Protest and the Urban Guerrilla, Guerrillas and Terrorists* and *Kidnap and Ransom*.

Alexander S. Cochran Jr is a historian whose area of research is modern Indochinese affairs with particular reference to the war in Vietnam since 1945. He is at present working in the Southeast Asia Branch of the Center of Military History, Department of the Army.

Colonel Peter M. Dunn is a serving officer in the USAF. His doctoral thesis is on the history of Indochina during the mid-1940s.

John B. Dwyer served both with the infantry and with armoured units in Vietnam. He was editor and publisher of the Vietnam veteran's newsletter *Perimeter* and has been a writer and correspondent for *National Vietnam Veteran's Review* for the past few years. His particular interest are Special Forces and Special Operations.

Brenda Ralph Lewis has specialised in political and military history since 1964. She's a regular contributor to military and historical magazines in both Britain and the United States.

Hugh Lunghi served in Moscow in the British Military Mission and the British Embassy for six years during and after World War II. He was interpreter for the British Chiefs of Staff at the Teheran, Yalta and Potsdam conferences, and also interpreted for Churchill and Anthony Eden. He subsequently worked in the BBC External Services and is a former editor of *Index on Censorship*.

Charles Messenger retired from the army in 1980 to become a fulltime military writer after 21 years service in the Royal Tank Regiment. Over the past 10 years he has written several books on 20th century warfare, as well as contributing articles to a number of defence and historical journals. He is currently a Research Associate at the Royal United Services Institute for Defence Studies in London.

Billy C. Mossman is a well-known American writer and historian. He is currently working on a volume on the Korean War for the US Army Center of Military History.

Bryan Perrett served in the Royal Armoured Corps from 1952 to 1971. He contributes regularly to a number of established military journals and acted as Defence Correspondent to the *Liverpool Echo* during the Falklands War. His recent books include *Weapons of the Falklands Conflict* and *A History of Blitzkrieg*.

Chapman Pincher is one of England's leading authorities on international espionage and counter-intelligence. He is the author of political novels and books on spying, the most recent of which is *Their Trade is Treachery*, which deals with the penetration of Britain's secret services by the Russian secret police.

Yehoshua Porath is a noted scholar at the Hebrew University in Jerusalem. He has made a special study of the Palestinian problem and is the author of two books on the subject, the most recent of which is *The Palestinian Arab National Movement 1929—39*, which was published in Britain in 1977.

Contributors

Antony Preston is Naval Editor of the military magazine *Defence* and author of numerous publications including *Battleships, Aircraft Carriers* and *Submarines*.

Brigadier-General Edwin H. Simmons, US Marine Corps, Retired, is the Director of Marine Corps History and Museums. At the time of the Inchon operation and the Chosin Reservoir campaign, he, as a major, commanded Weapons Company, 3rd Battalion, 1st Marines. Widely published, he is the author of *The United States Marines*.

Ronald Spector is an expert on Vietnam and has recently completed a book on that subject for the Center of Military History in the United States.

Andres Suarez served in the Cuban ministry of education from 1948—1951, took part in the Cuban revolution, and served in the ministry of housing from 1959. From 1965, he has been Professor of Latin American Studies at the University of Florida. Other publications include *Cuba and the Sino—Soviet Rift*.

Sir Robert Thompson KBE, CMG, DSO, MC is a world authority on guerrilla warfare, on which he has written extensively. He was directly involved in the Emergency in Malaya in the 1950s and rose to become permanent Secretary for Defence. From 1961 to 1965 he headed the British Advisory Mission to Vietnam and since then he has advised several governments, including the United States, on counter-insurgency operations Sir Robert Thompson is a Council member of the Institute for the Study of Conflict, London. His books include *Defeating Communist Insurgency and Revolutionary War in World Strategy, 1945—69*.

Patrick Turnbull commanded 'D' Force, Burma during World War II. His 29 published works include a history of the Foreign Legion.

Contents of Volume One

Introduction: an overview of
WAR SINCE 1945

With the dropping of atomic bombs on Hiroshima and Nagasaki in August 1945 the world entered the nuclear age and has been living uneasily ever since. The terrible destructive power of the new weapon first demonstrated in Japan, has overshadowed all military affairs since the end of World War II. At the same time the world has been divided into two hostile camps led by the two superpowers, America and Russia, each armed with nuclear weapons. Despite this division, however, and the tensions arising from the dissolution of colonial empires, the nuclear weapon has never been used as an instrument of war, although 'old-fashioned' conventional warfare has never ceased. There has been peace – an uneasy peace, it is true, but peace nevertheless – between the major powers since 1945. But there has not been a single day since then when fighting of some kind has not been going on somewhere in the world. At least 150 large-scale armed conflicts have occurred since World War II; somebody has always been fighting someone.

Wars have not only become more frequent under the umbrella of the nuclear stalemate; they have also become more diversified. The levels of fighting have ranged from the simple, impoverished guerrilla crouching in the bush with a stolen rifle, hoping that his ammunition will last out, to the fighter pilot flying at supersonic speeds and controlling highly sophisticated electronic equipment capable of delivering weapons costing millions of pounds. Some wars are fought by small groups of ill-trained but highly politically motivated men; their opponents are often well trained professional soldiers, inspired mainly by a sense of duty and discipline.

This is the first, central, paradox of modern war: that, although nuclear weapons have never been used, beneath the protective wing of 'mutual deterrence' conventional warfare has never ceased and has in fact become more frequent and more destructive as the years have passed. The relationship between these two forms of military power, the nuclear chiefly

In spite of the technical advances made since 1945, the human face of war has not essentially changed. In the front line, men still have to face death and be prepared to kill in their turn, like this Israeli in the Six-Day War (below). What has changed, of course, is the capability of the weapons systems, like the McDonnell Douglas Phantom (above right). Such aircraft can carry a payload that dwarfs that of whole squadrons of World War II planes.

latent, the conventional ever-active, has been a constant and so far unsolved puzzle.

A second paradox concerns other characteristics of modern weapons. On the one hand their destructive potential has increased immensely; obvious in the case of nuclear weapons, this is also true in the conventional arena, with new explosives, shaped charges and fuel-air explosives which spread and ignite vast aerosol clouds. Yet, at the same time, the capacity to control these weapons and to be selective in their use has also expanded greatly – for example, in the vastly improved accuracy with which weapons can be delivered, whether we consider the wire-guided anti-tank missile or the terrain-following Cruise missile with an accuracy of some 30m (35 yards) at intercontinental ranges. Such accuracy permits the limitation of damage and means that the need for indiscriminate attacks on civilian targets is much reduced.

Accuracy, however, is only one of several technological trends permitting the more discriminate use of weapons – new methods of reconnaissance and surveillance, for example, afford better target acquisition. But technology does not provide all the new

Supermarine Spitfire Mk 1X

type interceptor/close support fighter bomber **range (combat radius)** 700km (435 miles), with auxiliary tanks fitted 1577km (980 miles) **speed** 669km/h (416mph) **armament** 4 x 20mm cannon, rockets, 454kg (1000lb) bomb-load **crew** 1

Harrier GR 3

type V/STOL interceptor/close support fighter bomber **range (combat radius)** 667km (414 miles), with one in-flight refuelling 5560km (3455 miles) **speed** 1186km/h (737mph) **armament** 2 x 30mm Aden guns, rockets, gunpods, Sidewinder AAMs, flares, 2268kg (5000lb) bomb-load **crew** 1 (A full profile of the Harrier appears on page 63)

The changing shape of the fighter: from Spitfire to Harrier

The combat capabilities of today's air superiority fighters, such as the McDonnell Douglas F-15, would be beyond the wildest dreams of the Spitfire-flying pilot of the Battle of Britain. Nonetheless the Spitfire was arguably the finest fighter plane of World War II and much of its success lay in its ability to be updated in the light of new developments in aviation. Thus when most of the aircraft of 1940 had gone to the breaker's yard, the Spitfire was still in service in the late 1940s, seeing combat in the Greek Civil War and in Palestine.

However, the future lay not with the 'conventional' internal combustion engine that powered the Spitfire but with the new jet propulsion system. The dramatic increase in power and speed made possible by the jet engine brought about a transformation in the design and function of aircraft. This transformation was paralleled by equally rapid developments in weaponry that saw the gun replaced by the guided missile as an aircraft's main armament.

While the major trend in aircraft development was based on increased speed and armaments, a new development came into being during the 1960s. This was the V/STOL Harrier, a British plane capable of taking off from 'improvised' runways such as roads, or even vertically from small camouflaged clearings. Far more manoeuvrable in the air than more powerful aircraft, the Harrier proved its combat effectiveness during the Falklands conflict of 1982.

War in the streets

Rioters in Japan in 1981.

On one level modern warfare has involved ever-increasing destructiveness, yet on another there has been a steady increase in the incidence of rioting and crowd violence, often for clear political ends, which has led to armed clashes where casualties are quite light and the weapons less deadly than in conventional warfare. Phalanxes of policemen or troops armed with shields and clubs have taken on groups of rioters hurling bottles and stones. And although these confrontations sometimes seem reminiscent of the battles of the Roman Legions, they constitute one of the typical forms of 20th century conflict.

Riots have a long history as an expression of social discontent, but seldom have they been as common or as varied in cause as in the modern world – ranging from student demonstrations in Europe and race riots in the USA in the 1960s to political protests in Poland in the 1980s.

The way governments have responded to this problem has varied according to the seeming danger of the riot and its traditional level of 'tolerance' to such upheavals. In India, for example, where riots seem endemic, riot control is primitive but brutal and casualties are correspondingly high. In the communist world and in South America rioting is seen as a real threat to the authority of the state and repression is swift and massive. In the West, however, rioting is seen as an essentially civil problem, an occasional disorder to be dealt with by the truncheons of the police force rather than with the rifles and bayonets of the army. But the frequency and intensity of rioting in the West since the 1960s has forced the civil authorities to upgrade riot control measures.

A constant factor in the design of riot-control weapons is the need to make them effective in controlling and quelling rioters while, at the same time, ensuring that they are relatively 'harmless'. In view of this dichotomy one such development has been the baton round – commonly known as the rubber or plastic bullet – which has been used by British security forces in Northern Ireland. The two other major weapons used by police and paramilitary forces are CS gas and water cannon, weapons which cause few serious civilian casualties and yet are effective in breaking up concentrations of rioters.

Many other riot-control weapons have been less successful, however, either because they can affect the user as much as the rioter – for example, high-intensity sonic devices – or because they run counter to public acceptance, which is the case with the many types of electric shock weapons, whether in the form of simple 'cattle-prods' or as more sophisticated 'tasers', which fire electric contactors on a length of trailing wire to distances of 150m (165 yards) and can temporarily paralyse their victims. But if riots continue to follow a trend of increasing violence, then it seems likely that more extreme measures such as these will be introduced onto city streets.

sources of discrimination; in the area of military doctrine also, as in the now highly elaborated theory of limited war, the controlled use of military power has been raised to a major strategic principle. Clearly, leaders who can command warheads that could destroy whole cities with the explosive equivalent of 10 million tons of TNT, and missiles capable of hitting a single missile-silo at intercontinental range, possess dramatically alternative options as to how they would conduct even the most terrible forms of war.

Whereas warfare earlier in the 20th century had shown an almost automatic tendency to become as destructive as it could, exhausting or destroying those involved, this has not been so since 1945. War is as cruel as ever – but restrictions on escalation are always at work, from President Truman forbidding General MacArthur to attack mainland China in 1950-51 during the Korean War (even though Chinese troops were heavily engaged against the Americans in Korea), to the American decision not to invade North Vietnam during the 1960s. Indeed, Vietnam is a classic example of a great power (the USA) being unable to defeat a much less powerful enemy (the Vietnamese communists) primarily because it dare not apply its overwhelming resources. The war, therefore, was fought on terms that were advantageous to the insurgents. US commanders constantly bemoaned the limits placed on what they could do; but this was the nature of the war.

These limitations have meant that wars have carried on for several years, never surpassing a certain level of intensity, and various of these conflicts may even interlock. The Cold War of the 1940s and 1950s between the Soviet Union and the West might be seen, for example, as a war without a straightforward armed clash, but it provided an extra element in many of the anti-colonial 'hot' wars of the period. The Arab-Israeli Wars and the Iraq-Iran Gulf War came together when Israeli aircraft bombed the Iraqi nuclear reactor in mid-1981, thereby doing themselves a favour while ostensibly helping the Iranians.

Defensive nightmare
This is a very different strategic world from that which theorists foresaw in the months after those two bombs fell on Japan. At that time it was the crudely destructive power of the new weapons that dominated imagination. When a city-busting payload could be delivered by a single aircraft, the task of air defence or limiting the ravages of war seemed hopeless. A few imaginative thinkers concluded that defence was henceforth impossible and that security could only be

found in having the capability to reply to nuclear attackers in kind – that is, in what we would now call nuclear deterrence.

In the early postwar years, however, strategic preparations did not take that form at all. Of necessity, the military preparations of nations like the Soviet Union, which possessed no atomic bombs, had to be confined to conventional forces, though the Russians busied themselves to acquire the new weapons. Until they succeeded, the Soviet Union, like China after it, played down the significance of nuclear weapons and stressed the continued importance of the size of an army, industrial might and military skill. This in turn forced the United States to continue to devote some effort – albeit none too successfully – to preparations for conventional war, even when nuclear weapons were available.

As the wartime alliance broke up and the Cold War began in the late 1940s, the image of future conflict was the familiar one of steady mobilisation and attrition, not the spasm of global destruction we fear

today. Nor was this unreasonable at a time when nuclear weapons, however terrible, were nevertheless only fission bombs compared with today's thermonuclear weapons, when they were scarce and expected to remain so, and when only propeller-driven aircraft existed to deliver them.

The real nuclear strategic revolution occurred in the early 1950s. By that time the Soviet Union had exploded its own atomic bomb, so that a balance of terror, though as yet uneven, existed in fact as well as theory. Moreover, in 1952 both the United States and the Soviet Union tested thermonuclear devices – hydrogen bombs – of which the potential explosive yield was unlimited. Studies initiated by President

The nuclear bomb (below) has revolutionised many aspects of warfare. New weapons like RAF Vulcans (above left) were developed to deliver it, and infantry have had to train to fight on battlefields where tactical nuclear weapons are available (below left). With nuclear stalemate, the Soviet Union has had almost a free hand in eastern Europe (above, Soviet tanks in Budapest, Hungary, in 1956).

Smallarms design

Individual Weapon (experimental)

calibre 5.56mm
length 770mm
(30.3in) **weight**
4.98kg (10.97lb)
operation gas **feed**
30 round magazine
mode of fire single
shot, automatic
muzzle velocity
900m/sec (2953
ft/sec) **sight** optical
(The new breed of
smallarms is fully
examined in a
forthcoming volume)

At the end of World War II most foot soldiers were armed with bolt-action magazine rifles like the British SMLE. Such rifles, accurate at ranges above 1000m (1100 yards), had been the infantryman's basic weapon for 50 years. Since 1945, however, there has been a revolution in smallarms design with the introduction of smaller automatic weapons that attempt to combine both accuracy and firepower. Known as assault rifles, the first such weapons were developed during World War II in Germany, where the lightweight MP44 was produced. This gun was the model for the famous Soviet AK47 which became the standard infantry weapon for many communist armies.

In the West a variety of designs has been produced. The two most common weapons used by Nato forces are the Belgian FN rifle and the US M16. The high-velocity M16 makes widespread use of aluminium and

Short Magazine Lee Enfield (SMLE) Mk III

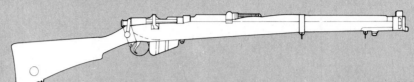

calibre .303in
length 1130mm
(44.5in) **weight**
3.91kg (8.62lb)
operation bolt **feed**
10 round detach-
able box **mode of
fire** single shot
muzzle velocity
628m/sec (2060
ft/sec) **sight** front
and back

plastic and is notable for having a calibre of 5.56mm. These smaller calibres represent the trend for the future, and the British Army has decided to adopt the 5.56mm Enfield Individual Weapon to replace its version of the FN rifle.

Harry Truman when the first Soviet nuclear test occurred suggested that, as the nuclear balance became two-way, it would at least partially neutralise American nuclear weapons. And so the conventional forces of the West had to be maintained at a level able to match the striking power of the Soviet Army.

The fears of the West were increased by the Korean War (1950-53), which seemed to prove communist aggressiveness and stimulated a considerable degree of Western rearmament. Korea was a conventional conflict on a large scale in which there were over a million casualties, and in which the masses of the North Korean and Chinese Armies were opposed by the technical expertise of Western forces. And the latter managed eventually to stem the communist tide. But the Korean War proved very frustrating to American public opinion; for if the confinement of the conflict to Korea was an important step towards evolving our modern ideas of 'limited war', it seemed to surrender the initiative to the aggressor, and the conventional military efforts put a heavy economic burden on both the United States and its European allies.

As a result, American strategy under President Dwight D. Eisenhower and Secretary of State John Foster Dulles, who dominated the 1950s, took the opposite course to that which the Truman studies suggested. Instead of playing down nuclear weapons and building up conventional forces, the United States adopted the policy of trying to throw an umbrella of nuclear deterrence over all its security interests. This was the doctrine of so-called Massive Retaliation. The United States broke with its diplomatic tradition and, trying to repeat the achievements of Nato, concluded a great number of alliances – notably the Southeast Asia Treaty Organisation and the Central Treaty Organisation – in an effort to indicate what the umbrella covered. American armed forces and, later, Nato commanders, were authorised

Guerrilla warfare has been the most prevalent form of conflict since 1945, especially in the countries of the Third World (such as Angola, above right). A ready supply of effective weapons and the nature of the country gave guerrilla fighters (opposite) definite advantages over the Portuguese in Africa. In such operations, sophisticated weaponry like helicopter gunships (above) are often of only limited use compared with adaptable and experienced ground troops (like these South Africans, top), skilled in guerrilla-type tactics.

to count on the use of nuclear weapons, which were put into the hands of both American and allied armies and navies for tactical use.

During the 1950s both American and European expenditure on conventional forces fell sharply. Nevertheless, dependence on nuclear retaliation even for lesser aggressions against American allies gave rise to considerable concern[*] – not least in the United States, where it was argued that such a threat was not credible, leading as it might to Soviet response against American cities, and consequently not an effective deterrent. Such objections came to a head when East-West tensions, which had relaxed after the death of Stalin and the end of the Korean War in 1953, increased again late in the decade. The chief source of political tension was Premier Khrushchev's reopening of the Berlin issue in 1958, accompanied by hints that small-scale Soviet military operations could cut off the city, leaving the weaker Western alliance to find a balanced and effective response.

Outside Europe, the limitations of strategy based primarily on nuclear weapons were demonstrated rather more decisively when consideration was given, in 1954, to using atomic bombs to help the French raise the siege of Dien Bien Phu in Indochina. The option was rejected on grounds of both danger (risking world peace) and probable military ineffectiveness (like taking a revolver to a swarm of bees). There was, it seemed, no substitute for fighting on the ground, and French defeat was soon followed by the prolonged American entanglement in Vietnam.

Nuclear weapons were quite clearly out of place in the wars that spread over much of Africa and Asia in the 1940s and 1950s. World War II had dealt a body blow to the power of the Western European nations that had once parcelled up the world between them, but the process of disengagement was painful and bloody as the Dutch, French, British and Portuguese fought their rearguard colonial actions. These were often accompanied by American efforts to shore up some regimes against revolutionary nationalism.

Guerrilla warfare

The example for the insurgents was in China where, during the 1940s, Mao Tse-tung had won the civil war against Chiang Kai-shek's forces by applying his vision of guerrilla warfare. His precepts were adopted by rebels and revolutionaries around the globe. From the jungles of Indonesia and Malaya to the mountains of the Yemen, and from the paddyfields of Vietnam to the Algerian desert there were cells and conspirators trying to be the revolutionary fish swimming in a sea of people.

Considerable friction arose among the Western powers about the wisdom and skill that the others displayed in these encounters, but all learned the difficulty of resisting guerrilla campaigns conducted by groups inspired by ideological fervour, particularly if they were associated with nationalism. And it was not only nuclear power that proved to be inapplicable to these wars. All the paraphernalia of modern military might could miss the enemy completely.

How could armies designed to fight a short, highly technical war cope with the debilitating task of holding down a countryside or an urban area where, at any moment, death could come from a booby trap or an assassin's bullet? How could armies whose basic procedures included isolating armed force from the civilian population deal with opponents who saw the general populace as their most important weapon?

The problems continued right down to the most basic tactical decisions, and are still of enormous importance today. What use is a helicopter gunship against a village in which there are a mere handful of activists out of a population of several hundred? As the Americans found in Vietnam in the 1960s and the Russians are now discovering in Afghanistan, the best-trained tankman in the most up-to-date tank can be as impotent as if he were in a Roman chariot when faced with a dedicated guerrilla army.

Arms and the man

To compound these difficulties, when a Western army did manage to bring guerrillas to battle on terms it could at least understand, the military task was by no means easy. Whereas in former times the European powers could expect decisive technological superiority, modern weaponry often proved very adaptable to insurgent use. A large quantity of weapons had been dispersed in World War II and much more was made available afterwards from surplus stocks. As the postwar years wore on, it became clear that many of the newer, so-called 'sophisticated' weapons were very useful to relatively simple armed forces. The missile and the shaped charge – which relies on chemical energy in the warhead to penetrate armour rather than the kinetic energy derived from a gun barrel – offered highly portable hitting power, and many of these weapons, complex in themselves, could be supplied pre-packaged, needing no maintenance and even little skill to fire them accurately.

The availability of these weapons to insurgent forces is the most obvious aspect of a major characteristic of the modern military world: the growth of a large international trade in arms. For this there are both economic and political reasons. Modern weapons are immensely expensive, the inflation of military prices having grown much more rapidly than that in the civilian sector. The Chieftain tank is about twice the price of a Centurion, a Jaguar aircraft three times that of a Hunter, and a Tornado or an F-15 costs well over $20 million. Even a simple anti-tank round of ammunition can cost more than $5000, while some

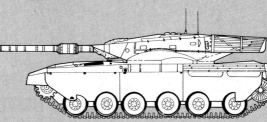

M4 A3 E8 Sherman Medium Tank

weight 32.3 tonnes (31.8 tons) **length** 6.27m (20ft 7in) **height** 3.43m (11ft 3in) **armament** 1 x 76mm gun, 2 x 0.3in machine guns, 1 x 0.5in machine gun, 1 x 2in smoke mortar **ammunition carried** AP **armour** 12-75mm (0.5 – 3in) **range** 160km (100 miles) **speed** 42km/h (26mph) **crew** 5

Merkava Main Battle Tank

weight 55.9 tonnes (55 tons) **length** 8.63m (28ft 4in) **height** 2.64m (8ft 8in) **armament** 1 x 105mm gun, 1 x 7.62mm machine gun, 2 x light machine guns **ammunition carried** APDS, HEAT, HESH, APFSDS, Phosphorous **armour** 105mm (4.13in) **range** 450km (280 miles) **speed** 46km/h (28mph) **crew** 4 (A full profile of the Merkava appears on page 303)

The changing shape of tanks: from Sherman to Merkava

Few tanks have had such a long career as the American-built M4 Sherman, which first came into use in 1942 and was still in service during the early 1980s.

Upgunned by the Israelis, the Sherman saw combat in the 1956 campaign, the Six-Day War and even the Yom Kippur War of 1973, although during the 1960s a new range of tanks came into service which totally outclassed the Sherman. They included the British Chieftain and the German Leopard I.

The Arab-Israeli Wars of 1967 and 1973 provided tank designers with many useful lessons and in 1979 the Israeli Merkava main battle tank came into operation. It embodied unusual design features with the engine at the front and the turret and crew compartment at the rear.

Besides its 105mm main armament, the Merkava has standard night vision equipment, a fire control system incorporating a laser rangefinder, and a nuclear, biological and chemical (NBC) warfare system.

The world has been flooded with smallarms like the Soviet AKM (left, in the hands of Afghan mujahideen) but this arms trade has sometimes rebounded on the producers. This expensive Russian helicopter (right) was brought down by those same mujahideen who found Soviet arms so easy to obtain.

The destructive power of modern weaponry was amply demonstrated during the Falklands conflict, when Britain lost several ships to weapons supplied by herself or her European allies – as when the frigate HMS *Antelope* exploded (above) when a team were trying to defuse a bomb lodged in the engine room. Far left: In spite of the cost of modern shells, during its advance into the Lebanon in 1982 the Israeli Army used lengthy bombardments against urban areas rather than risk its troops in street fighting.

air-to-air missiles can cost over $1 million each. One consequence is the search for export orders to share the cost of research and development, thereby helping the armed forces in their budgeting battles at home. Like any other exports, military sales overseas help the balance of trade. But many arms exports take the form of gifts – though decreasingly so as more Third World countries acquire the means to pay – because arms can buy influence, although it is often debatable whether donor or recipient acquires the greater leverage. That being so, the supply of arms has become a competitive business between adversaries.

A major milestone in this process occurred in 1955-56 when Nasser's Egypt broke out of a joint US-French-British effort to control the military balance in the Middle East by concluding arms deals, first with Czechoslovakia and then with the Soviet Union itself. As this episode illustrated, the arms

trade is not merely, or even primarily, a matter of suppliers forcing arms on recipients. The recipients believe they have serious security needs to fulfil. Wherever the suppliers have contemplated embargoes, the result has been resentment, a search for alternative suppliers and, ultimately, the appearance of indigenous arms industries in the Third World. By the 1970s Israel, India, Brazil and other countries outside the two main military blocs had become significant arms exporters themselves.

Arms sales and transfers have become very big business indeed, the total of air, ground and naval weapons delivered to Third World countries in the decade 1972-1981 being estimated at a total value of nearly $160 billion in 1972 prices. The bulk of these shipments has gone to the Middle East and South Asia, where they have found a ready use.

Whereas the 'first generation' of wars in the Third

World were generally to secure national liberation, there has since been a 'second generation' of struggles between the newly independent nations. These struggles have involved all aspects of conventional warfare. In the Middle East, for example, the Arab-Israeli wars have been on a massive scale, and have served as a testbed for much Western and Soviet military doctrine as well as for modern weapons. Since it became independent in 1948, Israel has been in continual conflict with its neighbours; the wars have ranged from the intense street fighting of 1948-49 to the World War II-style blitzkriegs of 1956 and 1967, when the precepts of mobile offensive warfare were brilliantly applied across the young state's borders.

The Arab-Israeli War of October 1973 raised – and only partly answered – important questions about the role of modern weapons in creating strategic and tactical surprise and whether the new precision guided munitions favoured the offence or the defence. Arab use of wire-guided missiles and new Soviet anti-aircraft systems seemed to have eroded some of the advantages that Israeli forces had previously enjoyed; but then in 1982 during the invasion

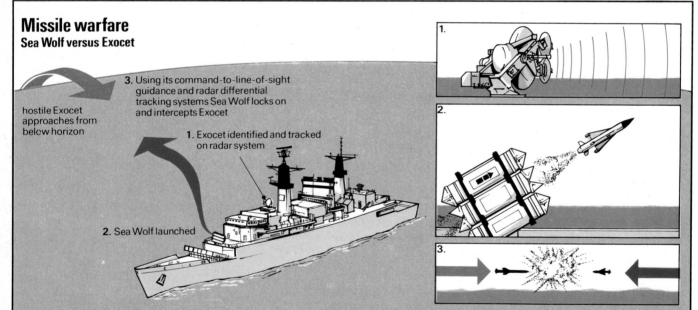

Missile warfare
Sea Wolf versus Exocet

hostile Exocet approaches from below horizon

3. Using its command-to-line-of-sight guidance and radar differential tracking systems Sea Wolf locks on and intercepts Exocet

1. Exocet identified and tracked on radar system

2. Sea Wolf launched

1.

2.

3.

The guided missile is arguably the most revolutionary weapon to have been developed since 1945. Although missiles had been used by the Chinese in the 13th century in the form of gunpowder-propelled rockets, they did not come into their own until the invention of advanced and miniaturised electronic guidance systems. Today the guided missile is generally acknowledged as the most fearsome weapon on the battlefield.

Such weapons are very expensive to produce and are primarily designed to knock out machines or other large objects rather than individual soldiers. Thus missiles have come to play a central role in the aerial and naval confrontations of maritime warfare.

The Falklands conflict highlighted the complexity and effectiveness of this form of warfare. The Argentine forces made good use of the French-built Exocet missile, which is capable of being launched from land, sea or air and has a range of over 40km (25 miles). It possesses an ingenious two-stage guidance system. The first, operated from the launching vehicle, directs the missile in the general direction of the target, while the second, inside the missile itself, comes into operation when the missile is a few kilometres from the target, so permitting final adjustments as it homes in on the target vessel at near supersonic speeds. The effect of such a weapon can be devastating, as shown when HMS *Sheffield* sank after being hit by one Exocet.

There are, however, a number of ways of countering these types of missiles, either by attempting to jam the electronic system within the missile (electronic countermeasures) or by attempting to shoot the missile down in flight. Although the tremendous speed of the Exocet, which skims towards its target at very low level, would seem to rule out the idea of shooting it out of the sky, the British Sea Wolf missile is capable of doing just that. The range of the Sea Wolf is relatively limited but, given the right circumstances, its advanced 'command' electronics allow it to hunt down and destroy the Exocet while in flight. In this role the Sea Wolf thus becomes an anti-missile missile.

The revolutionary nature of these weapons derives from the fact that they fight each other virtually independently of their crews. Sea Wolf versus Exocet is, fundamentally, a contest between electronic guidance systems – an aspect of modern war in which the sailor or soldier may be killed, but in which he can hardly influence the course of the contest.

of the Lebanon, the almost surgical precision with which the Syrian forces (and particularly their anti-aircraft missile systems) were neutralised provided overwhelming evidence to the contrary.

Elsewhere, too, wars between newly independent states have been on a large scale, as in the case of the struggle in the Horn of Africa between Ethiopia and Somalia (1977-78) and the still continuing Gulf War between Iran and Iraq. Where competing national interests are concerned, war seems to have become more rather than less likely in the last two decades, and with the widespread availability of sophisticated weaponry, radical changes in the world's political geography can be affected – as in 1971 when the state of Bangladesh (with a population of 75 million) came into being through an Indian invasion of East Pakistan that owed much to the provision of Soviet river-crossing equipment to the Indian Army.

Despite the significant differences of terrain and climate between Europe and much of the Third World, these wars afforded much food for thought within the two military blocs that face each other in Europe. Here the question of the relation of nuclear to conventional weapons still persists. It could be argued that it is in the conventional area that the pace of technological development has been most impressive. Indeed, much of the technology in 'nuclear weapons' – the guidance, fusing, accuracy and propulsion – is common to conventional weapons as well. Modern materials, explosives and fuels have all contributed to this technical revolution, but most important has been the micro-computer.

Precision guidance

This is the chief source of precision guidance, for sensors and computers enable weapons to use information received after launch, permitting them to correct course and thereby achieve the accuracy often summed up as 'if you can see it, you can hit it'. Great advances in surveillance and communication have also increased the ability to 'see'. For that reason interference with the ability to see becomes a major military objective, so that electronic counter-measures (ECM) and counter-countermeasures (ECCM) become a succession of competitive man-oeuvres. Rapid advances and counter-advances in electronics are thus not only a feature of the peacetime competition but can continue into wars and even into particular engagements, as the combatants adapt to the enemy's tactics and equipment.

It is often argued that the latest precision-guided missiles favour the defence, because cheaper missiles can destroy expensive aircraft and tanks as the latter make themselves conspicuous by movement in attack. This is, however, a gross oversimplification. The aggressor, or even the attacker in a particular battle, is not always on the move; he may have seized territory and gone on the defensive. And although anti-tank and anti-aircraft missiles are cheaper than tanks or aircraft, they are not cheap in absolute terms. Moreover, because the attack can concentrate, the defender needs considerable numbers of defensive weapons to cover his front. If the weapons are to be

New weapons and electronics have altered the battlefield. Hand-held missile launchers like the Shorts Blowpipe (top) give infantry a new punch, while (opposite) tanks are now seriously threatened by missile-carrying helicopters (above). And precise overall surveillance becomes possible using AEW planes like the Grumman Hawkeye (below).

Styles of command

One of the main themes in the story of warfare since 1945 has been the amazing strides made in weapon technology; its influence has been such, however, that it has obscured one of the most enduring factors in war – leadership. Whether at the level of section leader or army commander, the ability to motivate men to perform unpleasant and often dangerous tasks is the essence of military leadership and is, perhaps, the single most important element in securing victory on the battlefield. Confidence in its commander is the most important advantage an armed force can possess.

Since 1945 the style and type of leadership displayed by military commanders has been as diverse as ever, ranging from battlefield soldiers like Moshe Dayan, through ideological leaders such as Mao Tse-tung to the modern technocrats represented by Alexander Haig and Sandy Woodward.

These men all embodied the traditional virtues of leadership. They saw clearly what type of war they were fighting; they realised what their forces were capable of, and they worked out how to achieve their desired aim. Their solutions to the problems they were posed often involved what seemed to be great risks; but they were all proved perfectly adapted to the situation. Dayan's bold strike across the Sinai in 1956; Mao's decision to build his revolution on the peasantry rather than on the urban proletariat; and Woodward's defence of his aircraft carriers against the land-based Argentinian Air Force were all the basis of victory.

Moshe Dayan

Few modern soldiers have exemplified the concept of 'leading from the front' as well as Moshe Dayan, but in addition to being a dashing battlefield commander Dayan matured into an outstanding strategic and military planner.

Born on 20 May 1915 on an agricultural settlement in Palestine, Dayan was involved in the Jewish resistance movement from the outset and was an early member of the underground defence force, the Haganah.

During the 1948 war for Israeli independence Dayan was made commander of the 89th Commando Battalion which he moulded into a crack fighting force that acted as a mobile reserve able to cover trouble spots in the Israeli lines and to mount attacks against Arab strongpoints. Dayan's abilities as a battlefield commander came to the fore again during the campaign for Sinai in 1956 which he both planned and led: he flung his mechanised columns across the desert terrain of the Sinai, overwhelming the stunned Egyptians unused to such a mobile form of warfare.

Although Dayan went on to become a highly successful minister of defence – responsible for the direction of the Six-Day War in 1967 – he proved himself best as a gung-ho 'cavalry' commander in the tradition of such soldiers as Rommel and Patton. He died in 1981.

Mao Tse-tung

Born into a prosperous peasant family in Hunan province in 1893, Mao Tse-tung fell under the sway of Marxism while working as a librarian at Peking University and became a founder member of the Chinese Communist Party. Mao emerged as a controversial figure within the party, especially so when he proposed that the rural peasantry should be the motive force in a communist revolution and that the party should not rely on the small industrial working class of the cities. And it was as a theorist of revolutionary warfare that Mao proved to be arguably the most influential military thinker of the modern age.

Realising that the communists could not defeat the opposing Nationalist forces in immediate open conflict, he developed a three-stage plan of revolution that utilised the passive strengths of the peasantry. In the first stage the revolutionaries would be strategically weak but would concentrate on building up 'safe base areas', while during the second stage, using traditional guerrilla warfare techniques, they would wear down the enemy by harassing his forces and spreading out his army. The final stage was termed the strategic counter-offensive, when the revolutionaries would escalate their scale of operation towards mobile conventional warfare that would overthrow a weakened enemy. This three-stage struggle formed the basis for Mao's seizure of power in China as well as inspiring fellow left-wing revolutionaries such as Ho Chi Minh in Vietnam and Fidel Castro in Cuba. Mao died in 1976 but his military legacy lives on to the present day.

Sandy Woodward

Born in Cornwall in 1932, J. F. 'Sandy' Woodward was destined early on for a naval career; after graduating from the Royal Navy College at Dartmouth he went into the submarine branch where he assumed his first independent command, the submarine HMS *Tireless*, at the age of 29.

One of a new generation of naval officers, Woodward was brought up to consider nuclear engineering and computer systems to be as much a part of naval life as good seamanship. When captain of HMS *Sheffield* – to be sunk in the Falklands conflict years later – he played an important part in the installation and testing of the Sea Dart missile system. Besides his interest in the development of naval technology, Woodward proved himself an able administrator and naval planner. He assumed the position of Director of Naval Plans in 1978 where his chief function was to present the Navy's case for governmental funds. This is a crucial task in the British democratic system, and involves a clear grasp of strategic priorities and technical possibilities.

Woodward's real claim to fame came, of course, in 1982 when he was appointed commander of the British Task Force to retake the Falkland Islands from Argentina. The problem of logistics alone made Woodward's task a daunting prospect, and this was compounded by the limited number of vessels and aircraft at his disposal. But by sound planning and the careful husbanding of resources Woodward was able to carry out his prime function of putting the land forces ashore and keeping them supplied with food and ammunition until they were able to defeat the Argentinians. After his success in the South Atlantic, Woodward was knighted.

that would nullify any individual abilities and wipe out much of mankind. The complications of this relationship led to considerable scepticism about Nato's very nuclear-dependent strategy by the late 1950s, and in the following decade the Kennedy-Johnson administration, chiefly inspired by Secretary of Defense Robert McNamara, set about reversing this emphasis. In doing so, however, it became impaled on the nuclear-conventional dilemma that runs through all postwar Western strategy.

Hitherto, at the 'strategic nuclear' or intercontinental level, the overall American plan – the Single Integrated Operational Plan, or SIOP – had embraced three categories of target: Soviet (and Chinese) nuclear forces, military targets (especially logistics) and 'urban-industrial' targets. The last category had top priority.

The balance of terror

As intercontinental ballistic missiles (ICBMs) developed in the 1950s and became potentially more accurate, new possibilities emerged. On the one hand you might be able to hit the enemy's nuclear forces and disarm him. But he might do that to yours and so the necessary level of forces would cease to be, as had seemed possible, measured simply by the number of urban targets; the matching of 'orders of battle' familiar in traditional military balances might reassert itself. Thus, while a simple 'balance of terror' offered a chance of levelling strategic forces off at low levels, the creation of a counterforce, though it might buy you relative immunity if successful, also held out the possibility of an arms race.

It was obviously necessary to safeguard the forces for retaliation if cities were attacked and first the United States and then the Soviet Union deployed hopefully invulnerable weapons like the Minuteman ICBM in a silo and the Polaris submarine-launched ballistic missile. This, however, meant that to execute a counterforce strike was more difficult. Accordingly the United States, after flirting with the idea of a 'damage-limiting' strategy employing counterforce, ballistic missile defence and civil defence against fallout, reverted, in the interest of stabilising the balance, to a strategy of 'assured destruction'. It

Despite spectacular advances in the technology of war since 1945, the human element is of overriding importance in guerrilla operations. Above: Child soldier in newly independent Angola, 1975. Above left: A captured Viet Cong receives strong-arm treatment from a member of the US 1st Cavalry in South Vietnam. Below: In the uplands of Afghanistan, mujahideen guerrillas ambush Soviet invaders.

mobile, or proof against attacks or ECM, the price rises correspondingly. That a modern armed force needs such weapons is undeniable and it is clear that they have radically altered certain sectors of the modern land battlefield.

But although these enormous technical advances might seem to take warfare into a new dimension, they still have to be combined with the two variables that have always dominated military activity: leadership, and the quality of the troops involved. The ultimate British victory in the Falklands was the result as much of the superior abilities of the British ground troops as of British achievements in the 'electronic war'; and the Israeli successes in the Middle East since 1948 can be largely accounted for by the expertise and morale of the men of the Israeli Army and Air Force. The Israeli soldier has always been professionally superior to his Arab opponent. This continuing importance of the individual has been carried through to the highest levels of command.

Yet the central paradox remains; these conventional considerations of resolute leadership and well trained troops operate under the threat of a nuclear holocaust

During the Israeli advance into Beirut in 1982, the full weight of modern military might was on display. The city suffered heavily as it was bombarded (right) and many of its inhabitants were killed or made homeless (inset top). The main damage was done by heavy artillery (inset left, 155 mm self-propelled howitzers in action). Inset below left: An Israeli radio operator.

Inset right: Israeli mobile artillery moves along the narrow streets of West Beirut. The Israeli advance was not unresisted; PLO anti-aircraft guns (inset bottom centre) maintained a barrage against Israeli air strikes while rockets (inset bottom right) were used to answer the Israeli artillery, but in the end the PLO were forced to evacuate Beirut.

hoped the Soviet Union would follow suit.

There did follow a sharp fall in American spending on nuclear weapons but the strategy ran into two great difficulties. In the first place, the Soviet Union, which had launched a great rearmament effort after its humiliation in the 1962 Cuban missile crisis, showed no sign of accepting vulnerability to American strikes if it could be avoided. The threat of a race it could not afford as the United States began programmes for multiple warheads and cruise missiles, prompted the Soviet Union to accept the Strategic Arms Limitation Treaties (SALT) of 1972 and 1979, but these served largely to shift spending into other, as yet unprohibited, areas of strategic weapons.

The second great difficulty with an American strategy of deterrence using the threat of the 'assured destruction' of Soviet cities was that it immediately reopened the problem of how to match the Soviet conventional forces that might threaten America's allies, particularly in Europe. Initially the Kennedy administration approached this problem by asserting that the supposed superiority of the Soviet Army had been exaggerated, that the superior weapons and training of Nato forces made the balance much less uneven, particularly as an aggressor supposedly needs a 3:1 margin of superiority, and that a little more effort would provide, if not a completely adequate conventional defence, at least one to make the Soviet Union uncertain of success. The residual risk that nuclear weapons would be used in what would then be a large and prolonged war might also become rather more credible.

France under General de Gaulle rejected this notion and, having developed its own nuclear weapons, left the integrated Nato command (though not the alliance) in 1966. This paved the way for Nato to adopt a new conventional emphasis – the so-called 'flexible response', still Nato's official strategy. The three stages of this strategy are: (1) direct (conventional) defence, (2) 'deliberate escalation', including the limited use of tactical nuclear weapons in ways never fully, publicly agreed, and (3) general nuclear response.

Flexible response is thus still an ultimately nuclear strategy, and was adopted when Nato still possessed numerical superiority in nuclear weapons and a virtual monopoly of the so-called 'battlefield nuclear weapons'. These, it was thought, could be used to offset inferiority in firepower as well as making a clear step upwards on the ladder of escalation – a step that would deter because of the general terribleness of all-out nuclear war.

Submarines have assumed a new strategic importance since the days of World War II. HMS *Superb* (below) is a Royal Navy Swiftsure class nuclear-powered submarine commissioned in the late 1970s.

Since 1967 the Soviet Union has systematically eroded the basis of this strategy. Firstly, it has reached virtual parity at the 'strategic' level of weapons. It has also provided itself with a full range of tactical or theatre nuclear weapons, of which the SS-20 mobile multiple-headed nuclear missile of some 2000km (1250 mile) range, is only the most notorious. It is thus now far from clear that it would even be to Nato's military advantage to implement the escalation of flexible response, quite apart from the dire consequences possible for Europe.

Budgets and schedules

It has therefore become even more important to consider the conventional balance. Unfortunately for Nato, that also deteriorated after flexible response was formally introduced in 1967. Admittedly Nato forces improved greatly, especially in readiness. A series of exhortations produced some increase in Europe's efforts and the United States began rearming itself after the 'wasted years' of Vietnam. The Long Term Defence Plan, adopted in 1979, called for an increase of 3 per cent per annum in defence spending in real terms and identified 10 areas for specific improvement. But with the cost of weapons rising rapidly, resources are quickly consumed, and in 1982 the Nato supreme commander declared that the task of conventional defence was manageable only if spending could rise by 4 per cent annually.

The trouble is, of course, Nato's second problem: the immense improvement in Soviet and Warsaw Pact forces. From 1965 to 1980 the two blocs added some 35,000 major new ground weapons on the Central Front, chiefly tanks and armoured fighting vehicles (50 per cent), artillery, rocket launchers and anti-aircraft systems. Of these, 80 per cent were added by the Warsaw Pact, of which more than half were Soviet; of Nato's 20 per cent, less than half were American. Large increases in aircraft produce a ratio of 5:1 in favour of the eastern bloc.

The traditional reassurance for Nato was the superior quality of its weapons, but this is now not so clear cut. Assessments vary, but it would seem that in the main categories Soviet weapons have caught up with or even surpassed those of the West. That Soviet weapons are relatively much better than they were, and are well adapted to the Soviet Union's strategy of rapid penetration, seems undeniable. Particularly worrying for Nato, still very much dependent on warning, mobilisation and reinforcement, is the stiffening of the forces the Soviet Union has deployed forward in peace time and the number and quality of

such tools as ground attack aircraft, armed helicopters and airborne forces that could attack at short notice.

The best answer Nato has thought of for the 1980s is to train and equip its forces to use modern target acquisition and conventional precision guided or 'area' weapons – clusters of anti-tank bomblets and the like – to upset the tight time schedule that the Soviet strategy of attacking in 'echelons' requires. Certainly the Soviet Army is much obsessed with the time-scale of action and with having the correct 'norms' of force for each stage. A plausible ability to disrupt this plan by conventional means should thus be an effective deterrent.

It is this conventional confrontation, a direct result of the nuclear stalemate, that has done most to create the mass of destructive new weapons that are actually used in the wars of the Third World. The European conventional balance also has implications for the nuclear balance that are extremely disturbing.

It was always clear that Nato needed nuclear weapons if only to deter *Soviet* first use; for Soviet strategic writings gave the impression the Soviet Army itself would initiate the use of nuclear weapons if war broke out. It was for this reason that Nato maintained and refurbished its theatre nuclear arsenal – while reducing the numbers – and began to include some, such as the Cruise missile, that could deprive Soviet territory of immunity in a European nuclear war. In 1974 under Secretary of Defense James Schlesinger, the United States also tried to adapt its strategic policy for long-range nuclear weapons so that it could attack limited targets in the Soviet Union in retaliation for nuclear attacks on allies, without doing such damage as to leave the Soviet Union no reason for restraint in its response. Targets might be

neither cities, nor nuclear bases, but perhaps a limited set of other military targets, possibly directly related to the supply of a Soviet invasion of Europe. That such thoughts are possible is due to the accuracy of modern weapons and the improved capabilities for command and control. Indeed with accuracies of 30m (35 yards), it may be possible to destroy so-called strategic targets with *conventional* warheads.

Clearly these developments have ambiguous implications. By making nuclear war seem more 'manageable', the new strategic doctrines may enhance deterrence of any war at all; but equally, if deterrence nevertheless failed, the same doctrines and techniques could obviously hasten the combatants across the nuclear threshold and onto the ladder of escalation.

The horrible prospect of a devastated world has given renewed impetus to the idea of disarmament and arms control in the postwar era. In the 1960s and 1970s some significant agreements were achieved; perhaps most remarkable was the conception of 'arms

Confrontation between the two superpowers takes many forms. Intercontinental ballistic missiles such as America's Minuteman (top left) form the basis of nuclear deterrence. In Europe the forces of Nato and the Warsaw Pact remain alert for quick deployment. The might of Soviet armour (above left) is a constant worry to Western defence planners, and training for the nuclear battlefield continues apace (top right). To counter increasing Soviet presence at sea, the United States has recently given added priority to its naval strength (above).

How the Superpowers control the world

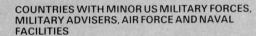 **COUNTRIES WITH LARGE SCALE US MILITARY PRESENCE**
West Germany, West Berlin (Nato), United Kingdom (Nato), Italy (Nato), Turkey (Nato), Spain, South Korea, Philippines, Japan, Panama

★ **COUNTRIES WITH MINOR US MILITARY FORCES, MILITARY ADVISERS, AIR FORCE AND NAVAL FACILITIES**
Holland (Nato), Belgium (Nato), Denmark (Nato), Norway (Nato), Greece (Nato), Portugal (Nato), Iceland (Nato), Canada (Nato), Bermuda, Puerto Rico, El Salvador, Cuba (Guantanamo), Morocco, Egypt, Somalia, Saudi Arabia, Oman, Bahrain, Okinawa, Midway, Guam, Australia, Ascension Island, Diego Garcia

✳ **COUNTRIES SUBJECT TO US MILITARY INTERVENTION**
Korea 1950-53, Vietnam 1954-73, Lebanon 1958, Cuba 1961, San Domingo 1965, Cambodia 1970, Laos 1970, Iran 1980

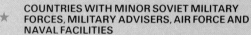 **COUNTRIES WITH LARGE SCALE SOVIET MILITARY PRESENCE**
Poland (Warsaw Pact), Czechoslovakia (Warsaw Pact), Hungary (Warsaw Pact), East Germany (Warsaw Pact), Afghanistan

★ **COUNTRIES WITH MINOR SOVIET MILITARY FORCES, MILITARY ADVISERS, AIR FORCE AND NAVAL FACILITIES**
Cuba, Algeria, Mali, Mauritania, Ethiopia, Congo, Angola, Libya, Mozambique, North Yemen, South Yemen, Iraq, Syria, India, Laos, Kampuchea, Vietnam

✳ **COUNTRIES SUBJECT TO SOVIET MILITARY INTERVENTION**
East Germany 1953, Hungary 1956, Poland 1956, Czechoslovakia 1968, Afghanistan 1979 –

World War II brought about a transformation in the world's power system: the major European states which had, until then, played a leading role in world affairs were supplanted by the emergence of the United States and the Soviet Union as two competing superpowers. Not only were the United States and the Soviet Union so much more powerful than other nations; more significantly they were able to establish spheres of influence throughout the world which ensured that few nations could remain outside the two armed camps of East and West. All warfare since 1945 has taken place in the shadow of this rivalry and has had, at the very least, to take account of it.

Both the United States and the Soviet Union have set up formal military organisations in opposition to each other. In Europe this is clearly brought into focus, with the Nato alliance of the West set against the Warsaw Pact of the East. But over the rest of the world also, groups of nations have been allied to the United States in organisations like Seato and Cento, while the Soviet Union has signed treaties of friendship and co-operation with various states.

Superpower influence extends to areas in less formal ways: the United States is very influential in South America, for example, while the Soviet Union supports regimes in the Middle East and Africa. Tension between the two superpowers arises when one believes that the other is overstepping the boundaries of its influence. Thus the United States is concerned about developments in Central America, where left-wing guerrilla forces are considered to be in league with the Soviet Union and its 'client state' Cuba, in attempts to undermine the dominance of the United States in that region. Both powers are prepared to help their own clients or allied governments when these require it – which led to American involvement in Vietnam and Soviet intervention in Afghanistan – and they are the main sources for the armaments that fuel the wars of the Third World.

Although the influence of the superpowers is far from total – China, possibly a third superpower of the future, is no friend of the Soviet Union, and in the West, relations between the European states of Nato and the United States are becoming increasingly fraught – the extent of their control shows no signs of diminishing. Indeed, in many ways their influence is expanding, an example being the way in which the Soviet Union has, since 1965, built up a navy that has given it a much greater capacity for global intervention than it possessed in the 1950s. In reply, the USA's rapid deployment force is designed to buttress US power in the unstable areas of the Middle East; and so the escalation of confrontation continues, over the entire world.

Superpower intervention at moments of acute tension. Above: US forces fly into Beirut in 1982 after Israel's sweep into the Lebanon. Below: Soviet T55s patrol the streets of Prague in 1968, crushing the Czechs' attempts at liberal reform.

control' itself, conveying the idea that it is more important to control the use and political effect of weapons than merely to reduce their number. But disarmament and arms control still suffer from the familiar problems of agreeing a fair balance, verifying compliance with agreements, and preventing the mere diversion of resources from one form of military power to another. Difficult though SALT has proved, the efforts to negotiate control of arms in Europe through the Mutual and Balanced Force Reduction talks in Vienna since 1973 have illustrated the even greater complexities of regulating conventional forces.

The 1970s also suggested that it would be premature to concentrate on disarmament in Europe to the neglect of the wider world. As we have seen, war continued briskly among the new states of Afro-Asia, much of it internal. With the international arms trade providing a ready supply of weapons, and mercenary forces providing ready-made trained troops, Africa in particular was the scene for long drawn-out wars. But in the 1970s the Soviet Union's greatly expanded and improved naval and airborne forces demonstrated their capacity to operate overseas, while the use of the Cubans in Africa opened up other novel possibilities. Such proxies, naval demonstrations, arms supplies, and training missions illustrated how much military power can do to provide underpinning for a more decisive conflict. In Angola, for example, Cuban troops rapidly achieved a victory for the communist MPLA in 1975. In response to Soviet policy the United States reactivated concern for its 'power projection forces', reversing the contraction of its navy, ordering more aircraft carriers, organising a task force for rapid deployment, and seeking additional military facilities in the Indian Ocean to refurbish the West's depleted network of bases.

Meanwhile the extension of Soviet-US rivalry in conventional forces to all areas of the globe was accompanied by another, possibly more ominous, development. The military power of the Third World itself was growing in size and sophistication and began to acquire capabilities previously possessed only by the Western and communist blocs. India's detonation of a nuclear device in 1974, the widely suspected Israeli possession of nuclear weapons, and the nuclear development programmes of such coun-

tries as Pakistan and Brazil raised fears of an increasing pace to what had hitherto been a rather slow rate of nuclear proliferation. It is now by no means impossible that nuclear weapons will first be used in anger not in Europe but in the Third World, the battleground of rival ideologies for over 30 years.

At the same time rivalry between the two superpowers has moved into the field of high technology and space. Enormous sums are being invested in the development of a 'third generation' of weapons making possible the more selective use of nuclear explosions. For example, scientists today foresee a weapon that could create a large magnetic pulse to destroy an opponent's communications system, and an X-ray laser capable of destroying enemy missiles. Even larger sums have been invested in the task of carrying war into outer space. Both the United States and the Soviet Union are rapidly expanding their military operations in space for communications, intelli-

gence-gathering, weather forecasting and mapping. Space is already an active theatre of operations.

The world is still in the uneasy age that began in 1945, and, although nuclear weapons have not been used since then, there are no signs that war is to be abandoned as an instrument of national policy. While the urge to limit and control military power, if not to abolish it altogether, is probably more widespread and more clearly articulated by political leaders and ordinary people alike than at any previous time in history, there is no guarantee of moderation in practice, and it remains to be seen whether the zone of stability, if not of true peace, established between the major blocs of developed nations can be extended to the Third World. Just as modern weapons simultaneously offer an unprecedented capacity for both destruction and discrimination, so the wider strategic scene embodies a potential for both control and catastrophe. **Professor Laurence Martin**

Israeli M48s and Centurions crossing a ridge in the Sinai in 1967. Tanks like the Centurion regularly proved their ability to be updated and were a match for their Soviet-built counterparts for 30 years.

Key Weapons
The TORNADO

The Tornado variable-geometry, all-weather Nato combat aircraft is produced by Panavia Aircraft GmbH, a tri-national company set up jointly by Aeritalia of Italy, British Aerospace in the UK and Messerschmitt-Bölkow-Blohm of Germany. The first prototype of the Tornado flew in August 1974, to be followed by eight more prototypes and six pre-series aircraft. Each country manufactures major components: the UK, front and rear fuselages; Germany, centre fuselages; and Italy, the wings. And each country assembles the aircraft for its own armed services.

The first batch of production Tornados consisted of two variants: the IDS (interdictor strike variant) and the ADV (air defence variant). Of the IDS variants, 212 aircraft were produced for the German Air Force, 112 for the German Navy, 100 for the Italian Air Force and 220 for the RAF; the 165 ADV aircraft were built solely for the RAF. The Tornado is intended to perform six major roles: battlefield interdiction; interdiction/counter air strikes; air superiority; naval

attack; interception/air defence; reconnaissance.

The Tornado is powered by two RB 199-34R afterburning turbofan engines, each delivering some 6800kg (15,000lbs) thrust, which provide a maximum level speed of Mach 2.2 at high altitude. This versatile engine also allows the Tornado to become airborne using short dispersed airfields; and with wings swept forward the Tornado can take off from strips of no more than 900m (2950ft) in length, in all weathers, day and night. For high-speed flight – at both high and low altitudes – the wings are fully swept back. Carrying a heavy weapons load the Tornado has a tactical radius of around 1400km (870 miles).

The advances in defensive weaponry, such as radar-laid anti-aircraft artillery and surface-to-air missiles, have greatly complicated the task of an advanced attack aircraft. In order to increase the chances of survival in this environment, the Tornado is designed to penetrate enemy defences at night or in bad weather at heights of 60m (200ft) at high speed. In visual conditions the aircraft can be flown even lower,

Previous page: Two prototypes bank over the English countryside on a test flight. Top: The Panavia Tornado 03 prototype armed with Kormoran anti-shipping missiles. Above: A Tornado 03 takes-off from Warton airfield. Suspended from the wings are two 1500 litre fuel tanks (with red tips) and the new Ajax ECM pods. Above right: A Tornado on a test flight in its role as a trainer aircraft. Right: The ADV prototype takes-off for a demonstration flight at the 1980 Farnborough Air Show.

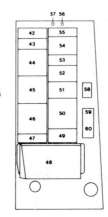

The complexity of the Tornado is demonstrated in these views of the cockpit interior, including that of the rear cockpit on the trainer model (top). Above right: Four pictures of ground-crew preparing a German Tornado for take-off. Below: Diagram of the navigator's controls. (NB: Numbers referred as 'blank' indicate spaces left on the control panels to incorporate future developments.)

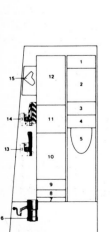

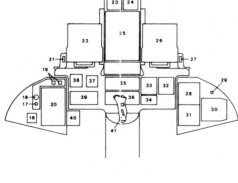

1 BLANK
2 MAPPING RADAR CONTROL PANEL
3 HEAD DOWN DISPLAY RECORDER (HDDR) CONTROL PANEL
4 BLANK
5 MAP-STOWAGE
6 WANDER LAMP
7 BLANK
8 OXYGEN CONNECTION PANEL
9 OXYGEN SUPPLY PANEL
10 BLANK
11 BLANK
12 BLANK
13 CANOPY JACK RELEASE HANDLE
14 INTERNAL CANOPY JETTISON HANDLE

15 ATTACK RELEASE SWITCH
16 LANDING GEAR POSITION INDICATOR
17 OXYGEN TEST BUTTON
18 OXYGEN CONTENTS INDICATOR
19 OXYGEN FLOW INDICATORS
20 WEAPON CONTROL PANEL 1
21 ATTENTION GETTER
22 LEFT TV/TAB DISPLAY
23 ALTIMETER
24 COMBINED SPEED INDICATOR
25 COMBINED RADAR AND PROJECTED MAP DISPLAY (CRPMD)
26 RIGHT TV/TAB DISPLAY
27 ATTENTION GETTER
28 BLANK
29 ACCIDENT DATA RECORDER (ADR) FAIL LIGHT
30 CENTRAL WARNING PANEL (CWP)
31 BLANK
32 BLANK
33 BLANK
34 BLANK
35 NAVIGATION MODE CONTROL PANEL
36 WEAPON AIMING MODE SELECTOR (WAMS)
37 ARTIFICIAL HORIZON
38 BLANK
39 BLANK
40 CLOCK
41 NAVIGATOR'S HANDCONTROLLER
42 COCKPIT VOICE RECORDER (CVR) CONTROL PANEL
43 MAIN COMPUTER (MC) CONTROL PANEL
44 INERTIAL NAVIGATOR (IN) CONTROL PANEL
45 SECONDARY ATTITUDE AND HEADING REFERENCE (SAHR)
46 INTERNAL LIGHTS PANEL
47 BLANK
48 BLANK
49 BLANK
50 BLANK
51 BLANK
52 V/UHF CONTROL PANEL
53 MISCELLANEOUS SWITCH PANEL
54 COMMUNICATION CONTROL SYSTEM (CCS) CONTROL PANEL
55 DOPPLER CONTROL PANEL
56 MICRO-DETONATING CORD (MDC) SAFETY PIN STOWAGE
57 SEAT SAFETY PIN STOWAGE
58 COMMAND EJECTION SELECTION LEVER
59 SEAT LOWER/RAISE SWITCH
60 LAMPS TEST PANEL

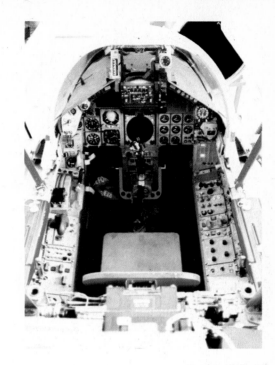

Above: A view of the pilot's cockpit on the final assembly line at the MBB works in Germany. The sheer complexity of the instrumentation makes flying modern aircraft such as the Tornado a daunting prospect. Below: Diagram of the pilot's controls.

1 ENGINE START PANEL
2 WING SWEEP LEVER
3 THROTTLES
4 MANOEUVRE AND AIRBRAKES SWITCH
5 PILOT'S HANDCONTROLLER
6 COMMUNICATION CONTROL SYSTEM (CCS) CONTROL PANEL
7 BOMB RELEASE SAFETY LOCK (BRSL) CONTROL PANEL
8 BLANK
9 WANDER LAMP
10 OXYGEN CONNECTION PANEL
11 OXYGEN SUPPLY PANEL
12 BLANK
13 CRASH PANEL
14 V/UHF CONTROL PANEL
15 COMMAND AND STABILITY AUGMENTATION SYSTEM (CSAS) CONTROL PANEL
16 AUTOPILOT AND FLIGHT DIRECTOR (AFDS) CONTROL PANEL
17 CANOPY JACK RELEASE HANDLE
18 INTERNAL CANOPY JETTISON HANDLE
19 EMERGENCY FLAP SWITCH
20 EMERGENCY AIRBRAKE SWITCH
21 FLAPS LEVER
22 ANTI DAZZLE LIGHTS SWITCH
23 TAXI THRUST SELECTOR
24 L.P. COCKS SELECTOR SWITCHES
25 LIFT DUMP INDICATOR
26 REVERSE THRUST INDICATORS AND OVERRIDE SWITCH
27 ARRESTER HOOK PUSH BUTTON AND INDICATOR
28 MASTER ARMAMENT SAFETY SWITCH
29 PILOT'S WEAPON AIMING MODE SELECTOR (WAMS) SWITCHES
30 PILOT'S WEAPON AIMING MODE SELECTOR (WAMS) SWITCHES LIGHTING DIMMER CONTROL
31 ATTENTION GETTER
32 LATE ARM SWITCH
33 ANGLE OF ATTACK (AOA) INDICATOR
34 ACCELEROMETER
35 ATTENTION GETTER
36 MANOEUVRE MONITOR WARNING LAMP
37 IFF MODE 4 WARNING INDICATOR
38 APPROACH PROGRESS INDICATOR
39 REHEAT OPERATING LIGHTS
40 CLOCK
41 FLIGHT REFUELLING LIGHTS
42 STANDBY COMPASS
43 LANDING GEAR EMERGENCY LOWERING LEVER
44 EXTERNAL STORES JETTISON CONTROL
45 SECONDARY CONTROL SURFACES POSITION INDICATOR
46 LAND/TAXI LIGHTS SWITCH
47 SERVO ALTIMETER
48 VERTICAL SPEED INDICATOR
49 COMBINED SPEED INDICATOR
50 LANDING GEAR POSITION INDICATOR
51 NOSE WHEEL STEERING MODE SELECTOR INDICATOR
52 RADAR ALTIMETER
53 AUTOPILOT ENGAGE INDICATOR
54 "B" RISK INDICATOR
55 E-SCOPE RADAR REPEATER DISPLAY (ESRRD)

56 ATTITUDE DIRECTION INDICATOR (ADI)
57 HEAD UP DISPLAY (HUD) CONTROL PANEL
58 HEAD UP DISPLAY
59 ENGINE FIRE EXTINGUISHER
60 BLANK
61 REMOTE FREQUENCY/CHANNEL INDICATOR
62 BLANK
63 ENGINE RPM INDICATOR
64 FUEL FLOW INDICATOR
65 ENGINE SPEED INDICATOR SELECTOR SWITCH
66 OXYGEN FLOW INDICATORS
67 HYDRAULIC PRESSURE GAUGES
68 FUEL QUANTITY INDICATOR AND SELECTOR UNIT
69 ENGINE TEMPERATURE INDICATORS
70 NOZZLE AREA INDICATORS
71 EMERGENCY POWER SUPPLY (EPS)
72 EPS SYSTEM ON LIGHT
73 HYDRAULIC PRESSURISATION SWITCHES
74 HYDRAULIC UTILITIES TEST SWITCHES
75 BRAKE SELECTOR HANDLE
76 BRAKE PRESSURE TRIPLE INDICATOR
77 CENTRAL WARNING PANEL (CWP)
78 REPEATER PROJECTED MAP DISPLAY (RPMD)
79 HORIZONTAL SITUATION INDICATOR (HSI)
80 HSI MODE SWITCH PANEL 2
81 WEAPON CONTROL PANEL 2
82 RAPID TAKE OFF PANEL
83 CONTROL STICK GRIP
84 RUDDER PEDALS

85 RUDDER PEDALS ADJUSTMENT HANDLE
86 LANDING GEAR SELECTOR LEVER
87 LANDING GEAR OVERRIDE BUTTON
88 KRUEGER FLAPS INDICATOR
89 BRAKES TEST BUTTON
90 THREE AXES TRIM INDICATOR
91 BLANK
92 TACAN CONTROL PANEL
93 HUD CAMERA CONTROL PANEL
94 ENGINE CONTROL PANEL
95 AIR INTAKE RAMPS CONTROL PANEL
96 TERRAIN FOLLOWING (TF) RADAR CONTROL PANEL
97 INTERNAL LIGHTS CONTROL PANEL
98 ENGINE TEST PANEL
99 BLANK
100 LAMPS TEST PANEL
101 BLANK
102 EMERGENCY UHF CONTROL PANEL
103 ENVIRONMENTAL CONTROL PANEL
104 IFF CONTROL PANEL
105 FUEL CONTROL PANEL
106 MICRO-DETONATING CORD (MDC) SAFETY PIN STOWAGE

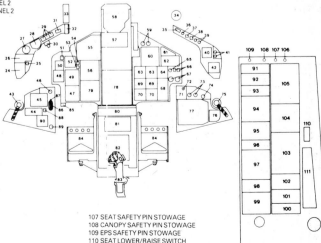

107 SEAT SAFETY PIN STOWAGE
108 CANOPY SAFETY PIN STOWAGE
109 EPS SAFETY PIN STOWAGE
110 SEAT LOWER/RAISE SWITCH
111 EXTERNAL LIGHTS PANEL

Tornado GR MK1 (IDS specification)

Type multi-role combat aircraft
Span minimum sweep 13.9m (45ft 7in); maximum sweep 8.6m (28ft 2in)
Length 16.7m (54ft 9in)
Height 5.7m (18ft 8in)
Weight empty 10,450kg (23,000lb); maximum take-off with full weapons load 27,200kg (60,000lb)
Powerplant Two 6800kg (15,000lb) Turbo Union RB 199-34R three-shaft afterburning turbofans with integral reversers

Performance maximum speed at sea level Mach 1.2 or 1300km/h (807mph); maximum level speed at 11,000m (36,090ft) over Mach 2.2 or 2335km/h (1450mph)
Range tactical radius with full weapons load 1390km (864 miles); ferry range 3890km (2417 miles)
Ceiling 15250m (50,000ft)

Armament two 27mm Mauser IWKA cannon and up to at least 8000kg (17,637lb) of stores, including Sidewinder, Sparrow, Aspide and Sky Flash air-to-air missiles, Maverick and Martel air-to-surface missiles, and Kormoran and P3T anti-ship missiles, plus almost all free-fall tactical bomb types, including a wide variety of cluster bombs, the MW-1 bomblet dispenser and Hobo and Paveway 'smart' bombs

TORNADO ARMAMENTS

GUN

Two 27 mm Mauser cannon + 360 rounds of ammunition

CONVENTIONAL BOMBS

Mk 83 1,000 lb bomb (ballistic and retarded)

Mk 13/15 1,000 lb bomb (ballistic and retarded)

Mk 82 500 lb bomb (ballistic and retarded)

BLU-1B 750 lb firebomb

JP 233

BL 755 cluster bomb (Mk 1 + Mk 2)

MW-1 dispenser

Lepus flare

250 kg MATRA (ballistic and retarded)

ROCKET LAUNCHERS

LAU 51A

LR-25

GUIDED WEAPONS

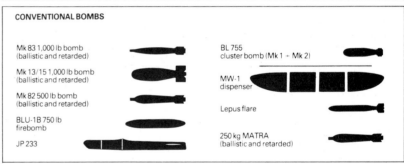

Sidewinder AIM 9B/9L

Kormoran AGGM

Maverick AGGM

P3T AGGM

Paveway laser-guided bomb

GBU 15 TV-guided bomb

EXTERNAL PODS

Recce pod

ECM pod

Data link pod

Chaff/flare dispenser

Pavespike

CARRIERS

Twin carriers

Triple carriers

EXTERNAL FUEL

330 Imp gal. tanks

220 Imp gal. tanks

Opposite above: An ADV prototype, fully armed with four Skyflash missiles slung under the fuselage as well as Sidewinder missiles suspended from the outboard wing pylons beside the long-range fuel tanks. Opposite below: An RAF Tornado practises low-level contour flying over the Scottish Highlands. Above: A Victor tanker aircraft refuels a Tornado in flight; such operations can extend the Tornado's operational range considerably. Above right: A Tornado fires its high-velocity 27 mm Mauser cannon. Centre right: A German Navy Tornado banks to reveal its MW-1 multi-purpose sub-munition dispenser. Below right: Tornados plugged into auxiliary power-unit equipment.

making it practically impossible to detect by ground-based radar and giving maximum protection from surface-to-air missiles and anti-aircraft artillery, due to terrain screening.

In order to achieve high-speed flight at these altitudes, the aircraft must have outstanding handling and control characteristics and, of course, advanced avionics. The Tornado is equipped with an automatic TF (terrain-following) navigation system which controls the flight path of the aircraft to a pre-set clearance height above the ground. Casting a probing radar beam in front of it, the Tornado's TF computer automatically pulls up the aircraft to pass obstructions in its way. Flight-director commands are relayed simultaneously to a visual display, enabling the pilot to override the automatic system at will and put the aircraft under manual control. The system is capable of operation at low-level speeds of up to Mach 1.2 with maximum flight safety. The Ferranti LRMTS (laser ranger and marked target seeker) allows the Tornado to make high-speed, single-pass attacks with extreme accuracy. In an increasingly hostile battle-field environment, the ability of an aircraft to execute successful single-pass attacks against enemy targets and then quickly return to the safety of its home base is of paramount importance if unacceptable losses are to be avoided.

The Tornado's main mission in the advent of war in Europe would be to attack sensitive targets such as airfields, command posts and second echelon concentrations in an interdiction role. The aircraft's speed and survivability, as well as its accurate bomb and missile stores delivery system, give it a high chance of achieving its designated tasks. Once its main stores have been released, the Tornado has an excellent air-to-air combat capability to fight its way back to base.

The ADV has been designed specifically to meet RAF requirements for a long-range interceptor to patrol the East German border and to be able to protect Nato shipping lanes (from the Arctic Circle to the English Channel) against enemy aircraft flying at both high and low levels.

One of the distinguishing features of the ADV – designated the F2 in the RAF – is an air-interception radar known as Foxhunter which is able to detect enemy aircraft at ranges of more than 185km (115 miles), while a long-range visual identification system will allow the Tornado pilot to sort out friend from foe. Although the ADV shares an 80 per cent 'commonality' with the IDS, it differs from the IDS in having an extended forward fuselage, extra fuel, different avionics and armament.

The ADV's extended range/loiter capability and quick supersonic acceleration make it well suited for its interception role. It can patrol for periods in excess of two hours at distances of up to 650km (400 miles) from its home territory, and carry out an interception mission including 10 minutes of air combat time. Provision is made for air-to-air refuelling from VC-10 tankers while on combat air patrol to extend its patrolling capability. The ADV is fitted with four Sky Flash medium-range missiles and has two Sidewinders and a single 27mm cannon for self-defence. Sky Flash missiles can engage targets at a range of 45km (30 miles) regardless of height.

Its high speed and operational flexibility, combined with sophisticated avionic equipment and powerful armament, make the Tornado a very potent attack aircraft. The Tornado will provide Nato with an effective all-weather counter to the forces of the Warsaw Pact, and it is likely to remain in service to the end of the century at least.

Top: The Tornado in full flight armed with a bomb-load of 1000 lb Mk 83 bombs, and with long-range fuel tanks and ECM pods. Above: A Tornado of the Italian Air Force carrying full external stores during a test flight over the sea.

Battle for Palestine

The Jewish fight for the Promised Land was the start of four decades of warfare

The modern state of Israel was born in battle, and its survival and expansion since its birth have to a large extent depended upon its military might. It is at the centre of the problems of one of the world's most important and turbulent regions, and is the major concern of its neighbours. Israel has owed its success to the unflinching willpower of its people and to the continuing expertise of its armed forces.

Even at the beginning of the 17th century Jews began to dream about returning to 'Israel'. But it was not until the end of the 19th century, in the heyday of nationalist sentiments in much of Europe, that an Austrian Jew, Theodor Herzl, first gave the Jewish dream a more tangible form in a pamphlet entitled 'The Jewish State', which advocated the creation of an independent country that would be populated by Jews alone.

During World War I the Zionist leader Dr Chaim Weizmann opened the first Zionist headquarters in London and gave the movement's support to the Allied cause. In return the British government gave its approval in November 1917 to the idea of a Jewish 'national home' in Palestine. Approval for the plan came in a letter from British Foreign Secretary Arthur Balfour to Lord Rothschild, chairman of the Zionist Federation. Later known as the Balfour Declaration, it was the most important single document in the history of the creation of the Jewish state.

After the war and the defeat of the Turkish Empire, the League of Nations gave the British government a Mandate to administer Palestine and to facilitate Jewish immigration and settlement there. It was by no means an easy task: it was in fact impossible to create a 'national home' for Jews in Palestine without doing anything which might, in the words of the Balfour Declaration, 'prejudice the civil and religious rights of existing non-Jewish communities in Palestine'.

The number of Jews who settled in Palestine rose very slowly up to the outbreak of World War I. From 24,000 in 1882 the Jewish population reached 50,000 by the end of the century, and 85,000 by 1914. Not until 1933, when Hitler came to power in Germany, did the number of Jews arriving in Israel show a marked increase. There were more than 42,000 immigrants in 1934, and over 100,000 arrived illegally in 1939. By 1946 the Jewish population of Israel had reached around 700,000; the Arab population then numbered 1,300,000.

Throughout the struggle for independence against the British, the Jewish resistance movement was never really united. There was a continual conflict of personalities and policies. The Haganah (defence force), which had been formed in 1920 to resist Arab attacks, was tolerated, though never officially recognised, by the British authorities. During World War II there was a truce between the British and the Haganah, members of which volunteered for service in the

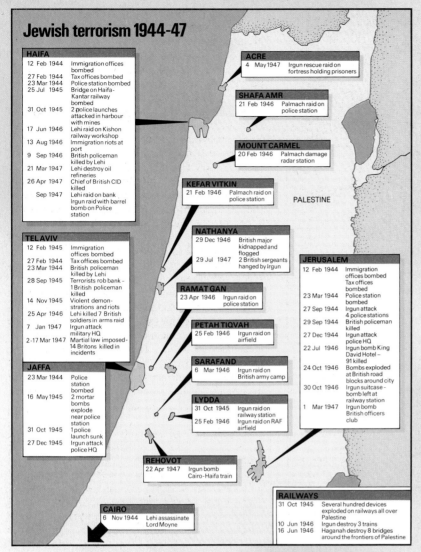

Jewish terrorism 1944-47

HAIFA

12 Feb 1944	Immigration offices bombed
27 Feb 1944	Tax offices bombed
23 Mar 1944	Police station bombed
25 Jul 1945	Bridge on Haifa-Kantar railway bombed
31 Oct 1945	2 police launches attacked in harbour with mines
17 Jun 1946	Lehi raid on Kishon railway workshop
13 Aug 1946	Immigration riots at port
9 Sep 1946	British policeman killed by Lehi
21 Mar 1947	Lehi destroy oil refineries
26 Apr 1947	Chief of British CID killed
Sep 1947	Lehi raid on bank Irgun raid with barrel bomb on Police station

ACRE

4 May 1947	Irgun rescue raid on fortress holding prisoners

SHAFA AMR

21 Feb 1946	Palmach raid on police station

MOUNT CARMEL

20 Feb 1946	Palmach damage radar station

KEFAR VITKIN

21 Feb 1946	Palmach raid on police station

PALESTINE

NATHANYA

29 Dec 1946	British major kidnapped and flogged
29 Jul 1947	2 British sergeants hanged by Irgun

RAMAT GAN

23 Apr 1946	Irgun raid on police station

PETAH TIQVAH

25 Feb 1946	Irgun raid on airfield

SARAFAND

6 Mar 1946	Irgun raid on British army camp

LYDDA

31 Oct 1945	Irgun raid on railway station
25 Feb 1946	Irgun raid on RAF airfield

TEL AVIV

12 Feb 1945	Immigration offices bombed
27 Feb 1944	Tax offices bombed
23 Mar 1944	British policeman killed
28 Sep 1945	Terrorists rob bank - 1 British policeman killed
14 Nov 1945	Violent demonstrations and riots
25 Apr 1946	Lehi killed 7 British soldiers in arms raid
7 Jan 1947	Irgun attack military HQ
2-17 Mar 1947	Martial law imposed - 14 Britons killed in incidents

JAFFA

23 Mar 1944	Police station bombed
16 May 1945	2 mortar bombs explode near police station
31 Oct 1945	1 police launch sunk
27 Dec 1945	Irgun attack police HQ

REHOVOT

22 Apr 1947	Irgun bomb Cairo-Haifa train

JERUSALEM

12 Feb 1944	Immigration offices bombed Tax offices bombed
23 Mar 1944	Police station bombed
27 Sep 1944	Irgun attack 4 police stations
29 Sep 1944	British policeman killed
27 Dec 1944	Irgun attack police HQ
22 Jul 1946	Irgun bomb King David Hotel - 91 killed
24 Oct 1946	Bombs exploded at British road blocks around city
30 Oct 1946	Irgun suitcase - bomb left at railway station
1 Mar 1947	Irgun bomb British officers club

RAILWAYS

31 Oct 1945	Several hundred devices exploded on railways all over Palestine
10 Jun 1946	Irgun destroy 3 trains
16 Jun 1946	Haganah destroy 8 bridges around the frontiers of Palestine

CAIRO

6 Nov 1944	Lehi assassinate Lord Moyne

British forces against Nazi Germany. In the 1930s the Haganah had formed its own mobile field force called the Chish and in 1941 the Palmach (shock troops) came into being. By 1947 the Palmach had 3200 members and the Chish, although poorly armed, numbered 7000.

In 1931 some right-wing Jews, dissatisfied with the Haganah's 'defencist' attitude to the Arabs, formed the Irgun whose main objective was, by means of terrorist attacks on police stations and government buildings, to make Palestine too hot for the British to rule. Getting the British out was, in the view of the Irgun leaders, the key to the creation of a Jewish state, whereas the Haganah was equally concerned with the defence of the new state against Arab attack.

In 1940 a split took place in the Irgun, resulting in the formation of the Lehi (Lohame Herut Israel – Fighters for the Freedom of Israel), better known as the Stern gang. The two groups now took the war to the British, while World War II was still continuing. Determined to assert Jewish rights, their attacks became more violent and two members of the Lehi killed Lord Moyne, the British Minister for the Middle East, in November 1944. This act horrified the British – and the majority of the Jewish population of Palestine. But the assassination had the effect of getting the terrorists the forum they wanted; and their motivation was clearly expressed in their chilling explanation: 'If we prove our ideals were right and just, then our deed was right and just.'

Begin's Irgun had decided to mount a spectacular series of attacks on the British to force them to take unpopular repressive measures. They had very few resources with which to mount such operations, but the core of the membership in the later years of World War II was fanatically determined – determined enough to be able to live the double life of the terrorist. As J. Bowyer Bell described it:

'Except for a few full time people, nearly everyone lived above ground, often in their own homes, under their own names, but always with another secret life. There was the daily round of quick meetings in dreary rooms with frightened hosts hovering at the door, tiny notes passed on street corners, rumours of disaster or arrests, or the headline in a paper that could not be acknowledged. There was never enough time or money. Everyone lived on nerves, coffee, and cigarettes.

'Later, it seemed to the members that the months and years slipped by in a delirium of heightened reality. Neither the later open wars nor the postponed careers would ever have the drama of life underground. There was the pulse of knowledge when, walking down the dark streets of Tel Aviv, one heard through a strange window the whistled bar of the Betar song as the Irgun's illegal radio began to broadcast.'

The first operations were against government buildings, and on a small scale, but as the security forces clamped down there were often gun battles – and both terrorists and policemen were killed, again to the consternation of the more respectable Jewish organisations.

The Haganah was by far the largest of the armed

Terrorist reprisal

The bodies of Martin and Paice in the eucalyptus grove.

Of all the many outrages that occurred in Palestine none aroused more controversy than the killing of two British Intelligence Corps sergeants, Clifford Martin and Mervyn Paice, by the Irgun in July 1947.

When three Irgun members were sentenced to death by a British court for terrorist activities, the Irgun determined to take hostages and on 12 July they achieved success. Sergeants Martin and Paice were unarmed and out of uniform when a car drew up beside them and out jumped an Irgun hit squad. Bundled into the back of the car they were taken to a specially constructed cell which was, in effect, a 3m (7 feet) cubed 'box' buried underneath a diamond factory. Lacking both light and air their requirements for survival consisted of a canvas bucket, a week's supply of food and two oxygen cylinders.

Martin and Paice and the Irgun awaited the British decision, which came on 29 July when the three Irgun terrorists were hanged in Acre prison. The terrorists reacted swiftly. Irgun commander Amihai Paglin and a squad drove to the diamond factory. One of the sergeants was dragged from the box and a hood was slipped over his head. After his hands and feet were tied he was stood on a chair, a noose placed around his neck, and then the chair was kicked away.

The second sergeant was similarly hanged. After hanging for 20 minutes the two corpses were taken to a nearby eucalyptus grove and suspended from a tree. A mine was placed beneath the bodies and the British authorities informed of the location. When the bodies were cut down they set off the mine which blew them to pieces. This shocking incident resulted in an immediate outcry in both Palestine and Britain.

On page 29 : Jewish soldiers train their Vickers Mk1 water-cooled machine gun on an Arab position in northern Palestine. Left: Terror in the streets, the aftermath of a bomb explosion in Jerusalem.

Jewish groups; its membership reached 45,000 in 1947. The Irgun, by contrast, never had more than 2800 members before Independence, while the Lehi had between 600 and 700. By late 1944, the Jewish Agency, under whose umbrella the main Jewish organisations operated, was so worried at the possible adverse effects of Irgun operations that it authorised the Haganah to break up the Irgun, and soon the Lehi too. This was in part a reflection of political differences; Irgun and Lehi were conservative and right-wing, whereas the Haganah contained many socialist elements. More than 1000 Irgun suspects were handed over to the British in the early months of 1945; but the Irgun managed to survive. By the summer, with the end of the war in Europe, Haganah operations against Begin's men ceased, and a potentially disastrous split among the Jewish groups was partially closed.

The British Labour government elected in the summer of 1945 was fully expected to give the Jews the state they had been seeking. But there was no firm announcement, and on 25 August the Colonial Office refused to raise the quota of Jewish immigration. This was a firm sign of intentions unacceptable to any of the Jewish organisations, and a revolt began all over Palestine. The Irgun and Lehi were now working in concert with the striking forces of the Haganah, the Palmach. During October and November 1945 joint operations destroyed refineries and railway lines, and the security forces began to lose control.

The underground war soon escalated. Arms raids led to shoot-outs; gun battles took place in small rooms and crowded streets. There were some British victories: in February 1946 they captured the Lehi radio transmitter and 20 insurgents. But throughout the early months of 1946, the Jews were the more successful. In April seven British paratroopers were killed in a Lehi operation; in May over £6000 was stolen from the Nablus branch of Barclay's Bank; in June there was a concerted attack on communications that destroyed 11 road and rail bridges.

As British security became tighter with the operations of Black Saturday, 29 June 1946 – in which 100,000 soldiers and 10,000 police occupied the Jewish Agency's headquarters and 25 Jewish settlements, confiscated files and detained 2700 people – so the resistance became more desperate and took hostages. Palestine became a land under siege as curfews and road blocks became the norm. Then, in July 1946, came the most audacious terrorist action of all. The King David Hotel, the social as well as administrative

The British presence

Britain's stance in Palestine has been described as resembling a 'police state with a conscience'. Certainly, self-imposed restraints and shortcomings in the coercive machinery were hardly conducive to success. The basic British problem was that they had little experience of such a situation and could not formulate a strategy that was effective in an underground war.

Government policy was unclear, leading to widespread unwillingness to cooperate with the security forces. Moreover, there was frequent capitulation to terrorism through the commutation of death sentences under duress. The resources available were limited and there was a tendency to equate the situation with normal imperial policing. The Palestine police, however, was chronically short of personnel and, as a paramilitary force, did not enjoy good relations with the population. Less than 4 per cent of its British members spoke Hebrew and the small Jewish component was unreliable. Much therefore depended on army units trained for conventional rather than guerrilla war. Static guards on important installations spared few for offensive actions, which mostly consisted of cordon and search operations – the isolation and thorough combing of given locations. Over 170 such operations were mounted, usually at battalion level after specific incidents. These operations were not always successful and exposed troops to false allegations, while reprisals were quickly seized upon by terrorists whose grasp of propaganda was always superior. Army strength totalled 100,000 in January 1947 and police numbered 20,000. In all, 223 British military personnel were killed in Palestine and 478 wounded.

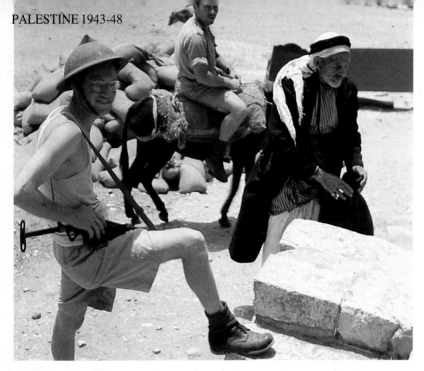

Above: A Jewish sentry stands guard in a village just taken by the Haganah. Below: Well armed Arabs on their way to the fighting at the Mount of Olives, 11 May 1948. Below right: Arabs in Jerusalem openly purchasing arms in the street in February 1948. The woman is inspecting ammunition to go with her Browning automatic pistol.

indeed as far as world opinion was concerned.

Finally, there was the affair of the two British sergeants, Paice and Martin, hanged by the Irgun on 29 July in retaliation for the execution of three Jewish prisoners. Once again, the Jewish Agency and the Haganah were horrified; but the hangings demonstrated to the British public in the clearest possible way just how control over Palestine had been eroded.

By the end of the summer of 1947 the British had lost all appetite for the struggle and had handed the problem to the United Nations, which decided in November on a partition of the country between Jew and Arab, to take effect from May 1948. There had always been simmering violence between the two communities and from the late summer of 1947 relations worsened. The war against the British had been unpleasant enough, but the gradual intensification of fighting between the two communities was even uglier. The slaughter of women and children was common; revenge and an almost casual acceptance of violence became the norm. The Arab practice of mutilating bodies horrified the Jews from Europe but the Arabs were convinced they had right on their side – that Palestine was theirs and should not be taken from them.

After November 1947 the fighting became widespread – in the cities where rival communities lived, around kibbutzim and Arab villages. In the first two weeks of December nearly 100 Arabs and almost as many Jews were killed. Arab volunteers from outside Palestine came in to attack the Jewish settlements. A kibbutz would be sniped at all day then, at night, members of the Haganah would slip out and perhaps blow up a house in a nearby Arab village in revenge.

Whereas the war against the British had been an undercover affair in which secrecy and evading detection had been the rule, the internecine warfare with the Arab community involved larger formations, and had to be directed by the Haganah if any success at all was to be achieved. But there were many problems in subordinating the Irgun to the Haganah. The Irgun was a small, battle-tested group, whereas the Haganah was a large, more amorphous body. Then there were the basic differences in approach. The Irgun was almost a religious sect; its members had a fanatical belief in the rightness of the Jewish cause. The Arabs were, to them, an irrelevance. If they got in the way of the Jewish state then so much the worse for them. To Ben-Gurion and the leadership of the Haganah, the Palestinian Arabs were a people, who had to be treated as such.

Acts of terror between the two communities multi-

centre of the Mandate, was attacked by the Irgun, and a whole wing was destroyed by carefully placed explosives. A total of 91 people – Britons, Arabs and Jews – were killed. Once again terror had done its work, and the whole world was made aware of the Jewish problem. With booby traps and assassinations abounding no British soldier or policeman in Palestine seemed safe. When convicted Irgun prisoners were whipped, Begin's men captured British troops and whipped them in return.

The war was now an intense strain for the British; troops had to be confined to safe areas to prevent more hostages being taken. Large-scale sweeps had failed to break the ability of the Jewish resistance to mount raids. The summer of 1947 saw three incidents that summed up the problems facing the British. First of all, in April, two captured terrorists, Meir Feinstein of the Irgun and Moshe Barazani of Lehi, blew themselves apart with a grenade that had been smuggled into their cell, thereby cheating the gallows by a few hours. This kind of fanaticism was something the British had no answer to. Then, in July, the ship *Exodus 1947*, carrying 4,500 Jews from France to Israel, was captured by the British Navy. Eventually the refugees were transported to Germany and Britain was seen to have returned concentration camp survivors to the hated land of their suffering. The episode put British policy towards Palestine in a very bad light

plied; a bomb near to Damascus gate in Jerusalem killed 15 Arabs at the end of 1947, and shortly afterwards the Irgun sent an oil drum full of explosives into a group of Arabs waiting at a bus stop, killing 17. In February, 52 people were killed as an Arab bomb exploded in Jerusalem.

These horrible acts could not decide the war, however. That was a question of whether the Arabs could cut off or destroy any of the Jewish communities – many of them isolated – that lay throughout Palestine. The big prize was Jerusalem, where a 100,000-strong Jewish community was surrounded by Arabs and could only be supplied along one road from Tel Aviv.

By February 1948 the battle was on in earnest. Ben-Gurion appointed David Shaltiel commander of the Haganah there and he had to cope with a rapidly deteriorating situation. By March there was no meat and no milk. The Arabs commanded the heights and threatened to overrun outlying settlements.

On 24 March a Jewish convoy set out to try and get from Tel Aviv to Jerusalem. It met a road block; a bulldozer trying to destroy the block was blown up by a mine. Of the 40 vehicles only 21 survived. The following day an 80-strong convoy was halted and the survivors had to be rescued by the British forces.

So far the Jews had fought a defensive war and had not wanted to take the offensive for fear of provoking the British authorities. The failure of the two convoys had changed the picture, however, and Ben-Gurion decided it was time to unwrap the plan for direct co-ordinated attacks on the Arabs.

Above: Arabs on the lookout for Jewish movements around the stronghold of Castel on the road to Jerusalem. Below: The call to arms – Jewish forces on the roof of a house in a village they have recently captured run for cover to reply to long-range fire from a detachment of the Arab Legion, 1948.

The first attack was to be on the Arabs blocking the Tel Aviv-Jerusalem road. The Haganah had an initial success when Abdul Kader, the Arab commander, was killed by a Jewish patrol. This temporarily dislocated Arab plans. The most critical moment came on 9 April, however, before the Jewish offensive was fully in gear. On that day a joint Irgun-Lehi operation against the village of Deir Yassin took place. After a day of fierce house-to-house fighting 254 Arabs – men, women and children – lay dead. The Haganah expressed its horror, occupied the village and buried the dead. But the road to Jerusalem was now open (temporarily at least). At the same time, Arab attacks on the coastal plain faltered when the Jewish settlement of Mishmar Haemek, the key to the area, resisted assaults.

With the Arab offensive having ended, a process that had been taking place since December began to gather pace: the flight of the Arabs from those areas designated as Jewish under the partition. The Arabs believed that they would be able to return when the Jews were defeated.

As the British began to withdraw, so the Arabs moved out too. In mid-April the Arabs quit Tiberias; at the end of the month 60,000 were evacuated from Haifa. The Irgun was now ready to take the offensive to capture any areas it could, and late in April took the city of Jaffa, from which the Arab civilians also fled. Haganah troops took Acre.

By the time the new Jewish state was proclaimed, on 14 May, the Jewish forces had defeated the British in an underground war and the Palestinian Arabs in the struggle for the land. But now they had to face the united armies of the neighbouring Arab states in open war to decide whether they could retain all their gains.

Ashley Brown

The Arab forces

Although the Palestinian Arabs outnumbered the Jews, and had access to considerable supplies of weapons, they failed to prevent the Jews establishing control over wide areas of Palestine by May 1948. This was mainly because there was no central Arab command. The Emir Abdullah of Transjordan controlled the best military forces of the region in the Transjordan Frontier Force, but his ambitions to dominate all Palestine were opposed by the Grand Mufti of Jerusalem, the spiritual head of the Palestinians; the mufti was supported by irregular troops under his cousin Abdul Kader. Meanwhile, in Galilee, Fawzi el Kaujki, a Lebanese, commanded a badly organised force known as the Arab Liberation Army, initially formed to counter-balance the schemes of the emir. Even the help from neighbouring states was biased towards their own interests – Egypt considered Gaza a suitable area for expansion while Syria and Lebanon had similar designs on Galilee. These internal conflicts considerably weakened the Arab cause, for there was no central authority to bring maximum pressure to bear on the Jews' weak points. So it was that the Haganah was able to take the initiative from April 1948.

OUTRAGE!

When the Irgun blew up the King David Hotel

After the British security operations of Black Saturday, 29 June 1946, involving the occupation of the Jewish Agency's headquarters and the detention of several thousand people, the Haganah realised that their future operations might now be jeopardised. Consequently on 1 July the Haganah authorised the Irgun to proceed with their proposed Operation Chick – the bombing of the British secretariat housed in a wing of the King David Hotel, Jerusalem.

Despite heavy security precautions around the hotel, barbed wire barricades, high nets to prevent an attack with grenades, and a central alarm system that would sound a general alert at the first sign of disturbance and cause the arrival of patrol cars, police and soldiers – despite all this the King David continued to function as a hotel, and as the social centre of the British community.

Amihai Paglin, who planned the Irgun raid, had noticed that people were making regular deliveries to the kitchen. Paglin calculated that a huge explosive charge detonated from the basement area under the secretariat would drop the entire southwest wing. He decided that the huge amount of explosives needed could be packed in milk churns and delivered to the hotel under the guise of a normal milk delivery. Furthermore, in order to draw attention from the 'milk delivery' two small bombs would be detonated in the hotel grounds. It was hoped that this would clear the area of civilians but not raise a general alarm.

At noon on 22 July these two small bombs were detonated. At roughly the same time a milk lorry turned into the hotel drive and pulled up outside the basement entrance. Fourteen people dressed as Arabs got out and began to unload seven unusually heavy milk churns, each packed with explosives.

A British officer strolling past the kitchens noticed that something unusual was going on, and on seeing the danger of the situation an Irgun man shot the officer, who fell to the ground. Two military policemen nearby heard the shooting and fired towards the

Above: A photograph of the hotel taken seconds after the explosion. Below: The main entrance before the bombing. The King David Hotel was the social as well as the administrative centre of the British Mandate in Palestine.

'I hated them [the British], we all did; all the young people were joining the Irgun or the Stern gang. My grandfather fled on foot from Egypt to come to freedom in Israel and I had relatives who perished in Europe. When I heard the British had turned back Polish refugees from our shores and that those Jews were later killed in pogroms, I decided I'd do anything to get the British out. I will always have blood on my hands. We never meant to kill anyone. But when I walk through these corridors now, I feel I did something worthwhile, something historical. I remember every detail of the operation and I think perhaps that my grandfather would be proud.'

Israel Levy, who participated in the King David Hotel bombing, in an interview, 1982.

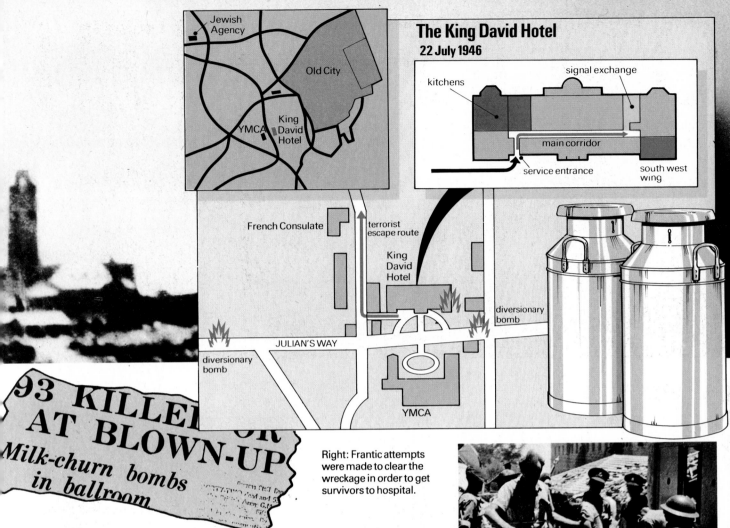

The King David Hotel
22 July 1946

Jewish Agency

Old City

King David Hotel

YMCA

kitchens

signal exchange

main corridor

service entrance

south west wing

French Consulate

terrorist escape route

King David Hotel

diversionary bomb

JULIAN'S WAY

diversionary bomb

YMCA

93 KILLED AT BLOWN-UP
Milk-churn bombs in ballroom

Right: Frantic attempts were made to clear the wreckage in order to get survivors to hospital.

kitchen entrance. Their fire was drawn by two or three of the Irgun party who were guarding the kitchen staff.

At 12.15 pm Police Inspector Taylor received some sort of alarm from the King David Hotel and despatched a patrol car to investigate. However, by this time the assault party had placed the seven milk churns around the central pillars of the southwest wing and escaped in a flurry of smallarms fire.

Shortly afterwards Inspector Taylor issued a general alarm, despatched his patrol cars and sounded the terrorist siren. At about this time at two-minute intervals a female member of the Irgun telephoned first the hotel switchboard, the *Palestine Post* newspaper and finally the French Consulate, each call explaining that bombs had been placed in the basement of the King David Hotel. In this way the Irgun hoped to clear the hotel of all personnel. But the messages were never properly relayed, and at 12.31 Taylor called off the general alarm.

At exactly 12.37 the milk churns detonated, the walls of the southwest wing bulged outwards and the entire wing collapsed. In one horrifying moment the hub of the British administration for Palestine became one huge pile of rubble. The explosion claimed the lives of 91 people and injured 45.

Alexander McNair-Wilson

Left: The charges were placed so precisely that the southwest wing was totally destroyed, but the rest of the hotel was relatively untouched.

Against all odds

The devastating impact of the guerrilla fighter in modern warfare

The war that the Jewish resistance fought against the British was not one of regular formations, formed to fight a setpiece battle. It was a small-scale war of terror against an occupying army, the sort of war the Spaniards fought against Napoleon's French armies and which they called the *guerrilla* – the little war.

Guerrilla warfare is nothing new. The use of small, irregular forces to ambush, harass and gradually wear down a large conventional army has been a recognised form of warfare since time immemorial. There are references to such tactics as early as 400 years before the birth of Christ, in the writings of the Chinese theorist Sun Tzu, and examples of their use may be seen throughout the centuries in all areas of the globe. In the modern age, such campaigns as those of the Boer Commandos against the British in South Africa (1900-02), of T. E. Lawrence in Arabia against the Turks (1916-18), of the various resistance groups against the Axis powers in World War II were classic examples. But it is only since 1945, in the host of liberation struggles in the former European colonies, that we have grown used to guerrilla warfare as an integral part of the military scene.

Guerrilla wars have been the most common form of conflict in the modern world, and they have naturally taken different forms. The war that the Viet Cong waged against the Americans in the 1960s was not the same as that fought by the Provisional IRA against the government in Ulster; Castro's bands in the mountains of Cuba were very different from the Afghan mujahideen who resisted the Soviet intervention in their country. Yet guerrilla armies do have something in common. They all operate from a position of weakness against a more powerful enemy, and they tend to use similar methods and procedures.

Confusion often arises over principles and definitions, particularly as guerrilla warfare is now widely regarded as part of political revolution. We hear constant references to such concepts as 'revolutionary guerrilla warfare' or 'urban guerrilla warfare', building up a picture of some complex development that only the experts can understand. This is unfortunate, for in reality it is not guerrilla warfare that has changed, merely the end results of its use.

Mao Tse-tung, the father of revolutionary guerrilla warfare, never advocated any new guerrilla tactics, but used his small, irregular bands of fighters gradually to undermine the strength of his Nationalist enemies in China preparatory to fighting conventional set-piece battles and winning political power. The same is true of urban guerrilla warfare, for although the scene of action may have changed, the principles and basic tactics remain the same. In both cases the need is to create military capability from virtually nothing and to attack the enemy with it. Lacking manpower, military skills and weapons, the guerrillas can hardly be expected to mount a conventional campaign. They must start from scratch, at the lowest level of capability, and build up their effort slowly, in line with the advantages they hold.

And such advantages do exist. Conventional armies tend to be large, unwieldy organisations, designed to overwhelm an enemy by force of superior arms. For this they need to be supplied, using roads, rivers or railways, and they need to control the country through which they move. As a result they garrison towns, occupy key positions and usually aim for a quick victory to minimise cost and losses.

All of this plays right into the hands of the guerrillas. They may be weak and poorly equipped by comparison, but they do blend into the surrounding countryside, enjoying local support and intimate knowledge of terrain. They are free from fixed lines of supply and can enjoy remarkable tactical flexibility. They do not need to garrison territory and they are under no restraints as to the duration of their campaign; indeed, the longer it goes on the more chance they have of building up their strength. Thus, by standing back and choosing their targets, the guerrillas can bring overwhelming local force to bear against vulnerable outposts, regardless of the overall strength of the enemy army.

The ever-changing image of the guerrilla – from T.E. Lawrence in World War I (above) to Che Guevara in the 1960s (top left). Centre: Fidel Castro chews thoughtfully on a cigar as he directs exercises for Cuban troops.

Regular armies may have superior equipment and ostensible freedom of movement by road and rail and air (above, an army security patrol in El Salvador in 1981), but guerrilla ambushes and mines are an ever-present threat (top, the remains of a government jeep in Biafra, the end of one such security patrol).

emerge spontaneously; they have to be created, nurtured and developed, and will always start from a position of frightening military weakness.

The key to ultimate success lies in the reasons for the birth of the guerrilla movement. The guerrilla feels he has a grievance of such importance that he is willing to risk his life for it, and the chances are that if he feels that way, a substantial part of the rest of the population may agree with him. A guerrilla army's greatest strength is the cast-iron devotion of its soldiers; and its second great strength lies in the support – even passive support – of some of the general populace. So in Palestine in the 1940s, the Irgun and the Lehi were organisations of ruthless, indomitable fighters, quite prepared to go to their deaths for what they saw as a just cause. And although most Jewish organisations might disavow these extremists, they sympathised with the cause and were not prepared to give the British forces the help they needed to put down the guerrillas.

The opponents of guerrilla armies nearly always label the insurgents as 'bandits' and treat them as they would murderers. But the guerrilla is often much more than a common criminal. He has sometimes to face difficult situations alone, with the knowledge that failure will result in certain death; and although it is true that he is also often a terrorist to whom atrocities may become second nature, this does not mean that he lacks military expertise. He may have to live a double life in a city for years; he may have to exist for months with little food and ammunition in desert, jungle or swamp.

Turning the raw material of a resentful populace into such soldiers is the task of the leadership. Leaders may come from a variety of sources. The right man could be found locally or may already be in a position of command through tribal or regional organisations; Mulla Mustafa Barazani of Kurdistan in the 1960s, leading the guerrilla campaign against Iraq, is a case in point. He may be a political leader, forced into military action by a lack of alternative courses, as Mao Tse-tung was in China after the failure of the Autumn Harvest uprising in 1927. Finally he may come from outside, bringing expertise and the promise of support, as Lawrence did in Arabia in 1916 and Che Guevara tried to do in Bolivia in 1967.

Essentially the leader has to embody the movement, to realise what it is capable of and to drive it to the goal. It is hardly surprising, then, that the great guerrilla leaders are so often charismatic figures like Castro and Ho Chi Minh or Mao himself. But irrespective of personal inspiration the leader has, as a preliminary step, to find a safe base where he can train and mould his forces.

Because of the nature of enemy occupation, with its emphasis upon the towns and lines of communication, the natural area for such a base is the countryside. A remote locality, of little apparent worth to the occupying authorities, has distinct advantages. Enemy presence will be minimal, particularly if the area is off the beaten track; the people will not have been intimidated into submission; local knowledge of difficult terrain such as mountains, forests or swamps will be deep. Examples include the Viet Minh bases in the mountains of northeast Tonkin in the early 1950s; Colonel Grivas's use of the Troodos mountains in Cyprus at much the same time; and Lawrence's dependence upon the vastness of the Arabian desert between 1916 and 1918. Admittedly it is

The enemy will feel obliged to defend everything he holds, spreading his forces thinly over ground he is intent on protecting, leaving the more flexible guerrillas to mount a campaign of attrition on their own terms. Moreover, as each guerrilla attack produces captured arms and enhanced prestige, the irregular forces will gain in strength as the conventional army faces demoralisation and weakened capability. Eventually a balance of forces will be achieved, after which the guerrillas may be able to attack to win.

It would be wrong, however, to assume that a guerrilla campaign is easy to effect. Problems abound, making good leadership and organisation essential throughout. Guerrilla movements, whether in response to enemy occupation of national territory, colonialism or indigenous political repression, rarely possible to create even safer bases outside the country, in a friendly neigbouring state – as, for example, ZANU guerrillas from Zimbabwe were able to do in Mozambique after 1975; and it is not unknown for guerrillas to find sanctuary in urban centres – as the Provisional IRA has done in Belfast and Londonderry since 1970. Traditonally, however, the countryside provides the most obvious location.

Having established his base, the next problem for the leader is recruits. Many local people may want to join, or he may have to persuade them with appeals to national identity or promises of long-term economic, social or political gains. In a colonial setting – as in Malaya in the 1950s or Angola and Mozambique 20 years later – the call for national independence may be enough; elsewhere it may need a popular cry along the lines of 'Land to the Tiller', a favourite among the more left-wing groups such as those now operating in Central America. Even so, care must be taken to recruit the best available people.

Guerrilla fighters need to be fit, particularly if they are to operate in difficult terrain, and capable of living rough for long periods. One of the reasons for Che Guevara's failure in Bolivia in 1967 was his recruitment of middle-class intellectuals who could not withstand the physical hardship of his campaign. Similarly, men with existing skills – gamekeepers, poachers or ex-soldiers – should be sought, even if they are not ideal physical specimens, for they can pass their expertise on to the younger fighters. This does not mean that the old, unfit or inexpert should be ignored; they can be organised to provide a passive wing – such as the communist Min Yuen in Malaya – to provide food, supplies, intelligence and shelter to

Right: Guerrilla armies depend on support throughout the population. Here, North Vietnamese women and children are taught weapons drill. Far right: A PLO guerrilla prepares to launch a grenade using a special attachment to his 7.62mm AK assault rifle. Bottom: The impedimenta of a modern army laid out in a Soviet camp in Afghanistan. The need to concentrate such equipment not only slows movement; it also provides a good target – in this case for the Afghan guerrillas (bottom right).

the active guerrilla gangs.

Guerrillas are not much use without weapons. Some may be left over from the conventional battles which preceded the enemy takeover; others may be available from the local people. Guerrillas in Vietnam, Malaya and the Philippines immediately after World War II were able to equip themselves with weapons left behind by the defeated Japanese, while Grivas called in a large number of privately-owned shotguns from sympathetic Greek-Cypriot families in 1956. Other arms may be imported from friendly states – the Soviet policy of providing weapons to national liberation groups in black Africa is a case in point – but quite often the guerrillas will be left to their own devices. Some may be able to manufacture their own crude weapons, as the Mau Mau did in Kenya in the mid-1950s, but for most the only accessible source is the enemy. Indeed, the capture of weapons may provide the incentive for the beginning of military action.

These initial attacks should not be over-ambitious. Isolated army outposts can be overwhelmed by a combination of surprise and force of local numbers, producing not only the required arms but also useful practical training. It is unlikely that the enemy will react with maximum force – such an isolated attack will probably be dismissed as banditry, leading to little more than replacement of the lost troops – and this allows the guerrillas to move on to the other outposts, with similar results. By the time the enemy realises the full extent of opposition he will already have suffered significant casualties, as the French did during the aptly-named War of the Posts in rural Tonkin in 1950.

Even if this realisation results in a major anti-guerrilla campaign, the enemy forces may still suffer disadvantages, entering unknown terrain and sticking rigidly to the tracks, roads and rivers. The guerrillas, enjoying local knowledge and support, can easily mount a series of ambushes, waiting for enemy troops at chosen defiles, choke-points or junctions. Using the weapons already captured, particularly portable items such as mortars, machine guns or mines, they should be able to achieve surprise and success, disappearing into the countryside before the enemy can recover. The Viet Minh ambush of a French mobile column in the Chan Muoung gorge, south of Phu Doan, in 1952 remains a classic example.

Faced with such disasters, the enemy will probably fall back onto his secure bases in the towns and try to contain rather than defeat the guerrilla threat. This gives the guerrillas a chance to expand by forming new groups in neighbouring rural areas, and to extend their attritional tactics close to the heartland of enemy rule. Sabotage, bombings and selected assassinations may take place in the towns – a policy favoured by Grivas in Cyprus – adding to the pressures and helping further to undermine enemy morale. Although the enemy might respond with ruthless force at this stage, normally the initiative would now lie firmly with the guerrillas. Every successful ambush or attack produces more weapons and greater expertise, slowly but surely wearing the enemy down and forcing him further into his bases. In the end, with guerrilla control of the surrounding countryside, the towns are besieged. The time is now ripe for the next stage of the campaign, moving away from guerrilla tactics to more conventional battles and the hope of eventual victory. **John Pimlott**

Weapons of terror

The underground arms industry that supplied the Jewish resistance

Above: British paratroopers survey part of the haul recovered during the massive 1946 security operation known as Black Saturday. The haul included 3in mortars, German MG34 machine guns, Bren guns, grenades, and other assorted home-made weapons. Right: Defending the Jaffa-Tel Aviv border – troops of the Irgun fire Sten guns while a girl prepares grenades. Note the Austrian 9mm Steyr M12 pistol at her knees. Far right: Members of the Haganah practise fire drill with a home-made mortar.

On 29 January 1946 a British jeep and a lorry packed with men in RAF uniform approached the rear gate of the RAF camp at Aqir near Gaza. The Arab Legion guards on duty at the gate saluted smartly as the vehicles passed into the camp – but they failed to check the identity papers of the two vehicles, which sped through the camp and pulled up outside the armoury. A Jewish worker was asked to get the keys. On refusing, he was knocked to the ground and the door forced open. Inside, four RAF airmen were quickly overcome before they could raise the alarm. Five Arabs standing nearby were press-ganged as loaders and, with the utmost speed, 20 Bren guns and hundreds of Sten guns were thrown into the back of the lorry. Once loaded, the convoy moved off down the runway, along an old sand track that took it away from the airbase undetected. The whole operation had taken less than 20 minutes. Jewish guerrillas of the Irgun had made another addition to their armoury.

This raid was typical of many carried out by the Jewish underground in their quest to obtain armaments. Although plenty of weapons were available at the end of World War II, with huge surplus arms dumps lying across Europe and the Middle East, the stringent security measures adopted by the British occupying forces severely limited the amount of arms that could be smuggled into Palestine. Such arms as were purchased abroad and illegally imported were usually concealed within machinery, in steamrollers or washing machines for example. In late 1947 the Haganah took its first delivery from Czechoslovakia of 20mm Hispano-Suiza light artillery pieces, which arrived concealed under a shipment of onions.

The branch of the Haganah responsible for the procurement of arms and ammunition was known as the Rekhesh, an organisation that maintained the highest level of secrecy – so much so that few in the Haganah knew of its activities. The dangers involved in either smuggling in arms from abroad or in stealing weapons from the British were many, and the price paid by the Rekhesh in loss of life was high.

Despite the success of the Haganah's smuggling missions, as a source of weaponry they were uncertain and could not be relied upon to guarantee a steady flow of arms and ammunition. And so, to gain the necessary weapons, the Jewish terrorists used the classic guerrilla tactic of turning the tables on the enemy by using his strength against him. As they needed weapons to fight the British so they took them from the British, and in operations such as the raid on the RAF camp at Aqir the Irgun, for example, was able to lay in large stocks.

Not all raids were casualty free, however. In one operation at the Ramat Gan police station, several members of the Irgun, dressed as Arab prisoners and British soldiers, gained entrance into the security of the compound. Once inside the police station they overcame the three policemen on duty, blew out the armoury door and made off with 30 weapons and 7000 rounds of ammunition. At that point other British policemen in the compound began to realise that something was wrong: captive Arabs had gone into the police station and yet armed Jews were coming out. The raiding party quickly came under fire from police on the rooftops and suffered heavy casualties as they made their getaway.

While the Irgun tended to specialise in such raids, the Haganah, less prepared to countenance direct confrontation with the British, turned to the produc-

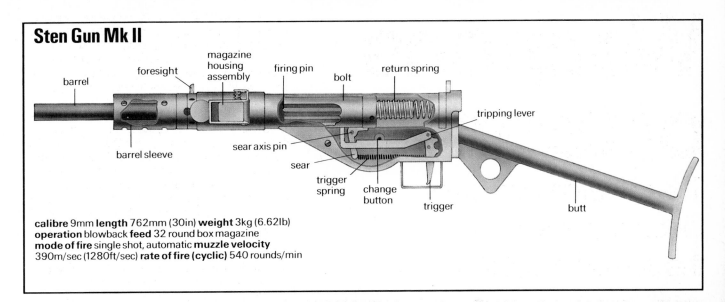

Sten Gun Mk II

barrel

foresight

magazine housing assembly

firing pin

bolt

return spring

tripping lever

barrel sleeve

sear axis pin

sear

trigger spring

change button

trigger

butt

calibre 9mm **length** 762mm (30in) **weight** 3kg (6.62lb)
operation blowback **feed** 32 round box magazine
mode of fire single shot, automatic **muzzle velocity**
390m/sec (1280ft/sec) **rate of fire (cyclic)** 540 rounds/min

tion of home-made weapons. The home weapons industry, called Ta'as, had begun life in the 1930s and consisted of a number of small and secret workshops scattered across Palestine. At first, weapon construction was fairly primitive – tin cans filled with explosives – but after 1945 manufacture extended to hand grenades and even sub-machine guns. The Sten was a particular favourite of the terrorists. It was extremely effective at close quarters, was cheap to buy and, because of its simple construction, easy to manufacture.

In the early days of 1946 ammunition was in short supply. Although some was produced by Ta'as in its underground factories, the production could not match the need. Consequently the Haganah was forced to look at the possibility of raiding British supply trains. By coincidence the Jewish Brigade of the British Army (which had fought in Italy during World War II) was used to guard the arms dumps stored in the rail yards, and with help from sympathetic Jewish soldiers the Haganah established a source for the regular supply of ammunition. During 1946 a terrorist unit was specially trained to jump onto moving trains and push crates of military supplies off at pre-selected locations.

Another example of the Haganah's versatility in supplying itself with arms was demonstrated in the way in which its members relieved the local Arab population of quantities of 'Chile potash', one of the constituents used in the manufacture of explosives. Traditionally, Imperial Chemical Industries supplied potash to the Arabs of Nablus and Hebron for firing cannon during the religious festival of Ramadan. A few members of Rekhesh, dressed as Arabs and bearing forged loading orders for potash, would drive into Nablus in a truck with false number plates, present their orders and depart with a substantial amount of the chemical.

As the underground arms industry established itself, so it extended its production to include 2 and 3in mortars and shells. The mortars were constructed to the highest standards, and when British security forces captured some examples they refused to believe they were locally produced and insisted that they were manufactured in the United States. These weapons were often trained on police or military establishments, usually concealed by being half-buried in the ground. The mortar would be armed with

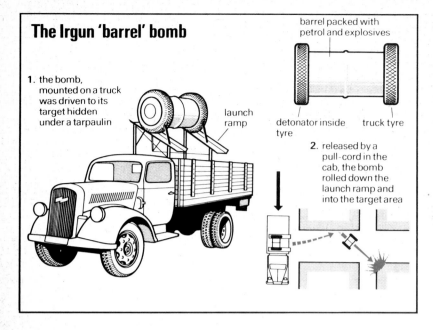

The Irgun 'barrel' bomb

1. the bomb, mounted on a truck was driven to its target hidden under a tarpaulin

launch ramp

barrel packed with petrol and explosives

detonator inside tyre

truck tyre

2. released by a pull-cord in the cab, the bomb rolled down the launch ramp and into the target area

a time-fused shell. The guerrillas would disperse and then a member of the underground would ring up the duty officer of the establishment under threat to warn of the imminent bombardment. The Haganah found that this was a useful method for occupying the time of the security forces, although the British eventually realised that the weapons were not accurate enough to warrant too much attention.

Apart from mortars, a string of improvised weapons were used to harass the occupying forces. As one British officer recalls: 'Typical incidents were the ambushing of army trucks and the mining of roads used by the trucks. They used a variety of means, of which the most popular was a bomb in a car detonated from the side of the road. They also used various ingenious devices, such as replacing the milestones along the road with dummy milestones filled with explosives and nuts and bolts. They had some original devices for bombing police stations: trucks fitted with a throwing arm which would hurl a forty-gallon drum of explosives over a high fence into the courtyard of a police station or an army barracks.'

It was not until the huge arms searches of 1946 and 1947 that the British actually realised the extent of the clandestine arms production. One such sweep uncovered 600 rifles, light machine guns, pistols and small mortars. Yet even the most stringent measures by the security forces could not contain the Jewish underground armaments programme. Ta'as even built one bullet-making factory 7m (23 feet) under the ground, the workers being given ultra-violet treatment and vitamins to reduce the skin pallor that otherwise might have made them look suspicious.

By May 1947 the Haganah had an arsenal of some 8300 rifles, 3600 Sten guns, 700 light machine guns, 200 medium machine guns, 600 2in and 100 3in mortars. But despite the effectiveness of these home-made weapons, Rekhesh increased their buying operations in Europe as the British departure from Palestine became imminent. The next round in the fight for a Jewish state of Israel would require much heavier equipment: terrorist activities against a departing colonial power would soon become transformed into open confrontation with the Arab states.

Simon Innes

Above right: A young religious student keeps guard on the Tel Aviv-Jaffa border at a heavily sandbagged Haganah checkpoint. In his hand he carries a 7.63mm Mauser pistol. Right: Two female members of the Jewish underground shock troops, the Palmach, assemble and arm grenades. As the Haganah began to increase its activities, so the need for better arms increased.

Key Weapons
The
ABRAMS M1 MBT

The Abrams M1 MBT (main battle tank) came into operation in 1980 and represents the latest thinking in American tank design. The M1 was named after General Creighton W. Abrams, the former Commander-in-Chief in Vietnam, and Chief-of-Staff, who approved the project personally in September 1972.

The United States had been a partner with Germany in the MBT-70 project, a joint-development effort begun in August 1963 aimed at helping standardise Nato's advanced tank requirements. Conceived and nourished by experience gained after World War II both partners were to invest jointly in designing what was intended to be the most advanced armoured fighting vehicle in the world. But although prototypes

were ready for combat evaluation in 1967 in the shape of a sleek 50-ton, three-man tank, problems soon arose.

While the Americans required the new tank for worldwide deployment, the Federal Republic of Germany favoured a design suited to warfare in central Europe. Differing firepower concepts were also a prominent issue. The Germans, from their World War II combat experience, favoured a high-velocity long-range large-calibre gun, while the Americans wanted to fit the Shillelagh 152mm gun/launcher system capable of firing a variety of ammunition types as well a Shillelagh missile.

The differences between the two nations seemed

Previous page: The M1 crashing through rough country at speed.
Above: The MBT-70 prototype – a highly unusual design with a hydropneumatic suspension system and a three-man crew, with the driver's position on the left side of the turret in a contra-rotating ring.
Below: The M1 as it finally appeared, with a 105mm main armament and a four-man crew.

irreconcilable and in 1970 the US Congress ordered the joint project to be abandoned and allocated special funds for a new national project. As a result, each country went its own way, the Germans ending up with their powerful 120mm-gun Leopard II, and the Americans going along the painful road which finally produced the M1.

The Americans began work on an 'austere' version of the MBT-70, to be known as the XM803, but this too was found to be unsatisfactory and the project was cancelled only a year after its inauguration. An urgent solution had to be found if the United States was not to be left far behind in modern tank warfare – and time was running out fast, as news of the new Soviet tank designs filtered through Allied intelligence channels. In February 1972 the US Army set up a special task force, which included user, trainer and development agencies aimed at cooperating closely in the development of the new MBT.

Following the presentation of proposals in 1972, contracts were awarded in 1973 to the Chrysler Corporation and General Motors, who both set about developing prototypes to be designated XM1. In 1976 both prime contractors presented their pilot vehicles for initial testing.

In November 1976 Chrysler was selected as the winner of the validation phase, and a full-scale engineering contract was awarded, worth $196 million. An interesting feature of the Chrysler power-plant was that it was an Avco-Lycoming gas-turbine engine, the first of its kind to power a battle tank. The turbine has better acceleration and power than conventional engines and is very economical from a field maintenance point of view, although present models consume more fuel than the high-powered diesel engines of other tanks.

In February 1980 the US Army accepted delivery of the first two production tanks in a ceremony held at

Above: An M1 with its gun traversed to the right. Below left: The pilot model of the XM1 prototype which was revealed to the world in 1978. Below right: The M1 showing its teeth, with the driver's position at the centre of the tank clearly visible.

the army production line at Lima, Ohio. Designated the M1, the US Army has ordered over 7000 of these tanks and they will provide the advanced edge of America's armoured might for the next two decades at least.

An impressive armoured vehicle, the M1 is also the most expensive tank ever produced, with its unit price surpassing $1.55 million. With a top speed of 72 km/h (45mph) on roads and up to 50 km/h (31mph) cross-country, the M1 is a fast-moving tank and a marked improvement over the existing M60A3. The same goes also for the silhouette, which is extremely low, enabling the tank to find better cover from hull down positions. The M1's ability to survive battlefield conditions has been enhanced by its quick acceleration – up to 32 km/h (20mph) in six seconds – which allows the tank to make sudden spurts from one piece of cover to the next. Also useful in this respect is the M1's comparatively low noise and smoke signature.

As in the German Leopard II and the British Challenger, the M1 is protected by compound armour technology. This covers the front hull and turret structure, balancing the rest of the tank with varying thicknesses of regular armour, ranging from 3.25mm (⅛in) to 125mm (5in). Spaced armour plating is added in vulnerable areas to decrease the effect from chemical action rounds such as HEAT and HESH.

The first production batch mounts the US 105mm M68 tank gun, which is a variant of the British 105mm L7 series manufactured under licence in the United States. Already fitted to the M60 tank it is capable of firing most ammunition types. However, it is planned to upgun the tank with a more powerful main armament in the mid-1980s, most probably the 120mm Rheinmetall smooth-bore gun as fitted to the German Leopard II.

The tank's fire-control system is very advanced: gun and turret drive are hydraulically powered with the gun's elevation and depression achieved by a hydraulic cylinder; turret traverse is powered by a hydraulic motor-gear box combination. The M1 features a Hughes laser rangefinder and a back-up solid-state digital computer, with an interior self-checking fault control. This allows the gunner to select the target, fix-it with the rangefinder and then press his

Above: The driving compartment with T-bar clearly visible. Below: The interior, showing the breach of the 105mm gun.

Left: A side-view of the tank with anti-shaped-charge plates protecting the suspension. Below: An XM1 ploughs across a field during its proving trials. The powerful 1500 horsepower gas-turbine engine and rugged torsion-bar suspension will provide production M1s with the ability to cross broken terrain at high speeds – a great advantage for survival on the battlefield.

fire switch. The computer then takes over and makes the necessary calculations and adjustments to ensure a hit.

A 7.62mm machine gun is mounted coaxially with the main armament and a second is fitted at the gun-loader's position on the turret. The commander has a 12.7mm anti-aircraft machine gun also fitted on the turret.

Crew protection against hits is improved by greater obliquity of the hull and turret surfaces and by armoured skirts over the suspension. Several protective innovations will improve the chances of survival following eventual penetration. Ammunition stowage has been compartmentalised with 44 main-gun rounds carried in the bustle behind sliding armour doors. Eight main-gun rounds are stowed in a compartment in the hull and three more on the turret floor, protected by spall plates. In the event of a hit, the blast of the explosion is vented upwards and out of the bustle by specially constructed blowout plates, thus directing the detonating rounds away from the crew compartment. During operational tests at the Aberdeen Proving Ground, a prototype XM1 was fully loaded with fuel and ammunition and subjected to various types of fire. Not only was it not destroyed – it was later driven away under its own power.

Although the shape of the turret is aimed at achieving a low silhouette over the hull, allowances for the crew's comfort and efficiency have prevented it from reaching the close-fitting dome shape of Soviet tanks. Moreover, there are resulting high-explosive pockets in front and at the sides, especially when the turret is traversed. The ability of the tank crew to work efficiently within the confines of an armoured vehicle under difficult conditions is of the greatest importance on the battlefield. The problem is to ensure that the tank's combat efficiency is not seriously impaired, and that costs do not become prohibitively expensive. The Soviet-built tanks of the Warsaw Pact are reliable and tough battlefield vehicles – as well as being relatively easy to produce – but the strains involved in operating them are considerable and would almost certainly have adverse consequences during sustained combat

The driver's position is situated at the front centre of the tank and is operated from a semi-reclining position when driving with the hatch closed. Steering is done by a rotating motorcycle-type T-bar which actuates the steering lever, with grips for throttle and fuel management. A centre periscope and image intensification periscope for night driving is provided.

Above: The XM1 prototype painted with the 1976 camouflage colour scheme in preparation for combat trials.

One of the most crucial questions arising on the present validity of the M1 is the effectiveness of its gun. While the fire-control system and advanced optical equipment may well ensure a high rate of first-hits at medium ranges, it remains debatable whether the present 105mm gun, even with its advanced ammunition, will cope with the frontal armour of the Soviet T64 and T72 tanks. However, the adoption of 120mm smooth-bore gun should improve the battlefield effectiveness of the M1.

Two more criticisms that have been levelled at the M1 are poor engine reliability and high fuel consumption. Exhaustive field testing seems to have proved the reliability of the Avco-Lycoming turbine, although information is far from complete. Tactical advantages outweigh the increased fuel consumption, especially in close or medium-range battle situations that would be likely to develop in central Europe, where movement is limited and staying power is emphasised. In fact, although the M1 was developed to meet American worldwide requirements, it will prove a highly effective weapon on the European battlefield should war break out between the Warsaw Pact and Nato. Alongside the German Leopard and the British Chieftain and Challenger tanks the M1 would become a central element in Nato's ability to block the Soviet tank assault and, of course, would form the spearhead of any Nato armoured counter thrusts.

The M1 has yet to prove itself in combat, but given its sophisticated electronic equipment, good armour protection and when armed with a 120mm main gun it should be a match for any main battle tank.

Abrams M1 Main Battle Tank

Crew 4
Dimensions Length (gun included) 9.77m (32ft); width 3.65m (11ft 11in); height 2.89 metres (9ft 1in)
Weight Combat loaded 54,432kgs (119,050lbs)
Engine Avco-Lycoming AGT-T 1500HPC gas turbine developing 1500hp at 3000rpm

Performance Maximum road speed 72km/h (45mph); maximum cross-country speed 50km/h (31mph); range (road) 450km (280miles); vertical obstacle 1.24m (4ft); trench 2.74m (9ft); gradient 60 per cent; fording 1.22m (4ft), with kit 2.36m (7ft 9in)

Armour Chobham compound type and spaced; details classified
Armament One 105mm M68 gun (55 rounds); one 7.62mm machine gun co-axial with main armament; one 12.7mm machine gun on commander's cupola; one 7.62mm machine gun mounted by loader's hatch; six smoke dischargers on either side of turret as well as integral smoke generators

A first in tank engine development, the Avco-Lycoming gas turbine has aroused considerable interest in tank-design circles. If the engine proves a success for the Americans then the Israeli IDF may well install the turbine in the Merkava MBT when it is due for upgrading. Although residual doubts still remain regarding its battlefield reliability, its advantages are many. Ease of maintenance is a particular feature and it has been claimed that the complete engine can be replaced in less than half-an-hour. A great advantage of the engine is that it allows a variety of fuels to be used, including petrol, diesel and even jet fuel. During confused campaign operations such flexibility would be highly beneficial, and – albeit to a limited degree – would help solve the logistical nightmare that bedevils Nato's heterogeneous organisational structure.

Storming the heights

The difficulties and dangers of mountain warfare

Warfare since 1945 has developed along sophisticated lines; the technological advances alone make training and preparation for war in Europe very different from what they were in the 1940s. But there are still certain constants on which technology has made only a minor impact. One of the most critical of these is mountain warfare. Since 1945 a number of the most important conflicts – from the Greek Civil War of the 1940s to Afghanistan in the 1980s – have been mainly mountain wars, while other struggles – the Korean War or Vietnam, for example – have involved large-scale mountain fighting.

Analysing the experience accumulated by the British Army in over 40 years of 'small wars' in rugged terrain, Colonel C.E. Callwell wrote in 1896 that such campaigns were generally 'rather against nature than against hostile armies'. A large part of that experience was gained in the mountains of the North West Frontier and, although weapons and equipment have altered radically since Callwell's day, the basic difficulties and principles of mountain warfare have not materially changed.

In physical terms alone, mountains still pose great problems for even the most sophisticated of modern armies. In the Korean War the modest 500m (1600 foot) Hill 800 in the Noname Line held by the US 2nd Infantry Division of X Corps in May 1951 required well over an hour's climb to reach the summit. In all

some 237,000 sand bags, 385 rolls of barbed wire, 6000 steel stakes and 39 55-gallon 'fougasse' drums had to be manhandled to the top to complete the defences. During the border war between India and China from September to November 1962, Indian troops were taking five days to march from the foothills to the defensive positions at heights of 4300-5600m (13,000-16,000 feet) around Tawang on the Tibetan frontier. All requirements had to be carried, since mules could not operate at such altitudes and, in any case, could not cross the flimsy rope, bamboo and log bridges that spanned the unfordable fast-flowing rivers.

Invariably such physical barriers are compounded by the inclement weather associated with altitude, especially in winter. In their operations in the Larissa region of Greece in April 1947, Greek National Army (GNA) troops found the bodies of 120 guerrillas from the communist Democratic Army (DSE) who had died of exposure in the mountains. Some four fifths of the 1300 dead suffered by the DSE around Pieria in March 1948 were also attributed to cold rather than government action. In its retreat through the mountains from the Chosin reservoir to the sea at Hungnam in Korea in December 1950 the US 1st Marine Division took between 59 and 79 hours to travel the first 22km (14 miles) from Chosin to Hagaru. The breakout from Koto-ri on 6 December took 38 hours

Below: The most feared mountain fighters have always been the Afghan tribes, who in the 19th century successfully resisted British invasions and in the 20th have stretched the capabilities of the modern Soviet Army.

to cover 18km (11 miles) in deep snow and with temperatures down to –18° Centigrade. Frostbite was a major danger and the 4400 battle casualties of the division were dwarfed by 7000 non-battle casualties, of which the majority were due to frostbite. Among Indian forces operating on the Tibetan frontier in 1962 lack of acclimatisation at high altitude led to large numbers succumbing to pulmonary oedema, a condition not unlike pneumonia which could prove fatal unless victims were immediately evacuated to a lower altitude.

In military terms mountains are ideal for defensive purposes. For this reason they have been most readily associated since 1945 with guerrilla warfare. The DSE forces in Greece sought refuge in more than 100 mountain villages in Thessaly and Macedonia during the winter of 1947-48 and concentrated their main base areas in the 1200-2100m (4000-7000 foot) Grammos and Vitsi ranges, which were convenient for sanctuary across the Albanian and Yugoslav frontiers. Fidel Castro's guerrillas took to the 6500 square km (2500 square miles) of the Sierra Maestra on Cuba while in Cyprus Colonel George Grivas's EOKA gangs – fighting for union with Greece – frequently found refuge in the Troodos and Kyrenia mountains, which ranged up to 1500m (5000 feet).

Such regions provide innumerable opportunities to harass opposing regular forces through sniping or ambush, particularly as most conventionally equipped armies will utilise what may well be a limited number of passes or valleys. Having imposed casualties the guerrilla then has the opportunity to escape, as Marshal Tito's partisans repeatedly demonstrated in the mountains of Yugoslavia during World War II. Grivas maintained that gaps could always be found in cordons. On one occasion, in June 1956, he escaped a British cordon in the Troodos

during a forest fire that killed 21 British servicemen; and on another, in December 1956, he escaped through mist.

In Greece the DSE guerrillas had had considerable experience fighting the German occupation forces, recording successes such as the destruction (with British and non-communist assistance) of the important railway viaduct over the Gorgopotamos gorge in November 1942. They were therefore able to adapt easily to the role once more in 1946. Railway sabotage remained a favourite tactic so that Greek engines were invariably preceded by a string of expendable waggons. In addition to the laying of land-mines, DSE forces booby-trapped trees, set booby-trapped mules to wander the hillsides, rolled bundles of explosives down slopes, and started landslides. The approaches to their mountain strongholds in the Grammos and Vitsi regions were barricaded with logs lashed together and, by the summer of 1949, with concrete bunkers and pillboxes.

At the same time, however, communist operations demonstrated the dangers that mountains could pose to guerrilla forces. Depopulation of the mountain villages by enforced government resettlement and fear of guerrilla intimidation effectively cut the DSE

Below left: Mules carry Chinese artillery during the civil war. Advances in military technology have meant that the problems of logistics and supply in unfamiliar terrain can now be more easily overcome. A Bell Huey helicopter (left) disgorges supplies and ammunition to US troops in Vietnam. Below right: The mountain forests of Central America give perfect cover from air attack for this guerrilla in El Salvador. Bottom: Soldiers of the 2nd US Infantry Division after having captured a ridge suitable for observation during the Korean War.

off from food and recruits. The GNA also had the same advantage as other regular forces in similar circumstances, possessing a formal line of communications that could keep them supplied with food and warm clothes. By contrast the insurgents were dependent upon precarious mule trains that were increasingly vulnerable to air attack. The ability of the GNA to continue its operations in winter was a principal factor in the DSE's failure, as was the communists' over-confidence in their ability to hold the mountain strongholds, which led the DSE to stand ground against GNA offensives in 1948 and 1949. Similarly, although forested or jungle-covered mountain regions could conceal the guerrilla – as in the Annamite mountains of Vietnam, the Sierra Maestra or Cyprus – bare mountain slopes as encountered in Greece or contemporary Afghanistan make guerrilla movement safe only at night.

Conventional forces operating in mountains must still adhere to basic age-old principles such as 'crowning the heights' with piquets in order to secure flanks against surprise and afford better observation. With

out such precautions operations can prove most hazardous, as in the case of the US 2nd Infantry Divison which lost 3000 casualties from mortar and machine-gun fire when caught in the Kunuri pass on its retreat to Chongchon in Korea in December 1950. Similarly the Chinese People's Liberation Army is believed to have suffered heavy casualties in rather crude frontal assaults through the mountain passes into northern Vietnam in February 1979. Chinese troops were ignorant of the existence of a second summit on Gao Bao Ling mountain, and several other neighbouring summits were simply not shown on their maps.

Modern weapons and equipment have eased many of the problems of mountain warfare, however. In Greece the Grammos and Vitsi strongholds of the DSE were overcome between June and September 1948 with the assistance of two squadrons of Spitfires, the majority of the 3128 dead and 6000 wounded suffered by the DSE in the Grammos operations being attributed to air attack. After the DSE returned to Grammos the following year, the GNA offensive of August 1949 was spearheaded by 52 Curtiss Helldivers as flying artillery. In its operations in Aden in the late 1950s and 1960s the British Army used armoured cars to fire on concentrations of tribesmen on reverse slopes obscured from advancing infantry while helicopters were used to establish control of the heights. During the Radfan operations of May 1964, for example, men of No 45 Commando were dropped onto the summit of 'Cap Badge' peak and were then able to move down the mountainside clearing snipers who had held up the advance.

In Vietnam the helicopter was a major factor in overcoming logistical problems. Task Force Remagen, which was drawn from the 1st Brigade of the US 5th Infantry (Mechanised) Division, was successfully maintained in the mountainous demilitarised zone for the 47 days of Operation Montana Mauler, from March to April 1969, by heavy Chinook cargo helicopters using specially designed A22 cargo slings to eliminate the need to land. Progress on the ground was assisted by two armoured vehicle launching bridges (AVLBs) wherever rivers were unbridged or where bridges had been destroyed.

But advanced equipment and airpower does not necessarily provide all the answers. In 1962 Indian Air Force Fairchild Packets simply could not fly slow or low enough to hit the confined dropping zone at Tsangdhar on the Tibetan frontier during the few hours each day when the area was not obscured by cloud. Helicopters cannot descend without a reasonably flat and firm landing zone, and even hovering requires a cleared area. Helicopter performance is also adversely affected with increasing altitude. At 900m (3000 feet) a helicopter requires a maximum approach angle to landing zone of 20 degrees while at altitudes over 1500m (5000 feet) an almost completely flat approach is required.

Helicopters and aircraft alike are also affected by the turbulence and wind currents associated with mountains. During Operation Mare's Nest on Cyprus, which concluded in January 1959, atmospheric turbulence prevented the RAF's Sycamore and Whirlwind helicopters from hovering over peaks and troops were unable to descend on ropes. As a result only two out of the 16 planned observation posts could be established on prominent features.

Above: A Soviet supply helicopter takes off from Kabul, Afghanistan. The helicopter's advantage in manoeuvrability over ground vehicles is often nullified by the problems it has in bad weather such as snowstorms. Below: Afghan guerrillas show how difficult a target they can present as they sit lodged amongst rocks in preparation for an ambush. Convoys are particularly vulnerable to attack from guerrilla forces sited above mountain passes.

Nor does airpower always have the desired military effect. In Cuba the forests of the Sierra Maestra were so dense and damp that bombs and even napalm dropped by government aircraft rarely had much effect beyond 45m (50 yards) from the point of impact. Bombing the 2400-3400m (8000-11,000 foot) forested slopes of the Aberdares in Kenya during the Mau Mau emergency in the 1950s proved so speculative that it was abandoned as counter-productive. During Operation Lam Son 719 in Laos between February and April 1971 the US and South Vietnamese forces made extensive use of helicopters, but few areas were suitable for landings in the mountainous area of operations and the rain, fog and persistent low cloud during the monsoon forced pilots of ground support aircraft to keep to low altitudes. As a result North Vietnamese Army anti-aircraft batteries were able, in many instances, to prevent effective air support. In all, the Americans and South Vietnamese lost seven aircraft and 108 helicopters with a further 600 helicopters damaged.

For the contemporary mujahideen guerrillas in Afghanistan there can be few more fearsome sights than the approach of the ubiquitous Soviet Mi-24 Hind helicopter gunship with its rocket pods, rotary cannon capable of firing 1000 rounds per minute, missiles and bombs. Such a machine can annihilate a whole village in seconds; yet even the Hind is not invulnerable to ground fire, and the guerrillas are believed to have shot down three or possibly four during the Soviet incursion into the Panjshir valley in August and September 1981. Nor has the massive Soviet superiority in equipment and firepower yet enabled them to destroy the guerrillas although, admittedly, Soviet strategy in Afghanistan may well be designed to control only the main towns and roads.

For the Soviet soldier, however, the pattern of mountain warfare in Afghanistan is not far removed from the experience of his British counterpart a hundred years ago. One Soviet soldier wrote in his diary of his experiences: 'There was some hard fighting and we could see mujahideen on horseback in the battle, riders who attacked our artillery positions and even fired at our planes. We were getting desperate.' Another, an artilleryman, wrote home: 'What a dump. It's always freezing or unbearably hot, and I still don't know when I'll be getting out.' Both documents were removed from the soldiers' bodies by guerrillas after a successful ambush on a Soviet convoy in Baghlan province, north of Kabul, in the early summer of 1981.   **Ian Beckett**

Greek against Greek

The desperate fight for the future of Greece

Not only was the Greek Civil War a desperate struggle between the forces of the left and right to secure power in Greece, it marked the first round of what was to become the Cold War – the continuing confrontation between the two rival world systems of capitalism and communism. The international dimension of the war remained constant: British and American aid ensured the survival of the Greek government while the drying-up of support from the neighbouring communist countries of Yugoslavia, Albania and Bulgaria was a fatal blow to the chances of the Greek left-wing guerrillas.

After the invasion of Greece by the German armed forces in April 1941, a number of resistance movements developed in the Greek mountains. Varying greatly in political outlook the Greek resistance groups fought as much amongst themselves as they did the Germans, and in October 1943 open warfare broke out between the left-wing National Liberation Front (EAM – Ethnikon Apeleftherotikon Metopon), with its military wing the Greek National Liberation Army (ELAS – Ellinikos Laikos Apeleftherotikon), and its centrist and right-wing opponents. Known as the 'first round' of the civil war, neither side achieved complete victory, although ELAS did gain an edge over its rivals. Although the Germans had lost the war in the Mediterranean, they hung on in Greece, regardless of guerrilla activities.

Despite Greek hopes of Allied intervention, the main weight of the Anglo-American offensive was directed against Italy; Greece became a sideshow and it was not until the Germans themselves were forced to withdraw in October 1944 that the British arrived. By this time EAM-ELAS was undoubtedly the most powerful of the guerrilla-political factions – it claimed to have two million supporters – and it expected to play a major role in the running of postwar Greece, following talks with the British and the Greek government-in-exile at Caserta in September 1944. The British had other plans, however, and Lieutenant-General Sir Ronald Scobie, the British commander, was ordered to maintain law and order in the country and install the Greek government-in-exile under Georgios Papandreou.

At this time ELAS had expanded its forces to over 50,000 fighting men under the command of General Stephanos Saraphis, a veteran soldier. Although not a communist he was a staunch left-wing republican. ELAS controlled the countryside but the main centres of population where British troops were stationed remained in government hands.

Confrontation sparked into open conflict on 2 December 1944: the 'second round' had begun. The central committee of the Greek Communist Party (KKE – Kommounisitikon Komma Ellados) was confident that the time was right to strike: the Papandreou government was weak and far from popular, and ELAS was at the height of its power. Fighting broke out all over Greece but the main action was centred on Athens, where fierce street fighting de-

veloped. During the first two weeks in December ELAS made impressive gains: the road from Piraeus to Athens was blocked and the British were forced back into isolated strongholds. Realising the situation was desperate Scobie called for reinforcements. On 20 December he went onto the counter-attack, and with the newly arrived 4th Division began a bitter house-to-house battle to recapture Athens from ELAS. Superior to the guerrilla forces and supported by rocket-firing planes from the RAF, the British were able to force ELAS from the city.

By 7 January 1945 Athens and Piraeus were firmly under British control: the guerrillas had lost the military fight and, when General Scobie offered fresh ceasefire conditions on the 8th, ELAS was prepared to listen. Within the ELAS camp a violent debate opened following Scobie's ceasefire offer. Many of the guerrilla leaders – the Kapetanios – who had been active in the mountain struggles during the German occupation wanted to fight on, but the KKE 'politicians', led by Secretary-General George Siantos, favoured a ceasefire as a respite from military operations which were obviously going against them. They argued that the 'war' would be best continued in the political arena. The 'politicians' won the day and on 15 January a ceasefire came into effect.

Both sides met to discuss peace terms and on the 12 February 1945 the Varkiza Agreement was issued. The terms stated that ELAS was to be demobilised and disarmed while there would be a general amnesty for political crimes, and that a plebiscite would be held to decide the future regime of the country, to be followed by a general election.

Above: Welsh Paras advance into the Omonia Square sector of Athens in an attempt to break up concentrations of ELAS guerrillas in late 1944.

Although in permanent opposition to the government, the Greek communists accepted the Varkiza Agreement and even expelled those members who wanted to continue the guerrilla war. The already complicated debate existing within the KKE was furthered by the arrival of Nikos Zachariadis, a leading communist who had survived World War II in a German concentration camp. Released by the Allies from Dachau he returned to Athens in April 1945, and taking over his old position of secretary-general he assumed leadership of the KKE.

The promised general election was held on 31 March 1946 but it was boycotted by the KKE who claimed that constant harassment by the forces of the right prevented a fair election, and that government promises had not been upheld. Whatever the truth of their claims the election represented a triumph for the right-wing. While the KKE was allowed to exist – in the interests of democracy, the British insisted on this – and continued to work in Athens under Zachariadis' control, an increasing number of disgruntled left-wingers crossed the border into Yugoslavia to prepare for the next 'round' of the civil war.

By mid-1946 not only was Yugoslavia under communist control, so too were Albania and Bulgaria. These were to become safe bases for those communists and left-wingers determined to further the guerrilla struggle. During 1946 the fighting was sporadic; confined mainly to northern Greece it consisted mainly of the assassination of government officials and assaults against police outposts.

In August, Markos Vaphiadis was selected by the central committee of the KKE to take overall command of the guerrilla bands operating out of Yugoslavia. Known as General Markos he was the best man for the task and although not a regular soldier he had a natural military talent, and, more to the point, he was respected by the other guerrilla leaders, whose traditional reputations for spirited independence rendered large-scale combined operations all but impossible. At first the guerrillas called themselves the Republican Army but in December 1946 they adopted the title of the Democratic Army of Greece (DSE – Dimokratikos Stratos Ellados).

The British forces remained in Greece but took no part in the fighting, confining themselves to training government forces and providing them with arms and equipment. Nevertheless the British authorities in Athens were concerned at the lack of progress made by the government in combating the guerrillas. Not only was the civil war becoming increasingly expensive to an impoverished postwar Britain – international attitudes towards Britain's relationship to the corrupt and oppressive Greek government were becoming ever-more hostile, and the embarrassment to

Above: Locals of the Kalabaka area of northern Greece are recruited to form a type of home guard to aid the GNA against guerrillas and choose their own weapons from a pile of rifles. Below right: Decapitation was a gruesome practice among right-wing civilian bands.

Supplying the Democratic Army

The DSE relied on two main sources of supply and support – neighbouring communist countries and its own underground organisation YIAFAKA. Yugoslavia, Albania and Bulgaria supplied a limited flow of rations, ammunition, small arms, mortars, explosives and transport while also providing refuge and training facilities. YIAFAKA, operating throughout Greece, gathered funds, intelligence, recruits and further supplies of food and clothing for the guerrilla forces.

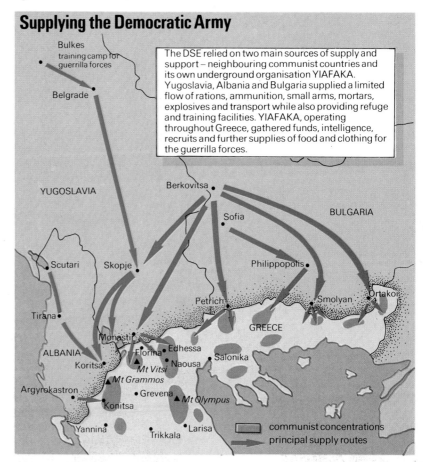

Bulkes training camp for guerrilla forces

Belgrade

YUGOSLAVIA

Berkovitsa

BULGARIA

Sofia

Scutari

Skopje

Philippopolis

Tirana

Petrich

Smolyan

Ortakoi

GREECE

Monastir

ALBANIA

Florina

Edhessa

Koritsa

Mt Vitsi

Naousa

Salonika

Mt Grammos

Argyrokastron

Grevena

Mt Olympus

Konitsa

Yannina

Trikkala

Larisa

communist concentrations

principal supply routes

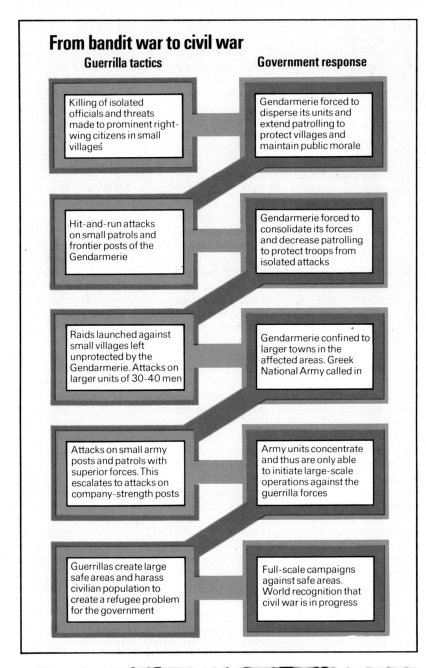

From bandit war to civil war

Guerrilla tactics	Government response
Killing of isolated officials and threats made to prominent right-wing citizens in small villages	Gendarmerie forced to disperse its units and extend patrolling to protect villages and maintain public morale
Hit-and-run attacks on small patrols and frontier posts of the Gendarmerie	Gendarmerie forced to consolidate its forces and decrease patrolling to protect troops from isolated attacks
Raids launched against small villages left unprotected by the Gendarmerie. Attacks on larger units of 30-40 men	Gendarmerie confined to larger towns in the affected areas. Greek National Army called in
Attacks on small army posts and patrols with superior forces. This escalates to attacks on company-strength posts	Army units concentrate and thus are only able to initiate large-scale operations against the guerrilla forces
Guerrillas create large safe areas and harass civilian population to create a refugee problem for the government	Full-scale campaigns against safe areas. World recognition that civil war is in progress

Britain's new Labour government was acute. Accordingly, Britain turned to her ally, the United States, for help.

At first the Americans were reluctant to become involved, but in March 1947 President Harry Truman went before the US Congress to ask for $400 million in aid for Greece and Turkey. Thus was born the Truman Doctrine: 'It must be the policy of the United States to support free peoples who are resisting attempted subjugation by armed minorities or by outside pressures.' The American commitment was to be crucial to the outcome of the conflict.

Meanwhile the war continued. The Greek government's plan for 1947 was code-named Operation Terminus, a large-scale offensive that was planned to clear Roumeli in central Greece in April. This was the first major operation by the Greek National Army (GNA) but it had little success. The guerrilla DSE forces escaped the GNA's clumsy attempts at encirclement and the government forces found it difficult to hold territory even after it had supposedly been cleared.

Although the GNA vastly outnumbered the 11,000 men in the DSE they were clearly unpractised in the arts of mountain warfare. Markos showed that he was a skilful irregular commander: he gave the generals of the GNA an unpleasant surprise early in June by an unexpected move southwards from western Macedonia, posing a threat to Ioannina – the main town of Epirus – before withdrawing northward to the safety of the Grammos mountains near the Albanian border. Government plans for a series of winter operations were abandoned, leaving the guerrillas in virtual control of northern Greece.

The main strategic problem facing the army was that if it was engaged in clearing the guerrillas across the mountains, a force would be needed to provide a static defence of the towns and villages. This function had been provided by a hastily organised civil guard in 1944, but, poorly controlled, it was little more than an armed mob. In October 1947 a National Defence Corps (NDC) was formed under army control. Initially 40 battalions of 500 men were authorised, though this was expanded to 100 battalions in 1948 to provide 50,000 men. Formed on a local basis NDC battalions were responsible for guarding the civil community from guerrilla incursions. As part of the army, the NDC would leave policing functions to the Gendarmerie – a paramilitary force that was rebuilt under British supervision to supplement the NDC in a purely police role.

Lastly there were the bands of armed civilians. Although the British and the Americans strongly disapproved of arming civilians, the Greek government tolerated them. Their origins lay in the right-wing bands that had fought ELAS and they were a useful if over-zealous force, capable of inhibiting the many communist sympathisers who were to be found in every Greek town and village. The most formally organised of these groups were known as May, who were enthusiastic 'head-hunters', as this extract from a training manual suggests: 'The bodies should be searched minutely. They should not be left until all weapons and identification have been removed. They should then be decapitated and their heads placed in a bag and taken to the nearest command post for public exposure.'

The quality of the GNA may have been low, but the guerrillas of the DSE were not a great deal better:

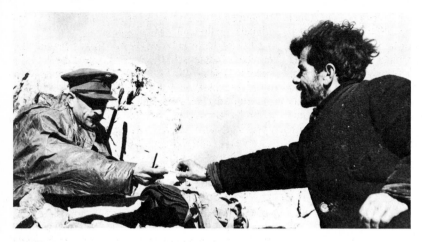

Below: Mopping-up operations along the Albanian border as troops of the Greek National Army clear a village. One such operation netted 500 guerrillas. Above: Captured along the Albanian border, a rebel is given a cigarette by a Greek Army officer before being led away for interrogation.

leadership was very variable in quality, morale could easily plummet in adverse circumstances, training was always rudimentary and, worst of all, the 'high command' was plagued by conflicting strategies of action. To a better army than the GNA, the DSE would have posed few problems.

Guerrilla numbers were never large. In 1946 operations had started with only 2500 men and at its height in 1948 the DSE rarely had a strength of more than 25,000. But unlike the government forces, almost all these men were fighters; logistical and other auxiliary troops were at an absolute minimum. This was both a strength and a weakness. The guerrillas were unencumbered by slow-moving support troops, but outside their immediate base-areas survival was difficult. Thus guerrilla units in central Greece and the Peloponnese had little strategic mobility or staying power. And, unlike the government forces, the DSE was incapable of fielding balanced forces. As a mainly infantry army the DSE was armed with rifles, light machine guns, mortars and a very few pieces of light artillery.

Besides the terrain the greatest asset possessed by guerrillas is the attitude of the people. During the war against the Germans, ELAS had gained support from Greek society as a whole, in so much as ELAS was a broad-based nationalist resistance movement. By 1946 not only were the Greek people sick of war – the Germans had systematically devastated the country leaving it virtually destitute – but loyalties were increasingly divided. Nevertheless, the DSE was also supported by an underground intelligence network

known as Yiafaka, some 50,000 strong, which was able to supply the guerrillas with information of GNA movements, supply aid and money and assist in individual operations. But the support of the people as a whole was ambivalent: although many Greeks detested the Athens government they had little sympathy for the DSE, who often acted more as bandit invaders than liberators. As the Gendarmerie and other paramilitary forces became more efficient in their policing duties then opportunities for collaboration with the DSE grew less and the influence of Yiafaka declined.

The strategic position of the DSE was further complicated by their decision to make full use of Yugoslavia – and to a lesser extent Albania and Bulgaria – as their centre of supply. Although the Balkan communists were prepared to help the DSE in their general aims, there existed a deep suspicion between the Balkan Slavs and the Hellenic Greeks – communists or not. Both Yugoslavia and Bulgaria had territorial designs on Greek Macedonia and Thrace respectively, and this was well known in Greece – a fact that made many Greeks suspicious of the DSE who had, in fact, been forced to agree to certain territorial concessions to their Balkan 'benefactors'. Despite this the guerrillas would never have been able to operate effectively without the sanctuary provided by Yugoslavia.

The DSE strategy of 1947 had been to contain the main enemy offensive and then to seize the initiative with classic hit-and-run guerrilla raids. This was to change, however, as an unintended consequence of increased government repression in Athens. In October the communist press was banned and Zachariadis and his fellow communists made their way to the mountains and joined Markos. Markos's freedom of action was curtailed by the new arrivals and a bitter personal feud developed between him and Zachariadis.

The influence of Zachariadis was soon felt in a change in the guerrillas' strategy: a politician rather than a soldier, he intended to take possession of a sizeable area of northern Greece – 'Free Greece' – and set up a government. To his mind a government – any government – was better than none at all, and more importantly he hoped that it would be recognised by the other communist Balkan states, thus giving greater legitimacy to his claims to represent Greece vis-à-vis the Athens administration. In December 1947 the formation of the Provisional Democratic Government of Greece was announced to the Greek nation; and to convert intentions into reality, on Christmas Day the DSE launched a full scale offensive against the town of Konitsa, the intended seat of the new government. Despite initial success the DSE forces were repulsed and casualties were heavy. The DSE, for all its success as a guerrilla force, was neither equipped nor trained for positioned warfare of this nature.

As the GNA prepared for its spring offensive of 1948 American aid and advice began to make itself felt. The American mission under the command of General James A. Van Fleet was determined on the most vigorous offensive action, and Van Fleet urged the GNA to quit the towns and fight in the mountains.

Operation Dawn opened on 15 April and was directed against DSE outposts in the Roumeli mountains. The GNA squeezed the guerrillas from their strongholds. After this success, the next stage was put

Below: As GNA troops closed in on the guerrilla strongholds in the north, lines of observation posts were established in order to prevent the rebels slipping clear.

into effect, namely Operation Summit – the direct assault against the heart of the DSE in the Grammos mountains on the Albanian border. Some 40,000 men were deployed in a three-pronged advance, but the assault soon got caught up in the ridges of the Grammos range and a fierce battle began to develop around Mount Grammos itself. Realising that the GNA was trying to grind his forces down in a battle of attrition, Markos began to disengage – no easy matter with about 3000 wounded to evacuate. But skilful as ever,

he guided his DSE forces through the GNA net and slipped into the safety of Albania.

During the autumn of 1948 Markos launched a number of attacks on GNA positions, but with little success. The position seemed one of stalemate – but events outside the conflict itself were to turn the scales of fortune decisively against the DSE.

In the summer of 1948 the growing rift between Josef Stalin and Marshal Tito came to a head, and the latter was expelled from the Cominform. At first this did not affect relations between Yugoslavia and the DSE, who still received aid from Tito and continued to use Yugoslavia as a sanctuary. But the pro-Stalin Zachariadis believed that Tito would eventually turn against the KKE. Tired of guerrilla tactics, he proposed that the DSE should convert to 'conventional' warfare as soon as possible and not rely on guerrilla bases in Yugoslavia. Markos violently opposed this plan but he was suspected of being pro-Tito and was adroitly outmanoeuvred; by the end of January 1949 he had been forced to relinquish his post. Zachariadis was finally in command.

The KKE's political policy was firmly pro-Soviet but, unfortunately for the Greek communists, they had backed the wrong horse: Stalin was not prepared to support what he saw as hopeless adventurism on the part of the KKE in the face of British and US determination to keep Greece under their control. And Tito, understandably, began to withdraw support from his 'ungrateful' guests. Albania and then Bulgaria followed Yugoslavia in isolating the DSE.

The political error was compounded by Zachariadis' decision to convert to conventional warfare and take on the GNS on their own terms. Inevitably, the DSE was doomed and the final battles in the Grammos and Vitsi mountains in August 1949 sealed their fate. The GNA victory was total. The left-wing and communist groups split into feuding factions, while in Greece the triumphant government was free to carry out its policies without opposition. The war left a deep and bitter legacy: the wounds – social as well as political – have been very slow to heal.

Adrian Gilbert

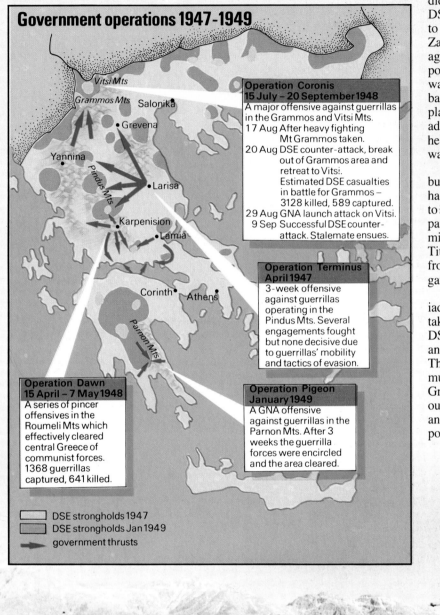

Government operations 1947-1949

Vitsi Mts
Grammos Mts
Salonika
Grevena
Yannina
Pindus Mts
Larisa
Karpenision
Lamia
Corinth
Athens
Parnon Mts

Operation Coronis
15 July – 20 September 1948
A major offensive against guerrillas in the Grammos and Vitsi Mts.
17 Aug After heavy fighting Mt Grammos taken.
20 Aug DSE counter-attack, break out of Grammos area and retreat to Vitsi. Estimated DSE casualties in battle for Grammos – 3128 killed, 589 captured.
29 Aug GNA launch attack on Vitsi.
9 Sep Successful DSE counter-attack. Stalemate ensues.

Operation Terminus
April 1947
3-week offensive against guerrillas operating in the Pindus Mts. Several engagements fought but none decisive due to guerrillas' mobility and tactics of evasion.

Operation Dawn
15 April – 7 May 1948
A series of pincer offensives in the Roumeli Mts which effectively cleared central Greece of communist forces. 1368 guerrillas captured, 641 killed.

Operation Pigeon
January 1949
A GNA offensive against guerrillas in the Parnon Mts. After 3 weeks the guerrilla forces were encircled and the area cleared.

☐ DSE strongholds 1947
▨ DSE strongholds Jan 1949
➤ government thrusts

Behind rebel lines

Kenneth Matthews had two spells with the communist-led Democratic Army in the Greek Civil War, once in winter in northern Greece as a journalist accompanying a UN Commission, and once in autumn in the south, when he was kidnapped by a rebel raiding force and held captive by the guerrillas for 16 days.

66 Greek mountains . . . the words might call up pictures of thyme-scented mountain paths and shepherd boys with pan-pipes on the slopes of Parnassus. But what I chiefly remember is the play of moonlight on bare screes and wastes of thorny scrub, as the sixth, seventh, eighth hour of a guerrilla night march prolonged itself to the point of utter exhaustion. A guerrilla must be for ever on the move, and night is safer for movement than day.

For equipment, a guerrilla needs no more than a gun, a grievance, and a mountainous country. No problem about the gun in Greece, after several years of world war. He might dispense with the grievance if he simply liked the guerrilla life, as many of the Greek rebels did. But he cannot do without the mountains, which give him the chance of shaking off all pursuers.

The mountain villages offer temporary shelter or sanctuary – primitive habitations of timber or stone, clinging precariously to the cliff, they are all but inaccessible to police cars or army transport. Even so, they must not be used as a base. When I was a prisoner of the rebels, I slept – when I was allowed to sleep – in a shepherd's hut, in a cave-mouth, on the floor of a ruined chapel. Only in the last phase of my captivity, on a village bed.

At first the government tried to maintain gendarmerie posts in the larger villages. What happened? The rebels could easily muster a superior force, cut the telephone wires (if there were any) and lay siege to these posts, knowing that no help could arrive for hours, perhaps days. I stumbled by accident on the scene of one such raid, while the blood was still wet on the cobbles of the village street. The rebels had brought up on mule-back a Piat anti-tank gun and had spent the night knocking chips off the gendarmerie building and calling on the handful of defenders to surrender. On that occasion it was the attackers who had suffered casualties, and they had retreated at daybreak, carrying away with them the headmen of the little community, who were never heard of again.

The government finally withdrew these vulnerable outposts of law and order; and at the height of the civil war the whole of the mountainous interior of Greece was abandoned to the rebels. It was the rebel 'zone' and it was 'blockaded'. Those outside who wanted to go in, for example 150 foreign journalists, were prevented from doing so (one, the American George Polk, was murdered in the attempt); those trapped inside could not get out. But thousands had already fled to become refugees in the big cities; and any young and active people left were conscripted by the rebels. The Greek countryside was not only rebel-controlled but practically depopulated.

The blockade deprived the rebel zone of basic

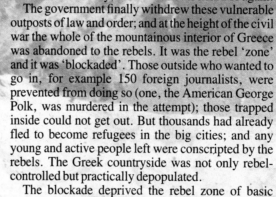

Below: The lonely mountains of Greece provided perfect terrain for guerrilla operations. Inset below: Welcome refreshment for rebels in a taverna in occupied territory. The price of holding on to territory could be high, however. Inset below right: Rebel captives are led away.

foods. There was no bread. When the United Nations made their privileged entry into the zone in the season of snow, the delegates were astonished and dismayed to find the menu in the coffee-house reduced to a tot of spirits and a dried fig; they hastily assembled a mule-train to return to government territory and fetch supplies. I was lucky in suffering my kidnapping in October, the month of harvest; we ate – sparingly – eggs and tomatoes, walnuts and currant-grapes. The rebels on the northern frontiers were provisioned by their communist neighbours, Yugoslavia, Albania and Bulgaria.

I spent two days in an army camp near the Yugoslav frontier, exposed to spasmodic shelling from an artillery piece on Mount Belles; a rebel deserter told us that the gunners drew a daily ration of 50g (1¾ ounces) of bread from their Yugoslav allies. A rebel band on Parnassus, alarmed by the approach of winter, slaughtered a flock of sheep and pickled the meat in 12 old cheese barrels, but then, cumbered by their hoard, from which they could not bear to be parted, they forgot the first principle of guerrilla warfare, which is instant mobility, and were captured, barrels and all, by the pursuing army.

The army made these occasional punitive sallies, especially if provoked; but for long periods the rebels were left to their own devices. They set to work creating a state within a state, copying the institutions of their communist neighbours.

On the second day of my captivity, I faced an interrogation by a village soviet, three men and a woman, across a kitchen table; I learnt that there were 400 of these soviets, or 'people's councils', in southern Greece alone. To each village was assigned a 'people's policeman' – those I had to do with were surly youngsters, strolling about aimlessly with a gun. There were also 'people's courts', largely occupied with confiscating and re-distributing the property of 'monarcho-fascist' owners. A communist newspaper circulated. The seat of this unconstitutional government was on the frontier, a rebel metropolis in the shape of an agglomeration of wooden huts, camouflaged by the oak and chestnut of the northern forest. Here the 'ministers' met; here the 'generals' planned their strategy; and a telephone exchange kept

them in touch with their comrades and sponsors in the adjoining states.

Although fortifying themselves with all the apparatus of a communist society, the rebels were not much occupied with ideology. Their propaganda appealed mainly to nationalism, independence: 'British out!', 'Americans out!' – these were the slogans shouted in the mass demonstrations. I must have talked to hundreds of the disaffected and their motives were as varied as their characters. The leaders had their minds locked on the prospect of political power. The professional soldiers mostly had personal injuries to avenge; if some were ambitious, was there not a revolutionary tradition in Greece? The tragic elements of the rebel army were the children, the boys and girls of school age or only a little older, who were flocking to the rebel ranks as if they were going to a banner-waving march through peaceable city streets. They were making a life-or-death choice on the strength of a teenage impulse.

Ironically, the very expansion of the rebel army contributed to its undoing. When recruits began to be numbered in thousands, true guerrilla warfare went out of fashion. The recruits had to be 'trained', formed into 'battalions' and 'brigades'. The rebel chieftain into whose hands I fell assured me that in face of a full-scale army offensive, his forces would scatter and give ground and so neutralise the enemy's superior firepower. It did not work out like that. The 'brigades' were too unwieldy; they could not scatter quickly and effectively; they were cut to pieces when the offensive came. In the far north, two or three squadrons of American-built Helldivers proved the decisive instrument, bombing the rebel gun-emplacements and strongpoints in the mountains. The rebel 'capital' in the forest was overrun; the remnants of the rebel army streamed back over the frontier as refugees, and when Tito closed the frontier a little later, it was all over.

The surprise was that after all the killing (the death toll exceeded 50,000 – I lost more friends in the Greek Civil War than in Britain's war against Hitler), the end when it came was so sudden and complete. Peace settled back on the Greek mountains, absolute peace, and has not been disturbed again. **"**

Showdown in the Grammos

How the communists were destroyed in the mountains

By the end of February 1949, the Greek National Army (GNA) was in a position to make an effective effort to wipe out the communist-led Democratic Army (DSE). The United States, determined that the communists should not succeed, had been pouring military aid into Greece since mid-1947, and by early 1949 the GNA had received some $170 million worth of equipment. There had also been a substantial alteration in the structure of the GNA's high command. More importantly, under the guidance of General James A. Van Fleet, chief of the US military advisory group, a change was made in the tactics used against the communists. Rather than occupying a few key villages and allowing the guerrillas to employ hit and run tactics against them, the GNA decided that concentrated sweeps of communist strongholds would be far more effective and might force the insurgents into static defence positions.

Under General Alexandros Papagos – who had commanded the Greek Army in 1940 and was prob-

During the final five-day offensive against the communists in the Grammos mountains in August 1949, the Royal Hellenic Air Force (RHAF) flew 826 sorties and unleashed some 250 tons of napalm, bombs and rockets on the guerrilla positions. Throughout the war, air superiority had never been in question yet it had taken the RHAF several years effectively to exploit its advantage.

In early 1947 the RHAF consisted of 58 obsolete aircraft and 291 pilots. Despite the delivery of 250 war-surplus aircraft from Britain later that summer, the air force was still faced with a chronic shortage of skilled maintenance personnel, essential spare parts and suitable aircraft. The RHAF deployed its aircraft in reconnaissance, target location, resupply in the field and direct air attack against troops and guerrilla positions. One of the main advantages of complete control of the air was that it severely restricted daylight movement by guerrilla forces; it also enabled the RHAF to harass Democratic Army forces that were either withdrawing from action or evading government encircling operations. Aircraft were particularly advantageous in the mountainous terrain, which limited the use of artillery, and they substantially increased efficiency in command liaison and communication on the battlefield.

The introduction in August 1949 of 52 Curtiss SB2C Helldivers, purchased from the US Navy, gave the RHAF the edge it needed and effectively decided the outcome. Since 1947 the air force had relied mainly on Spitfires and converted C-47 Dakotas for its ground attack and bombing operations, neither of which was particularly suited to the task. The new Helldivers, flying in 18-plane formations and fitted with dive brakes, enabled the RHAF to make concentrated steep-angled dive attacks and high-angled strafing and rocket assaults on guerrilla positions. They also had the advantage of a low stall speed and the ability to operate from short runways.

Jonathan Reed

ably the most able soldier available to the Greek government – a small war cabinet of six members was formed, a more efficient body than the unwieldy 36-member National Defence Council. Because of US aid the size of the army was increased by 20,000 men to 150,000 effectives. The DSE, by contrast, numbered around 19,000.

For all the disappointments that the GNA had suffered during the 1948 campaigns, they had cleared the DSE strongholds in the Peloponnese, and so by early 1949 the GNA was free to make a concentrated sweep from south to north of mainland Greece. The aim was to reach the Grammos and Vitsi mountains in the northwest sector, stronghold of the DSE. In the spring and early summer the GNA began an offensive by seizing peaks and passes to the south and northwest of Athens, while commando units followed up and eliminated remaining pockets of resistance. The government further reduced guerrilla operations by depriving the communists of valuable intelligence through the arrest and detention of suspected sympathisers. Thus the back-up organisation Yiafaka, the basis of so much guerrilla success, was snuffed out. The guerrillas were by now losing the initiative. Forced back into their most remote strongholds by the government offensive they were dealt a further blow in July when Marshal Tito decided to close the

Yugoslav frontier. They no longer had a safe area into which they could escape and regroup.

At the beginning of July government forces launched what they hoped would be the final phase of operations with an offensive against a communist brigade of 1200 men holding the Kaimakchalan mountain east of Florina on the Yugoslav border. The GNA hoped that these guerrillas would defend their territory and not fall back to join other guerrillas who were then being forced to withdraw to the Grammos area near the frontier with Albania. The plan was to divide and isolate the guerrillas and then destroy them piecemeal.

Within a week the operation in the Kaimakchalan had succeeded. The insurgents were overcome and lost more than 400 men, the remainder escaping over the border into Yugoslavia where they were disarmed and interned. Thus the GNA had driven a wedge between the guerrilla forces. The insurgents were now compelled to fight on two fronts. Their main force was concentrated in the northwest and they also had a division, entirely isolated, in the Beles mountains on the Bulgarian border in the northeast.

The DSE was now facing major problems of supply and communication, for the regular military tactics of fighting static defences that the insurgents had adopted since the early months of 1949 amounted to

Opposite: Close to the Albanian border, Greek soldiers await an attack from guerrillas advancing across the frontier.

Air support
Reconnaissance, liaison, strafing and dive-bombing

Operational tasks

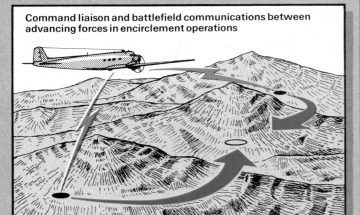

Command liaison and battlefield communications between advancing forces in encirclement operations

Resupply of troops in the field in terrain with poor roads

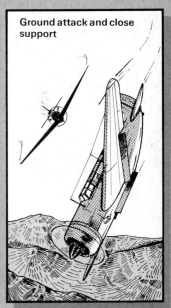

Ground attack and close support

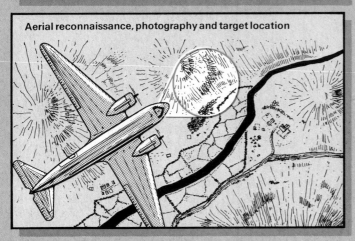

Aerial reconnaissance, photography and target location

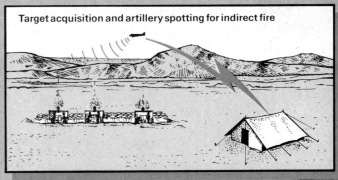

Target acquisition and artillery spotting for indirect fire

Operation Torch
August 1949

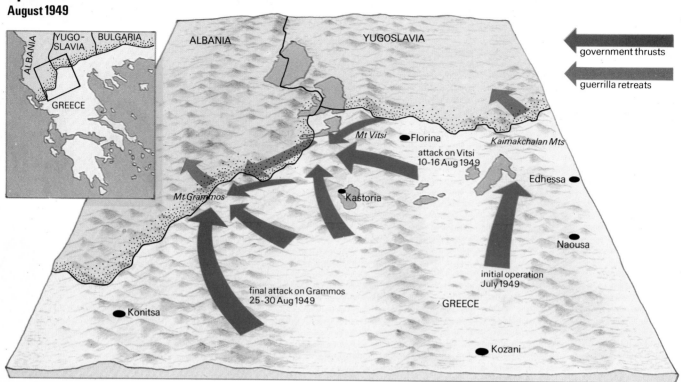

Above: A machine gun post above the town of Kalabaka. The high peaks and rocky terrain were easily defended and commanded excellent views over the surrounding areas.

the greatest mistake their leaders could have made. During the summer months Nikos Zachariadis, the new commander of the DSE, fortified some 650 square km (250 square miles) of mountain country around the Vitsi massif, so presenting the GNA with a known guerrilla location and the DSE with a front 65 km (40 miles) long. Zachariadis concentrated about 7000 troops in the area and approximately 5000 to the southwest in the Grammos range.

On 1 August 1949 Operation Torch was launched. This, it was hoped, would finally crush the communists. Initially it was intended that there should be a diversionary attack against Grammos followed by a sudden switch to Vitsi. Because the rest of Greece had been cleared, Papagos was able to employ six of his available eight divisions in the operation. On 5 August II Corps moved against the Grammos guerrillas but after a week there was a stalemate.

On 10 August the three divisions of I Corps moved against the Vitsi fortifications where they met stiff resistance from the communists, who held fast to their positions, but the guerrillas were now using tactics to which they were not accustomed and the weight of artillery fire and aerial bombardment against their positions was too much for their meagre forces to withstand. By 16 August Vitsi had fallen. The guerrillas suffered 2000 casualties although 4000 insurgents escaped to Albania. Once over the Albanian border these guerrillas re-formed and began to filter back. A further 1000 crossed into Yugoslavia but were disarmed and detained.

Meanwhile, further east, III Corps had taken the Beles range within a few days, though once again the bulk of the guerrillas (about 1000) escaped – this time over the Bulgarian border – and only some 10 per cent of the defending force were killed or captured.

Following their success in clearing the Vitsi and Beles areas the GNA returned to the problem of defeating the guerrillas in the Grammos mountains. It

was at this point that the 52 Curtiss Helldivers supplied by the United States proved their worth. With their heavy armament of cannon and machine guns, and the two tons of bombs they could deliver very accurately, the Helldivers were of crucial importance in the GNA's efforts against the communists.

On 25 August, three divisions of the GNA supported by Helldivers launched a final offensive against the Grammos stronghold. In a pincer movement with one division attacking from the north and one from the south, the government pushed the guerrillas back and by the 26th several key positions on the heights had been taken. In order to prevent any attempt by the guerrillas to escape across the Albanian border, the GNA moved quickly along the frontier. The rain of artillery fire (using both incendiary phosphorous and high explosive shells) combined with the firepower of the Helldivers and the sheer number of government troops proved too much for the ill-equipped guerrillas. Now engaged in a static defence, the guerrillas were forced to fight a conventional-front war against the GNA, but it was not a tactic that they could successfully hope to continue.

By the 27th Mount Grammos itself had fallen. The following day GNA forces blocked the Starias and Boukas passes, the two main routes into Albania. By the morning of 30 August the Grammos range was effectively taken. In the final days of the fighting approximately 1000 insurgents had been killed or captured; despite the efforts of the GNA, the remaining 8000 had escaped into Albania, but as an effective fighting force they were finished and Albania by then had followed Yugoslavia's lead and denied them further assistance.

For the DSE Grammos turned out to be the final defeat. On 16 October 1949, under direction from Moscow, its leaders declared a ceasefire in order, they said, to 'prevent the complete annihilation of Greece'.

Alexander McNair-Wilson

The
HARRIER

The Harrier is the only V/STOL (vertical/short take-off and landing) jet aircraft in operational service anywhere in the world. Its nearest rival, the Soviet Union's Yakovlev Yak-36MP Forger naval strike fighter, is capable of vertical take-off and landing only. Curiously enough, the Harrier's short take-off capability is more useful in a military aircraft than VTOL alone. This is because an aircraft using a short take-off run can carry a greater weight of fuel and weapons than one lifting-off vertically. Therefore, the Harrier usually flies a STOVL (short take-off, vertical landing) mission to enable a useful warload to be carried.

The key to the Harrier's V/STOL performance is its Rolls-Royce Pegasus vectored-thrust powerplant. This has been developed in parallel with the Harrier's airframe, progressively improved versions powering the Hawker P1127 technological demonstrator in 1960, the Kestrel military trials aircraft in 1964 and the Harrier itself in 1966. The current version of the Pegasus develops 9752kg (21,500lb) of thrust. It is a turbofan engine with a low fuel consumption which channels its exhaust through four swivelling nozzles, in contrast to the conventional jet engine with a single fixed exhaust pipe to the rear. For a vertical take-off the nozzles are rotated through 90 degrees to point straight downwards, and once airborne they are progressively swivelled back to the aft position for conventional wingborne flight. For a short take-off the nozzles are rotated to an intermediate setting during the take-off run and then gradually swivelled aft.

During vertical flight the normal aerodynamic controls – tailplane, rudder and ailerons – are ineffective and their place is taken by the RCS (reaction control system). This system comprises valves in the nose and tail and at each wing tip, through which high-pressure air bled from the engine is fed. The air jets thus produced can control the Harrier in pitch and roll during hovering flight. Although the controls themselves are both simple and reliable, their operation requires careful training; one experienced pilot has likened flying the Harrier in the hover, to balancing at the top of four wobbly bamboo poles.

The Royal Air Force uses the Harrier in the close air support and battlefield interdiction roles and, in addition, it can also carry out battlefield reconnaissance. The aircraft's V/STOL characteristics make the Harrier virtually independent of fixed air bases with their vulnerable concrete runways and taxiways. Such installations are likely to be primary targets of Warsaw Pact attack aircraft in wartime and conventional close air-support aircraft could find themselves trapped on their airfields because the runways have been extensively cratered. Not so the Harrier, which can lift a warload of 2270kg (5000lb) over a tactical radius of 150 nautical miles using a short take-off run from 610m (2000ft) of runway. If even this length of runway is unavailable the Harrier can take-off vertically with a 1134kg (2500lb) warload and operate over a 50 nautical-mile radius.

However, in time of crisis it is intended to deploy the Harrier force away from its permanent peacetime bases to preselected dispersed sites. These would be carefully camouflaged so that the Harriers could operate unmolested by enemy attack. The ideal dispersed site would provide woodland in which camouflaged aircraft hides and storage dumps could be built with a stretch of roadway nearby for take-offs. However a grass meadow with a 396m (1300ft) unobstructed and level take-off strip could serve just as well. Urban sites could be used as easily as those in rural districts. Defence of the site from air attack or commando-style raids is provided by a detachment of the RAF Regiment.

Close support

Logistic support and maintenance during dispersed site operations present many problems. The two Harrier squadrons based at RAF Gutersloh in Germany require over 400 vehicles to establish dispersed sites. Even the minimal spares holdings required to support 10 aircraft over a two-week period weigh seven tons, and during sustained air operations the Harriers sites would require regular resupply of fuel and ordnance. Helicopters, such as the Puma, or the RAF's new Chinooks, could be used for this task, but in wartime helicopter lift will be a scarce asset greatly in demand from many users. The aircraft itself has been designed to be easily maintained in the field, and with a built-in auxiliary power unit, it is completely independent of ground support equipment apart from that needed for rearming and refuelling.

Apart from the value of operating from secure, concealed sites, the Harrier's unique abilities enable it to respond to army requests for close air support more rapidly and efficiently than conventional aircraft. This is because the Harrier's dispersed sites can

Previous page: A Sea Harrier is guided down onto a carrier deck. Although broadly similar to the land-based Harrier GR Mk3, the Sea Harrier has a new forward fuselage and more advanced avionic equipment. The success of the Sea Harrier in the Falklands aroused new interest in the concept of V/STOL aircraft. Below: A Harrier takes-off from a wooded forward-deployment base. The fan air nozzles (one visible below the wing) are pointing downwards to provide the necessary uplift. Bottom left: The two-seater Harrier prepares to make its flight down a short take-off runway. Bottom: A Harrier is moved into its hiding-place in northern Germany.

Right: A flight of Harriers maintains perfect formation while on exercise trials. Bottom right: A Harrier of No. 4 Squadron taxis out of its lair ready for take-off. No. 4 Squadron is based at Gutesloh, the RAF airbase nearest the Iron Curtain, and in the advent of a full-scale European war its Harriers would be in the thick of combat from the outset.

Above: The Harrier in action – a fighter launches its rockets from an underwing dispenser.

be established close behind the battle front, perhaps as near as 16km (10 miles) to the forward edge of the battle area. The aircraft can then stand at readiness on the ground, awaiting orders to take-off. A conventional CAS (close air support) aircraft would need to be airborne on a 'cab rank' patrol to respond with the same speed as a 'ground-loitering' Harrier to a demand for air support. Consequently the Harrier's method of operation conserves fuel and reduces aircrew fatigue – both valuable bonuses to any air force in wartime.

The Harrier's primary navigation sensor is the Ferranti FE541 inertial navigation and attack system, which provides positional information projected onto the pilot's head-up display and drives a moving map display inside the cockpit. The Harrier's nose-mounted laser rangefinder and marked target seeker can pick out targets fixed by a ground controller's

laser designator and can also supply very precise target ranges.

The aircraft can carry a wide range of weapons on four underwing hardpoints and a fuselage centreline station. These include free-fall bombs, rocket launchers, flares, cluster bombs and firebombs. Two 30mm cannon are mounted beneath the fuselage and Sidewinder air-to-air missiles can be carried on the outer wing pylons. The two-seat operational training version of the Harrier has the same weapons capability as the single-seater.

The first operational Harrier squadron was formed within the RAF in 1969, and in 1982 three front-line units operate the aircraft. In RAF Germany Nos. 3 and 4 Squadrons are based at Gutersloh, while in the UK No. 1 Squadron at RAF Wittering is part of RAF Strike Command. Wittering also houses the Harrier training unit, No. 233 Operational Conversion Unit.

The United States Marine Corps is the other major operator of the Harrier, with three light attack squadrons (VMA-231, 513 and 542) flying the single-seat AV-8As and two-seat TAV-8Bs. It was the Marines who pioneered the use of 'viffing' (vectoring in forward flight) in air-to-air combat. This technique involves the deflection of engine thrust to produce rapid decelerations or high pitch rates which would be impossible with a conventional aircraft, thereby making the Harrier all the more manoeuvrable in combat.

The Sea Harrier

The Marines have operated their Harriers aboard aircraft carriers and amphibious assault ships and a squadron of AV-8As (re-christened Matadors) serve with the Spanish Navy aboard the World War II-vintage aircraft carrier *Dedalo*. However, it is the Royal Navy's Sea Harrier which has made the greatest impact on naval aviation. Derived from the RAF's Harrier GR Mk 3, the Sea Harrier FRS Mk 1 is intended for fighter reconnaissance and attack/strike

A Sea Harrier is launched into the sky thanks to the revolutionary 'ski-jump' device that allows the Harrier's payload to be increased by 1134 kg (2500 lb), and makes the Sea Harrier a truly effective combat aircraft.

missions. While the airframe and powerplant are substantially those of the Harrier, the avionics have been almost completely replaced. A raised and redesigned cockpit canopy provides the good all round visibility required for air-to-air combat, and in the nose a Ferranti Blue-Fox radar is fitted for the air interception and air-to-surface search and strike roles. Other new equipment includes a radar altimeter, a simple autopilot and a self-aligning attitude and heading reference platform for navigation. The Sea Harrier can carry all the weapons used by its RAF counterpart, including the AIM-9L advanced, 'all-aspect' version of the Sidewinder air-to air missile. It is also to be armed with the BAe Sea Eagle sea-skimming, anti-shipping missile when this becomes available in the mid-1980s.

The significance of the Sea Harrier is that it can be operated from warships such as the Royal Navy's Invincible-class vessels, which would normally be regarded only as helicopter carriers. A 183m (600ft) flight deck – insufficient for the operation of conventional fixed-wing aircraft – allows the Sea Harrier a short take-off run. Its warload has been further increased by the invention of the ski-jump launch from an inclined ramp. This technique, which was first proposed by Lt Cdr D. Taylor, allows the Sea Harrier to lift 1134kg (2500lb) more weapons or fuel than its maximum load taking-off from a flat deck. HMS *Invincible* and HMS *Illustrious* are fitted with a ramp inclined at seven degrees, while HMS *Ark Royal* and HMS *Hermes* have a 12-degree ramp.

The Fleet Air Arm intends to operate some 50 Sea Harriers, assigned to three operational squadrons and a training unit. The first Sea Harrier trials unit was formed in 1979 and No.800 Squadron, the first front-line unit, became operational in 1980. The Indian Navy has ordered the Sea Harrier FRS Mk 1 to replace its obsolete Sea Hawks aboard the carrier INS *Vikrant*.

The FAA's Sea Harriers and the RAF's Harriers were blooded in combat during the Falklands conflict in mid-1982. A total of 28 Sea Harriers took part in the fighting, flying over 1500 sorties, while the small force of 14 RAF Harriers flew about 150 sorties. The

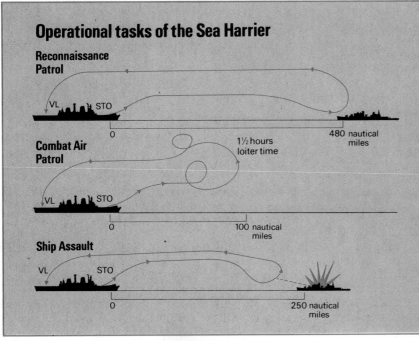

Operational tasks of the Sea Harrier

Reconnaissance Patrol

VL STO
0
480 nautical miles

Combat Air Patrol

1½ hours loiter time

VL STO
0
100 nautical miles

Ship Assault

VL STO
0
250 nautical miles

One of the Sea Harrier's greatest advantages is its tactical flexibility; able to carry out a variety of missions, it employs the now standard procedure of STO (short take-off) and VL (vertical landing) to ensure the best payload/range performance. On reconnaissance patrols the Sea Harrier can be fitted with a built-in nose-mounted camera and an optics pod containing five cameras slung on an underfuselage pylon. On CAP (combat air patrols) drop tanks are carried to extend loiter time and the aircraft's armament consists of two Sidewinder air-to-air missiles and twin 30mm Aden cannon. For attacks against naval targets on the surface the Harrier dips below the target ship's radar to deliver the latest Sea Eagle air-to-surface missile.

Above: A Sea Harrier keeps watch over a Soviet Kiev-class carrier sailing through the English Channel. Two Yak-36 'Forger' aircraft are visible on the carrier's deck and are still the Harrier's only VTOL rival.

Sea Harriers are credited with the destruction of 31 Argentinian aircraft in air-to-air combat and both versions of the aircraft undertook ground-attack sorties with bombs and rockets. The average sortie rate for the Sea Harrier was six flights a day, a strenuous schedule that the Harrier was able to carry out with considerable success. The aircraft's performance in this conflict was undoubtedly impressive, although it should be remembered that the theoretically more potent Mirage III fighters of the Argentinian Air Force were operating at extreme range from their bases and their pilots showed little inclination to engage in air-to-air combat.

A successor to the first-generation Harrier, the AV-8B Harrier II (RAF Harrier GR Mk 5) is now in an advanced stage of development. The US Marine Corps plans to procure some 340 AV-8Bs to replace its earlier AV-8A Harriers and A-4M Skyhawk light attack aircraft. The RAF's requirement is for 60 aircraft. The new Harrier is to be jointly built by McDonnell Douglas (60 per cent) and British Aerospace (40 per cent), with engine manufacture split between Rolls-Royce and Pratt and Whitney.

The Harrier II is powered by an improved version of the Rolls-Royce Pegasus, which although no more powerful than the present engine has a longer life before overhaul, and is more reliable and uses less fuel. The major change is the fitting of a larger wing, which is 14 per cent greater in area than that of its predecessor. It has a supercritical aerofoil to improve manoeuvrability and reduce transonic drag and it carries more internal fuel. Structural weight is reduced by using carbon-fibre composite materials instead of metal in many parts of the airframe. The

aircraft's turn rate has been improved by fitting leading-edge extensions on the wing, and lift-improvement devices give a better VTOL performance. Finally, a new raised cockpit has been designed for better visibility for the pilot. The Harrier II therefore offers considerable advances in range and payload over the current Harrier, but an improvement in performance enabling supersonic V/STOL operations will have to await the arrival of a Harrier III.

Harrier GR Mk 3

Type V/STOL attack aircraft
Dimensions Span 7.7m (25ft 3in); length 13.91m (45ft 9in); height 3.43m (11ft 3in)
Weight Empty 5580kg (12,300lb); maximum take-off (short take-off) 10,500kg (23,000lb)
Powerplant One 9760kg (21,500lb) static-thrust Rolls-Royce Pegasus 103 vectored-thrust turbofan

Performance Maximum speed at 300m (1000ft) Mach 0.95 or 1160km/h (720mph); cruising speed at 6000m (20,000ft) Mach 0.8 or 900km/h (560mph)
Range Combat radius with 1360kg (3000lb) warload 667km (414 miles); maximum ferry range 3330km (2070 miles)
Ceiling Over 16,760m (55,000ft)

Armament Two 30mm Aden cannon and up to 2270kg (5000lb) of stores on four wing hardpoints and fuselage centreline, including Sidewinder air-to-air missiles, 250lb, 500lb and 1000lb free-fall bombs, Snakeye retarded bombs, fire bombs, rocket pods, and flares

The bleeding heart of Asia

Since 1945 the Far East has never known peace

The signing of the formal document of Japanese surrender on board the USS *Missouri* in Tokyo Bay, 2 September 1945. General Douglas MacArthur is about to append his signature on behalf of the US government.

The Japanese surrender in August 1945 may have seemed to resolve the future of the world as far as the Europeans and Americans were concerned; but in one sector of the globe it raised more questions than it answered, and the conflicts it opened the way for are still with us today. This area of the world was the southeastern corner of Asia and the archipelago of islands that stretches out from it – Indochina, the Malay peninsula and what became known as Indonesia. All the nations in this region, with the possible exception of Thailand, have been involved in serious internal or external struggles since 1945. And it is perhaps not coincidental that Thailand was the only one not to have been part of a colonial empire in 1941 when the Japanese attacked.

The wars in this part of the world have seen some of the most intense conflicts ever between ideologies, races and religions; they have seen the imposition of a national identity on often unwilling minorities; they

have seen the expansion of some new states fiercely resisted by others; and they have seen some of the most hideous examples of man's inhumanity to man, in the slaughter of hundreds of thousands of communists in Indonesia and the deaths of millions in Kampuchea.

These wars can be divided into a number of categories. First of all there were wars against the colonial powers. In Vietnam and Malaya the communists soon dominated these struggles, but this was not always the case: Indonesian nationalists under Sukarno, for example, were not swallowed by their communist allies. These wars were fought by relatively badly equipped forces against much more technically advanced European forces; but the Dutch in Indonesia and the French in Vietnam had certain factors restricting their ability to deal effectively with the insurgents.

Secondly, there were wars concerning the consolidation of the newly established nations, against separation or break up. The Karen revolt that erupted in Burma in 1948 was one such war, as was the longstanding guerrilla campaign in the Moluccas

Below: The face of American involvement in Asia as US troops man an M60 7.62mm machine gun in Hue, February 1968.

against Indonesian authority. The Thai government's persistent attempts to destroy the power of the semi-independent warlords in the north of the country might be accounted another. In this regard competing national and minority interests could sometimes be resolved peacefully, as when Singapore became independent of the Malaysian Federation in 1965. But generally, such level-headed statesmanship has been lacking, and the position of national minorities – be they the hill tribesmen in Vietnam or the Chinese in Java – has been fraught with risk since 1945.

The third category of war might be termed one of communist containment. The success of Ho Chi Minh in the northern part of Vietnam in the early 1950s was a great boost to communist parties all over Asia, and it was inevitable that South Vietnam would have a serious problem in surviving. The intervention of the USA and the subsequent spread of war to all of the former French colonies made this one of the biggest wars fought anywhere in the world, a story of great heroism, of the most sophisticated weapons, but

also of horrifying brutality and complete disregard for human life. Indonesia, too, had its war over communism; in 1965 after more than a decade of small-scale activities, there was a spasm of violence against the left that resulted in a death toll whose proportions will probably never be known, but certainly numbered hundreds of thousands.

The final category of wars in the region are those attempts at aggrandisement by one state against another. These may be disguised as struggles for national unification – Indonesia's 'confrontation' with Malaysia in the 1960s, for example, or her conquest of East Timor in 1975. They may also be connected to ideology, or to fears about the stability of a neighbouring state. Vietnam's invasion of Kampuchea in 1978 may be put down to this cause. Nevertheless, they are classic examples of one state using its military power to extract concessions from, or to dominate, another.

Little of all these future developments could have been foreseen in 1945, when the surrender of the Japanese ended the war. The British, Dutch and French were all eager to regain their former possessions; the raw materials – rubber from Malaya, oil from the Dutch East Indies and the agricultural and mineral wealth of French Indochina – made them very attractive prizes.

Reasserting control over such a vast area would have been difficult in any case, but in 1945 it was compounded by other factors. The first of these was the attitude of the Americans. The US government had never felt comfortable about traditional European colonialism and, during the last two years of World War II, official American policy was to encourage a redistribution of power. In Vietnam this took the form of help to the nationalist guerrillas who were fighting

Above: The tension and alertness shows as British troops set out on patrol in the Malayan jungle, searching for insurgents during the Emergency of the 1950s.

suspicious (as Sukarno did in Indonesia) they had at least been given a taste of power. Then again, in Vietnam, the fact that the Vichy French administration initially collaborated with the Japanese gave the nationalists who took up arms against both foreign conquerors great moral weight.

On a practical level, too, the Japanese takeover gave nationalism a significant push. As Europeans left or were imprisoned, Asians took over parts of the administration that had previously been closed to them. They now had a vested interest in independence. And the experience of not having to undergo the almost ritual recognition of white superiority in social or professional situations made many unwilling to have it reimposed.

The final factor that made the smooth resumption of the colonial situation impossible was the suddenness of the Japanese surrender. Although ultimate Japanese defeat had been foreseen, the atomic bombs were not. Europe was expecting a campaign of three months to a year against obdurate resistance when the news of the end of the war came. Over enormous stretches of the world, the Japanese armies gave up, but the British army was still fighting its way out of Burma while the Americans were not interested in re-establishing colonial control – and so the nationalists took over.

Sukarno proclaimed the republic of Indonesia on 17 August 1945; Ho Chi Minh's forces marched into Hanoi on 19 August; the communist Malayan People's Anti-Japanese Army (MPAJA) took over the Japanese munitions all over the hinterland of the Malay peninsula, disarmed the Japanese forces and set up people's committees – and its political wing failed to declare independence only because of hesitation and prompt British action.

This was a period of confusion in which the seeds of future wars were born. For after taking such control, the nationalists were not prepared to go back under European rule. British forces reached Kuala Lumpur on 12 September; they moved into Saigon on 13 September and landed in Java later that month. Meanwhile, as agreed at the Potsdam conference, Chinese Nationalist troops marched down to Hanoi. But these measures could not alter the fact that nationalists were already in control in many areas. There were inevitable clashes, and within six weeks of the Japanese surrender there was fighting again in Southeast Asia – wars of colonial re-conquest that were the preamble to four decades of conflict. **Ashley Brown**

the Japanese, and a definite policy of no return as far as the French administration was concerned. The Americans even asked the Nationalist Chinese whether they would like to take over the northern part of Vietnam rather than suggest the French go back.

The second factor was even more important. This lay in the nationalist aspirations of many of the former subject peoples. The Japanese had shattered the myth of European invincibility, and although their administration had been hated because of its grasping, selfish brutality, by their very conquest they gave local nationalists a considerable fillip. Often they tried to work with nationalist politicians (as in Burma and Indonesia) and even when the nationalists proved

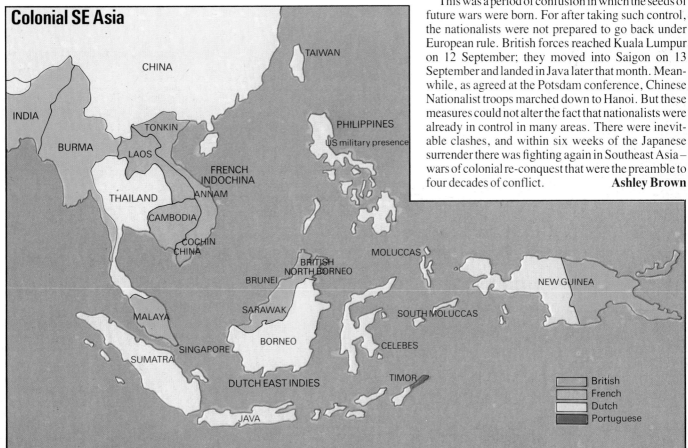

Colonial SE Asia

CHINA

TAIWAN

INDIA

TONKIN

BURMA

LAOS

PHILIPPINES

US military presence

FRENCH INDOCHINA

THAILAND

ANNAM

CAMBODIA

COCHIN CHINA

MOLUCCAS

BRITISH NORTH BORNEO

BRUNEI

NEW GUINEA

SARAWAK

MALAYA

SOUTH MOLUCCAS

BORNEO

SINGAPORE

CELEBES

SUMATRA

DUTCH EAST INDIES

TIMOR

JAVA

British
French
Dutch
Portuguese

Attack on Java

When British forces went into Indonesia

By the end of 1944 it had become clear to the Indonesian underground that the Allies would inevitably succeed in both Europe and Asia. The Japanese high command had also, somewhat reluctantly, realised that a complete Allied victory was imminent. With this in mind, the Japanese adopted a policy of promoting nationalism wherever they could in areas under their occupation. This was an attempt to frustrate the Allies should they consider re-colonising areas of Southeast Asia, for it was hoped that by encouraging independence movements the Allied armies would encounter well-organised guerrilla armies capable of substantial defence actions.

However, the Indonesian underground, realising the Japanese were desperate, had no intention of allowing them to dictate the format that any independence movement might take. Despite Japanese offers of independence in return for fighting against the Allies, the Indonesians were more concerned with the development and consolidation of their movement than in the death-throes of the weakened Imperial Japanese.

As the movement grew stronger the Japanese were almost powerless to resist the rise of the Indonesian Independence Preparation Committee and, indeed, somewhat limply encouraged its formation in a final attempt to curry favour with the developing independence movement. On 11 August 1945 Field Marshal Hisaichi Terauchi, Commander of the Japanese Southern Army, promised the Indonesians independence. He set the official date for 24 August. Sukarno, the leading nationalist figure, was urged by his subordinates to declare independence prior to the date proposed, but he doubted that the underground forces were strong enough to overcome the occupying Japanese. When the Japanese suddenly surrendered to the Allies on 15 August, however, a power vacuum was created: the Japanese were now a defeated power, yet there were no Allied forces to take their place.

Sukarno had continually insisted that independence should only be declared by agreement with the Japanese, but on the night of 16 August he was informed that the defeated Japanese now considered themselves mere 'agents' of the Allies and could not possibly entertain a declaration of independence. It was this information which finally convinced Sukarno that independence should be declared without delay. Accordingly, on the morning of 17 August, Sukarno proclaimed the independence of Indonesia.

The Allies had previously promised the Dutch that if their possessions in Southeast Asia were taken by the Japanese then the Allies would re-occupy and

Above: Dutch troops return fire from a nationalist sniper in Malang, East Java. Above right: New Year's Eve 1945 as British troops of the 12th Battalion, Yorkshire Regiment, search suspected rebels. Right: The attack on Surabaya. An infantryman gives covering fire as British tanks approach the eastern outskirts.

administer them until the Dutch could once again take over. Since their offensives in the Pacific were now over, the British had both troops and ships with which to occupy the former Dutch East Indies.

The first British troops arrived in Java in late September, by which time the disarming of the Japanese by the Indonesians was almost complete. The Indonesians had enjoyed some minor military successes against the demoralised Japanese troops and had, for six weeks, attempted to govern their 'illegal' republic. However, the arrival of British troops meant that war would be likely. The aim of the British was twofold: primarily they intended to establish an administration sympathetic to the Dutch and, secondarily, they wanted to halt the continued persecution of Dutch and European internees who had been initially imprisoned by the Japanese.

Initial occupation of west Java was accomplished fairly easily, but it was the concentration of Indonesian rebels around the area of Surabaya in the east that presented the greatest threat to the resumption of Dutch sovereignty over Java. Under the direction of Lieutenant-General Philip Christison, Commander-

Death in the jungle

The British Empire and Commonwealth forces found the fighting in the jungles of Java a vicious and dangerous experience, as this episode illustrates.

In November 1945 an RAF Dakota, bound for Semarang with a crew of four and 21 Indian soldiers, developed engine trouble shortly after take-off and was forced to crash land in a paddy field some distance from the nearest military base. The pilot had managed to radio for assistance and an RAF Thunderbolt was diverted to the area. The Thunderbolt quickly located the wreckage of the Dakota and the survivors standing nearby. A search party was sent out from Batavia under Wing-Commander B. R.

McNamara. On arriving at the scene of the crash, the three men were confronted by the horrifying spectacle of about 100 Indonesians, armed with knives, swarming round the plane. Hopelessly outnumbered, the party were forced to return to Batavia to fetch reinforcements.

By the time the search party – supported by tanks – returned, the Indonesians had dispersed. There was no sign of the survivors, either. But as the party began to sweep the area, the fate of the survivors became all too clear. Not far from the wreckage of the plane lay the headless body of a Sepoy. And in the surrounding jungle was found an assortment of limbs that were scattered around to such a degree that it was impossible to estimate the number of victims.

in-Chief of Allied Land Forces, Netherlands East Indies, General E.C. Mansergh issued an ultimatum to the rebels in east Java that the full weight of the British would be brought to bear against them unless hostilities ceased forthwith. The Indonesians defied the ultimatum and troops were moved against Surabaya in early November.

The initial landings at Surabaya were without casualties and Mansergh's Fifth Indian Division managed to establish a bridgehead around the harbour area. This facilitated the landing of tanks and artillery. In addition eight Thunderbolts and four Mosquitoes were landed at Surabaya, and destroyers stood by in the harbour, ready to provide a naval barrage. Yet despite this overwhelming display of military strength, the fanatical Indonesians were far from discouraged. In one attack 200 Indonesians equipped with smallarms charged British positions, but the combined strength of mortar and machine gun fire from Sherman tanks caused heavy casualties. In one day the British troops captured 80 Japanese 3-ton lorries, 70 field guns and 67 troop-carriers. Although the Indonesians actually managed to bring captured Japanese tanks into the battle, the combined firepower of the British 25-pounders, Sherman tanks, RAF Thunderbolts and Mosquitoes, supported by a constant naval barrage, inevitably forced the rebels to withdraw from Surabaya, but it was not until late 1945 that the British could claim to have finally gained effective control.

After this battle the British decided to put pressure on the Dutch to negotiate with the nationalists. But despite protracted talks no concrete agreement was reached, though continual prodding from the British backed by Australia and the United States was inexorably pushing the Dutch into recognition of the Indonesian Republic. It was not until November 1946, however, that the British finally withdrew – by which time the steady build-up of Dutch troops had reached a level sufficient to effect a takeover. Yet the continued presence of 'foreign' troops was a constant thorn in the side of Indonesian leaders and a solution seemed far off. Indeed, there was yet more fighting to come, though this next period of military intervention would be against the Dutch. **Simon Innes**

Britain's Vietnam War

How Saigon was occupied by the Gurkhas

Above: Scanning the horizon in the lower reaches of the Mekong Delta as French-led Vietnamese look out for Viet Minh guerrillas. Right: Major-General Gracey (far right) confers with Japanese officers at Saigon docks early in 1946 while a Gurkha watches in the background.

Wars in Indochina have captured much of the world's attention during the last 35 years. France's unsuccessful nine-year conflict there (1945-54) and America's equally unsuccessful involvement (which ended in 1973) are often referred to as the First and Second Indochina Wars. The more recent conflict in Kampuchea, sparked by the Vietnamese invasion of 1978, is now often called the Third Indochina War. They are actually misnumbered by one, for the first war in Indochina after World War II was a brief but important conflict that grew out of the British occupation of Saigon in 1945. That conflict produced well over 3000 deaths as a direct result of fighting and contained the interesting spectacle of British troops fighting alongside their erstwhile enemies the Japanese.

At Potsdam in July 1945 the Allied leaders decided to divide Indochina in half at the 16th parallel to allow Chiang Kai-shek to receive the Japanese surrender in the north and Lord Louis Mountbatten to accept the surrender in the south. To carry out his task Lord Mountbatten, Supreme Allied Commander Southeast Asia, formed an Allied Control Commission to go to Saigon. A military force, built around an infantry division, was designated Allied Land Forces French Indochina (ALFFIC). This force was meant, among other things, to ensure civil order in the area surrounding Saigon, enforce the Japanese surrender, and render humanitarian assistance to Allied prisoners of war and internees.

The Control Commission itself was concerned primarily with winding down the Supreme Headquarters of the Imperial Japanese Army in Southeast Asia and rendering assistance to prisoners of war. The head of the Control Commission was to be a major-general, whose own division would make up most of the force of ALFFIC; he thus 'wore two hats'. Major-General Douglas D. Gracey was named to head the mission, and his crack 20th Indian Division was to follow him to Vietnam.

In late August 1945, British occupying forces were ready to depart for various Southeast Asian destinations, and some ships were already at sea, when General Douglas MacArthur caused an uproar at Southeast Asia Command by forbidding reoccupation until he had personally received the Japanese surrender in Tokyo. This was set for 28 August, but a typhoon caused the ceremony to be postponed until 2 September.

This decision by MacArthur had enormous consequences, for Allied prisoners of war in Japanese camps were in a ghastly state and the additional delay before Allied troops arrived enabled revolutionary groups to fill the power vacuums that had existed in Southeast Asia since the announcement of the Japanese capitulation on 15 August. The chief beneficiaries in Indochina were the communists, who exercised complete control over the Viet Minh, the nationalist party founded in the north by Ho Chi Minh in 1941. In Hanoi and Saigon they rushed to seize the organs of government, liquidating or intimidating their rivals as they did so. While the Allies stated that the French had sovereignty over Indochina, American policy in practice was to oppose the return of the French to their possessions; but there was no such official American animosity towards the communist-led Viet Minh groups. Although the desire for independence was strong among the Vietnamese, it is doubtful whether the creed of the communists held much universal appeal. Their power derived from their ruthless efficiency.

MacArthur finally had his ceremony on board USS *Missouri* on 2 September, and three days later the first Allied medical teams parachuted into prisoner of war camps. On the following day a small advance party of support personnel and infantry escort from Gracey's forces arrived in Saigon to check on conditions and report back; on the 11th the fly-in of the first brigade, who came from Hmawbi field in Burma via Bangkok, began. When these advance Allied units landed in Saigon they found themselves in the unique position

Right: Nationalism in Vietnam had been a growing force from the 1930s, and the problems encountered by the British and French in 1945 were foreseen by many observers.

Roots of revolt
Uprisings against the French before 1945

Bac Son uprising 1940
Communists assume leadership of Tho tribesmen in revolt against French and gain their first strategic foothold in Vietnam. French disperse insurgents but guerrilla forces continue to operate in the Viet Bac

Ngeh-Tinh soviets 1930-31
12 Sept 1930 column of peasant demonstrators attacked by French aircraft. 216 killed. 16 village soviets established. Communist attacks on Vietnamese officials. French set up 122 security posts and successfully break soviet network

Mekong Delta uprising 1940
Communists block roads from Saigon into the delta and attack public facilities in countryside. 3 French, 30 Vietnamese soldiers killed. 6000 arrested during French suppression of revolt

CHINA
Cao Bang
Lao Kai
TONKIN
Bac Son
Red River
Dien Bien Phu
Haiphong
Hanoi
HAINAN
Vinh
LAOS
ANNAM
Hue
Da Nang
16 parallel
Mekong River
THAILAND
Qui Nhon
SOUTH CHINA SEA
CAMBODIA
Phnom Penh
Saigon
Vinh Long
COCHIN CHINA

areas where communist-lead peasant uprisings occurred

Viet Bac guerrilla zone

Above: Communist nationalism in 1944. Vo Nguyen Giap (left) addresses a unit of his forces during the campaign against the Japanese.

of being welcomed and guarded by fully armed Japanese and Viet Minh soldiers, the French having been disarmed and interned six months earlier, on 9 March, by the Japanese, who feared an American landing in Indochina after the fall of Manila and did not trust the French.

Gracey, who arrived on 13 September, immediately realised the seriousness of the situation. Anarchy and murder were prevalent, the administrative services of Saigon had collapsed, a loosely-controlled and communist-led revolutionary group had seized power and were even guarding his own office building; the Japanese were still fully armed and capable of undermining the Allied position. Furthermore he could barely communicate with his higher headquarters in Burma, his American signals detachment having been abruptly withdrawn by the United States for political reasons at the very last moment; it was a loss that could not be rectified for several weeks. A serious riot had occurred 10 days before Gracey arrived and bad weather was slowing the fly-in of his own troops.

Gracey wrote that unless something was done quickly the state of anarchy would worsen. The position was exacerbated by the Viet Minh's lack of strong control over some of their allied groups. So Gracey was persuaded by the French – in a move which exceeded the authority of his orders from Mountbatten – to rearm their local colonial infantry regiment, who until recently had been prisoners of war. They, with a nucleus of newly arrived 5th Colonial Infantry Regiment (RIC) commandos, would then evict the Viet Minh from what hold they had on the administration of Saigon. Gracey saw this plan as the quickest way to allow the French to reassert their authority while letting him get on with the job of disarming and repatriating the Japanese.

Gracey had other problems too, for relations with Mountbatten were never easy. In September Gracey drew up a proclamation that declared martial law and stated that he was responsible for law and order throughout Indochina south of the 16th parallel. Mountbatten took issue with this, claiming that Gracey was responsible for public security in key areas only. The proclamation was published throughout Saigon on 21 September and, although the Supreme Commander disagreed with its wording, the Chiefs of Staff and the Foreign Office later supported Gracey.

During the next few days Gracey gradually eased the Viet Minh from their grip on the city, replacing their guards on vital points with his own troops, who then usually gave way to the French; the Viet Minh would never relinquish their positions directly to the French. By 23 September, less than half a dozen positions still sported Viet Minh guards, and on this date the French regained control of Saigon. Gracey allowed about 1000 French former prisoners of war to be rearmed and, aided by fresh 5th RIC troops, they ejected the Viet Minh in a noisy but relatively bloodless coup in which two French soldiers, and no Vietnamese, were killed.

The Vietnamese reaction was predictable, if horrifying. On the night of 24/25 September a howling mob – not under Viet Minh control – butchered, abducted, mutilated and outraged scores of French and French-Vietnamese men, women and children. On the 25th the Viet Minh attacked and set fire to the central market, while the Gurkhas repelled an attack on the Tan Son Nhut airfield perimeter where one of Gracey's soldiers and half a dozen Viet Minh were killed. The British now had war on their hands, something which Mountbatten had sought to avoid.

For the next few days armed Viet Minh parties fought British/Indian patrols, with the Viet Minh suffering mounting losses. The British forces were highly experienced troops who had recently battled their way through Burma against the Japanese; many officers and soldiers had experience in internal security and guerrilla warfare in India and the North West Frontier. The Viet Minh, by contrast, courageous as they were, were still learning about war.

In early October Gracey held talks with the Viet Minh and a fragile truce began. On the 5th the senior French commander, General Philippe Leclerc, arrived in Saigon where he and his troops came under Gracey's command. However, on 10 October the state of semi-peace with the Viet Minh was broken by an unprovoked attack on a small British engineering party inspecting water lines near Tan Son Nhut. Most of the party were killed or wounded. Gracey accepted the fact that the level of armed insurrection was such that he would first have to pacify his key areas before he could afford to repatriate the Japanese. His hand

Below: Oil tanks burning in the Mekong Delta after shore fire was returned by a French naval patrol. Left: British and French troops on operations in the Mekong Delta in October 1945. Above: French troops manning captured Japanese tanks, mostly Type 89 Mediums and Type 94 Lights.

had been strengthened by the arrival of his second infantry brigade, the 32nd, under Brigadier E. C. V. Woodford; he had only recently completed the build-up of his first brigade, the 80th, under Brigadier D. E. Taunton. The third brigade, the 100th (Brigadier C. H. B. Rodham) would arrive on 17 October. On the day following the ambush, Gracey deployed 32 Brigade into Saigon's troublesome northern suburbs of Go Vap and Gia Dinh. The Viet Minh fell back before this force, which included armoured car support from 16 (Indian) Light Cavalry.

Spitfire reconnaissance sorties revealed that the approach roads to Saigon were blocked: the Viet Minh were attempting to strangle the city. On 13 October Tan Son Nhut airfield came under Viet Minh attack, their commandos and sappers reaching to within 275m (300 yards) of the control tower. They were at the doors of the radio station before the desperate attack was blunted by Indian and Japanese troops. As the Viet Minh were pushed back from the airfield perimeter, the Japanese were ordered to pursue them until nightfall, when contact was broken.

The fighting took on characteristics which later became only too common: ambush, assassination, hit-and-run raids, sweeps by security forces, and so on. This was the first of the modern unconventional wars and, although the Viet Minh had sufficient troops to sustain a long campaign, they were beaten back by well-led professional troops who were not alien to Asia. By mid-October 307 Viet Minh had

been killed by British/Indian troops; 225 more were killed by the Japanese (including 80 on one bad day in Dalat). British, French and Japanese casualties were small by comparison.

The Viet Minh next assaulted Saigon's vital points. There were attacks against the power plant, docks, airfield and even the city's artesian wells. Saigon was periodically blacked out at night, and the cacophony of smallarms, grenades, mines, mortars and artillery became familiar throughout the city. On one occasion the Japanese repulsed an attack on their headquarters at Phu Lam, killing 100 Viet Minh. Unable to overwhelm Saigon's defences, the Viet Minh intensified their siege tactics. The task of the first troops from France was to help to break the siege while aggressive British patrolling kept the Viet Minh off-balance.

On 25 October came the only known evidence of direct Soviet involvement in the area when a Japanese patrol captured a Russian near Thu Dau Mot. He was handed over to Lieutenant-Colonel Cyril Jarvis, commanding the 1/1 Gurkhas at Thu Dau Mot. The Russian had been sent down from China, but Jarvis's attempts at interrogation were fruitless so the intruder was given to the Sûreté, and from there he disappeared from history.

On 29 October the British formed a strong task force with the objective of pushing the Viet Minh main units further away from Saigon. This force was called Gateforce, after its commander, Lieutenant-Colonel Gates of 14/13 Frontier Force Rifles (FFR). Gateforce contained Indian infantry, artillery, armoured cars and a Japanese infantry battalion. In operations at Xuan Loc, east of Saigon, it killed between 160 and 190 of the enemy; the Japanese killed 50 in a single incident when they surprised a Viet Minh group in training.

Another notable operation occurred in November, involving the only kukri (Nepalese knife) charge of the campaign. On the 18th a Gurkha unit set out for Long Kien, south of Saigon, to rescue French hostages held there. The force was not strong enough to overcome the Viet Minh en route, and on the 22nd a stronger force was despatched. Japanese deserters were seen leading some Viet Minh parties. According to a Gurkha platoon commander, at one point the Gurkhas were held up by determined Viet Minh defenders occupying an old French fort. The Gurkhas brought up a bazooka and blew in the doors, then without hesitation drew their kukris and charged the position, putting the defenders to the knife. Long Kien was finally reached on that blistering hot day,

Gremlin Task Force

Japanese pilots surrender to the Allies.

The late Air Chief Marshal Sir Walter Cheshire was appointed, after the end of the war in the Far East, to be Air Officer Commanding French Indochina. He arrived in Saigon in September 1945 to join the Allied Control Mission which had a twofold task: to act as a link between Admiral Mountbatten, the Allied Supreme Commander, and Field Marshal Terauchi commanding the Japanese forces which had surrendered; and to supervise the disarming and repatriation of the Japanese troops in the southern part of French Indochina, now known as southern Vietnam and Kampuchea (Cambodia).

❝After we had established ourselves in Saigon we discovered that violent differences were developing between the French and their former colonial subjects. It was proving more and more difficult to prevent an armed conflict. Eventually, however, the Vietnamese appreciated that the French would in due course assume full and unfettered control and, in retaliation, the Vietnamese proceeded to mass armed forces on the approaches to Saigon. The build-up of our own forces had been delayed because of operations elsewhere, and it was questionable whether in their present reduced numbers they were in a position to resist the advancing rebels. It was at this point that it occurred to me that we had at our disposal a possible source of reinforcements in Indochina itself – the Japanese prisoners we had been sent to disarm.

The Japanese still had a number of fully armed divisions awaiting repatriation. After some hesitation it was decided to summon them to assist us in the maintenance of law and order. In practice the Japanese accepted their new role without demur and were immediately allocated a number of defensive tasks, including the protection of the vital road connecting Saigon with its main airfield.

They performed their duties with competence and, when necessary, fought with courage and determination. Had they been Indian or British troops they would undoubtedly have earned decorations.

The Royal Air Force in Indochina was also in difficulties but, unlike the army, it was not short of men but of fuel. After some discussion it was decided to make limited use of the Japanese Air Force. The planes were to be flown and serviced by their own crews and would be used only for transport and unarmed reconnaissance duties.

The next stage in the creation of this special force was to obliterate the Japanese markings on the aircraft and replace them with Royal Air Force roundels. Finally I decided to give this force a special designation to distinguish it from the RAF and the French Air Force. Inspired by the US example set in the Pacific, I chose the term 'Task Force' with the prefix 'Gremlin' because of its popularity in the RAF at the time. Thus the Gremlin Task Force, the GTF was born. Once the GTF was launched it quickly got into its stride with the main effort directed to transport operations.

The last major operation carried out by the GTF was to help in the transfer of an RAF squadron from Saigon to Bangkok. That was virtually the end of the GTF. In the course of its very brief existence the Japanese crews had completed more than 2000 successful sorties. They had filled a real gap in our logistic organisation and at little cost to the British Treasury.

As I left Saigon I reflected that when I accepted my appointment I had not expected to command a sizeable component of the Japanese Air Force on operations or to fly several of their aircraft. And I had certainly not expected to be guarded and protected by the very force we had set out to disarm. ❞

but though no hostages were recovered, about 80 Viet Minh had been killed on both sorties.

By early December Gracey was able to turn over Saigon's northern suburbs to the French, when 32 Brigade relinquished responsibility to General Val-luy's 9th Colonial Infantry Division (DIC). On Christmas Day, the brigade embarked for Borneo.

Many of the newly arrived French soldiers were ex-Maquis (French Resistance), not accustomed to strict discipline. Many, too, held the same attitude towards Asians as did some Americans a generation later. It caused Gracey to write a blistering letter to Leclerc. In it Gracey lashed out at those French who looked down upon his Indian soldiers. Wrote Gracey, 'Our men, of whatever colour, are our friends and not considered ''black'' men. They expect and deserve to be treated in every way as first class professional soldiers, and their treatment should be, and is, exactly the same as that of white troops . . . it is obvious our Indian Army traditions are not understood.'

On 3 January 1946 occurred the last big battle between British and Viet Minh forces. About 700 Viet Minh, including a cadre of nearly 200 from the north, hurled themselves on the 14/13 Frontier Force Rifles positions in Bien Hoa. The fight lasted through-out the night, and when it was over 80 attackers had been killed without the loss of a single FFR man. Most of the damage was done when supporting machine-gunners caught the Viet Minh in a murderous crossfire.

In mid-January, with the Viet Minh now avoiding large-scale attacks on the British forces, 80 Brigade handed over to the French and 100 Brigade withdrew into Saigon. Gracey flew out on the 28th. On his departure control of French forces passed to General Leclerc. On 30 March 1946 the *Islami* took aboard the last two British/Indian battalions in Vietnam. Now only a single company of 2/8 Punjab remained to guard the Allied Control Mission in Saigon, and on 15 May they left, the mission having been disbanded a day earlier as the French became responsible for getting the handful of remaining Japanese home.

For Britain's Vietnam War the official casualty figures list 2700 Viet Minh killed. The real total may be twice that figure, given the efficiency with which the Viet Minh recovered their dead and wounded; about 600 were killed by British/Indian forces, the rest by the Japanese and French. Forty British/Indian soldiers were killed; French and Japanese casualties were substantially higher. The long Indochina wars had begun, with a victory for Western forces. Four decades of fighting lay ahead.

Colonel Peter M. Dunn

Top: French Marines wearing 'borrowed' US army uniforms on operations in the Mekong Delta. Above: French representative General Leclerc meets Prince Sihanouk of Cambodia in 1946.

79

Mao and revolution

The beginning of China's civil war

The Chinese Civil War, which lasted from the summer of 1945 until October 1949, was the last violent spasm of a century of turmoil. It was the decisive phase of the struggle between the Chinese Nationalist Party or Kuomintang (KMT) and the communists. The communist victory, when it came, had immediate and violent repercussions in East Asia and intensified the hostility between the United States and the Soviet Union.

The armed conflict between the communists and the KMT began in 1927. Both these revolutionary movements had their origins in the decay of the old order in China. In October 1911 the last Manchu emperor was overthrown. Central authority vanished and, in northern and central China, warlords (military governors) strove fruitlessly to dominate each other. Their efforts were encouraged and sustained by foreign governments and concerns seeking to consolidate their own spheres of influence and prevent the emergence of an effective national government.

In the south, radical Nationalists set up a Chinese Republic. The Kuomintang, founded in 1912, was the first modern political party in China. Its leader, Sun Yat-sen, based his policy on the ideals of nationalism, representative democracy, and social and economic reform. After failing to persuade the warlords to accept his ideals he transformed the KMT into a mass movement. Assisted by Chiang Kai-shek

Above: The enthusiastic peasant guerrillas of Mao Tse-tung (inset) were honed into the tough infantry of modern China (right) in the war against Japan (below, Japanese troops on the offensive in 1937) and during indoctrination and training in the safe base areas of Yenan (below right).

The Long March – 1934

Mao's 10 Principles

- Attack dispersed and isolated enemy forces first, concentrated forces later
- Win control of extensive rural areas and small and medium-sized cities first; take big cities later on
- The main objective is to wipe out the enemy's effective strength
- In battle employ superior numbers to annihilate the enemy; in this way inferior numbers overall will ultimately triumph
- Do not go into battle unprepared; fight no battle you are not sure of winning
- Fear no sacrifice or hardship
- Use mobile warfare to defeat the enemy, and pay attention to the tactics of positional attack
- Seize those cities first that are weakly defended
- Use captured arms and troops to replenish strength
- Use the periods between engagements to rest, regroup and train

he organised the recruitment and training of an army whose task was to unite China by force. The success of the Bolsheviks in Russia in 1917 impressed Sun Yat-sen, and he adopted their forms of organisation for his own party. For their part the Bolsheviks willingly gave aid to the KMT, which Lenin regarded as a progressive movement. The KMT army was trained and indoctrinated according to the Soviet system – but the KMT leaders never accepted the ideology of communism. Sun Yat-sen remained a liberal democrat until his death in 1925, and Chiang Kai-shek gradually drifted towards reactionary militaristic views.

The Chinese Communist Party, meanwhile, was founded by a group of intellectuals in 1921. Under Soviet advice it aligned itself with the KMT against the warlords and set to work to build a power-base among factory workers of the big cities. The KMT, a broad coalition of progressive movements, allowed the communists to join as individual members.

After the death of Sun Yat-sen, Chiang Kai-shek emerged as leader of the KMT and regarded the communists' activities in the cities and the KMT army as subversive. In 1926 he dispatched the army on a northern expedition to crush the warlords, unite China, and free the country from all foreign influence. As the army advanced, the communists spread their ideas to the soldiers and to the people in the newly liberated areas. Chiang decided he had to consolidate his position within the KMT and so, in the summer of 1927, the communists were purged. Their immediate response was to foment uprisings in several cities. The insurrection was swiftly crushed. Some communists went underground in the cities while others fled into remote and desolate parts of the countryside, accompanied by their meagre bands of

armed partisans. The KMT armies resumed their advance and captured Peking (now known as Beijing) in 1928. That year Chiang was declared president of a National government in Nanking (Nanjing).

But the communists and the forces of warlords who had been compelled to adhere to the KMT, survived and revived. Their leaders, advised from Moscow, attempted a new wave of urban risings in 1929. As before, however, the workers in the cities and towns failed to respond, and many communists were killed. Meanwhile, in the Chingkang mountains, Mao Tse-tung had by study, reflection and practical experiment, devised a theory of revolution in which destitute peasants would be used as a revolutionary force. By combining armed force with intensive political work, Mao and his supporters were able to indoctrinate and organise the peasants. Mao aimed to win the favour of the rural poor so that they would be a reliable source of intelligence, food, recruits and other essentials to his guerrilla troops. By 1930 the Maoists had created a number of base areas in southern China, areas within which they and their adherents could move with impunity and evade or ambush their enemies at will. At the end of 1931 Mao was proclaimed president of a communist republic at Juichin (Ruijin).

Chiang now resolved to wipe out the communist threat by military action. To this end he launched five successive encirclement campaigns. The first four were conducted by ex-warlord troops, and failed. The tactics were clumsy and predictable, and the soldiers were vulnerable to communist propaganda. The fifth campaign, in 1934, was effective, being carried out by KMT main-force units. Communist guerrilla tactics were countered by using field works and obstacles to inhibit their mobility. The communists were

The Nationalist government never managed to capture the allegiance of the mass of the Chinese people. Their rule was always based on force – and often in the most obvious and unpopular manner. The public execution of petty criminals (above) in Shanghai in the 1940s was not the act of a secure government based on general consent.

forced into pitched battles where their inferiority in training and equipment led to defeat. They now faced the prospect of annihilation so, in October 1934, a column of 100,000 men headed west on the Long March, a strategic retreat of some 9500 km (6000 miles) across mountains, valleys and deserts. A triumph of endurance and resolution in the face of natural adversity and enemy attack, the Long March guaranteed the survival of the Communist Party and its army. Having outrun their pursuers and reached north Shensi province by the summer of 1935, the communists set about the creation of a new secure base area with its capital at Yenan (Yanan). A regular Red Army was formed for defence.

Chiang assembled his armies for another encirclement campaign, but was unable to carry it out. His commanders were reluctant to attack the communists at a time when a Japanese invasion seemed imminent, and in 1936 he was forced to agree to the formation of a 'united front' of KMT and communists against the Japanese. The communists were able to take advantage of this truce to recuperate and reorganise.

The Japanese began their campaign of conquest in July 1937. Many of the best KMT troops perished in last-ditch stands against the onslaught. The KMT attempted to defeat the invaders with conventional tactics, and it was overwhelmed. Chiang was forced to retreat far inland to Chungking (Chongqing), his refuge for the rest of the war against the Japanese. The defeated KMT, incapable of effective action against the Japanese, became demoralised and corrupt.

The communists did not attempt conventional operations against the Japanese invaders; they resorted to guerrilla warfare instead, concentrating their attention on the vast and ill-protected rear areas of the Japanese forces. Their activity made little impact on Japanese strategy, but it did maintain communist morale and attracted the sympathy of Chinese patriots. So, as the KMT sank into sloth and discredit, the communists established networks of political and military support in the countryside behind Japanese lines. The Red Army's only attempt at a large scale operation was the '100 regiments campaign' of 1941. This offensive, which used peasant volunteers to

assist the guerrillas and regular forces in attacks on isolated garrisons, ended in failure. The Japanese response was so brutally efficient that the communists took four years to recover and Chiang seized the opportunity to denounce the united front and order attacks on the few communist forces that lay within reach of his own.

However, when Japan surrendered in the summer of 1945, the communists in China were ready for action. The Red Army called up its trained peasants and was doubled in size in a fortnight. Guerrillas stripped the Japanese troops of their weapons and kit. The 4th Field Army was created under the command of Lin Piao and moved north to seize Manchuria, the industrial heartland of China. Soviet forces who had already overrun Manchuria assisted the communists' advance. As 4th Field Army occupied key ground, the 2nd and 3rd Field Armies took up blocking positions in north and central China to delay the advance of the KMT armies from the southwest. Put at a disadvantage by the communists, Chiang sought help from the United States. The Americans provided sea and air transport facilities, and as the KMT occupied the industrial cities in Manchuria, the communists vanished into the surrounding countryside.

At this stage, both the United States and the Soviet Union would have preferred to see a settlement by compromise. The Americans were as yet not hostile to Mao and had grown weary of Chiang during his long period of inactivity in Chungking. They were also suspicious of his anti-democratic tendencies, and had been favourably impressed by the communists' small-scale but persistent attacks on the Japanese. They tried to promote the idea of a coalition government of national unity, but neither Mao nor Chiang trusted the other. Stalin favoured a partition of China into two states, because he did not believe the communists were strong enough to beat the KMT. Neither of the emergent superpowers favoured a decisive armed clash, but they were unable to prevent it. Mao and Chiang were convinced that the future of China must be settled irrevocably by force of arms. They were able to wage war – and to force their stronger friends to take sides.   **Nigel de Lee**

Key Weapons

The
MIL Mi-24 HIND

The Mil Mi-24 Hind helicopter came into service in the early 1970s and has since become an important element in the Soviet Union's aerial ground-support armoury. The development of this helicopter had been shrouded in secrecy and its arrival on the military scene was greeted with particular interest by observers from the West. At first it was thought that the Hind was to be a simple troop-carrying helicopter, not dissimilar to the earlier Mi-8, but it subsequently became clear that the Hind was to have a far more extensive role, becoming in effect a 'helicopter battle-cruiser'. An expensive weapon by any standards, the Hind is a far larger helicopter than its equivalents in the armouries of the West; thus, for instance, the American helicopter gunship the Huey Cobra has an empty weight which is less than half that of the Hind.

The Hind is powered by two 1500shp (1119kw) Isotov turboshaft engines mounted side by side above the cabin area. The 1500 horse power engine gives the Hind a very fast maximum speed of 320km/h (200mph) and a cruising speed of 260km/h (160mph). The main rotor has five blades with flapping and drag hinges as well as swivel dampers and an automatically adjustable flapping-angle regulator. This system allows the helicopter to be extremely stable against side gusts or jet turbulence, enabling it to manoeuvre effectively within areas where low-flying jet aircraft are operating.

Coming into service in East Germany in 1974 the Hind-A has a four-man crew and is capable of carrying eight fully-equipped infantrymen in the main cabin. Armament is provided by a 12.7mm machine gun, mounted in the nose of the gunner's compartment, and a whole array of external weapons. Three weapon systems can be attached on each of the Hind's stub-wings: four missile pods containing 32 57mm hollow-charge rockets, capable of penetrating 200mm of armour at 1200m range; paired-rails for carrying up to four anti-tank missiles such as the AT-2 Swatter; and gun pods capable of carrying 23mm GSh-23 twin-barrelled cannon, also fitted to the MiG-21. Since 1980 the Swatter anti-tank missile has begun to be replaced by the more lethal Spiral system

Previous page: A flight of Mi-24 Hind helicopters at a Soviet air-base in Afghanistan. Below: A Hind-D is prepared for flight. Bottom: An early version of a Hind-A; unlike later A-series models this Hind has its tail rotor positioned on the starboard side.

Top: Maintenance crewmen work on a Hind-D. Beneath the four-barrel turret-mounted cannon is the sensor bubble, while the UB-32 rocket pods are visible under the Hind's wings. Above: Side and rear views of Hinds in flight over Afghanistan.

– a tube-launched 'fire-and-forget' anti-tank missile which is guided onto its target by laser illumination, and is reported to have a range of up to 16km (10 miles).

The Hind-A was followed by the Hind-C (the Hind-B did not enter service), a variant that lacked a nose gun and the ability to carry anti-tank missiles. In 1975 the Hind-D came into service. It was a substantial redesign on previous models and extended the role of the helicopter to that of a gunship. The fuselage has been rebuilt so that the pilot and weapons operator have separate canopies: the pilot's canopy is situated above that of the weapons operator giving both of them an unobstructed view forwards; the canopies have bullet-proof windscreens, and the crew has better armour-protection overall. The other major redesign feature was the installation of a Gatling cannon with four barrels, mounted in a turret in the helicopter's nose (the exact calibre of the gun is believed to be either 14.5 or 20mm).

A major production model, the Hind-D has been joined by the Hind-E which incorporates a number of other improvements. The calibre of the nose-mounted cannon has been increased to 30mm and has its own laser target-seeker; this development was probably intended to counter the 30mm armour-piercing gun installed in the US Air Force's A10 Thunderbolts. Avionic equipment in both D and E versions is of considerable technological sophistication: besides the low-airspeed probe (which juts out from the forward gunner's windscreen), new all-weather sighting systems have been installed, including infra-red sights and low-light TV, which will make the Hind especially effective in the flying conditions likely to be encountered in central Europe.

In East Germany the arrival of yet another variant has been reported; known as the Hind-F details remain scarce but the helicopter will be able to carry six anti-tank guided missiles (ATGM). This increase in ATGM capacity would tend to suggest that Soviet planners envisage an increasingly important role for the Hind as an anti-tank platform to bolster its conventional forces in Europe.

Whereas in the West it is normal practice to design and build separate types of helicopter to carry out differing roles, the Hind has been constructed as a multi-role combat helicopter. Besides being a troop carrier, it is equipped with rockets for a defence-suppression and ground-attack role, and its guided missiles allow it to be employed as an anti-tank aircraft. On the one hand, this makes the Hind an extremely flexible tactical weapon, but on the other, it can be argued that the Hind is too ungainly a helicopter to fulfil any of its allotted roles with real efficiency.

Not only does its large size make it vulnerable to ground fire, its lack of agility in combat situations would put it at a grave disadvantage if faced by an enemy possessing advanced weapons technology. Another telling disadvantage is its exhaust system, which is completely 'open' from all aspects and so makes the Hind very vulnerable to attack from even the simplest of infra-red missiles.

Despite these problems the Soviet Union has a long tradition of designing and building multi-role combat vehicles. One can compare the Hind concept to that of the BMP-1, a multi-mission armoured personnel carrier which operates a variety of complementary weapons from one mobile platform, while at the same time carrying out its primary role as a troop transporter. There, the question of the effectiveness of such a system has brought about a prolonged controversy, both within the West and in the Soviet armed forces themselves. This debate has now been extended to the Hind as a multi-role weapon system – though this controversy would require the outbreak of a major war to be fully resolved.

In Europe, Hinds would be expected to operate against enemy tanks and armoured vehicles; organised into flights of four helicopters they would work in coordination with fixed-wing aircraft in delivering mutually-supporting air strikes. If war did break out in Europe, then the intensity of the first few days of fighting would place the value of assault helicopters like the Hind at a premium; casualties would be severe, however, and it is quite possible to imagine whole units being wiped out in the first days of full-scale combat.

Above: The sand and green camouflage scheme of this Hind-D can be readily observed in this photograph, as can the array of rockets slung under the stub wings. Left: Flight crews of a Hind unit newly returned from a training mission. Right: A Hind-A cuts through the thin mountain air of Afghanistan while on an anti-guerrilla patrol.

Three views of a Hind-D, armed with a multi-barrel machine gun housed in the nose-turret as well as 'Swatter' anti-tank missiles and UB rocket pods – each capable of holding 32 57mm rockets.

Although primarily designed for a role in a Warsaw Pact-versus-Nato war, the Hind has first been used in combat as part of the Soviet forces in Afghanistan. The Soviet Army has had to reorganise its conventionally structured forces to take on the Afghan tribesmen as part of a guerrilla war, and consequently the Hind has played an increasingly important role. The Hind has two important advantages that the guerrillas fear deeply: firstly, it can suddenly fly over a mountainside and deliver a great volume of well-directed fire against a surprised ground target, and secondly, it is able to land a squad of fully-armed troops in advanced positions; and given the inhospitable terrain and poor communications systems encountered in Afghanistan this is of considerable value. For while the Soviet Army has no shortage of men, the Hind is able to save Soviet troops from some of the worst rigours of conducting foot patrols, the cause of a high rate of attrition in all but the toughest units.

On the debit side the Hind has proved vulnerable to ground fire and a number have been reportedly shot down by guerrillas using nothing more than 12.7mm anti-aircraft machine guns (ironically of Soviet manufacture). On the basis of Soviet experience in

Afghanistan it should be expected that later models of the Hind will be redesigned to improve flaws revealed in combat. And although the Hind is unwieldy and cumbersome, it remains a highly potent weapon – one not to be discounted by any opponent.

Mil Mi-24 Hind

Type Assault helicopter (Hind-A and C); helicopter gunship (Hind-D and E)
Main Rotor Diameter 17m (55ft 9in)
Length 17m (55ft 9in)
Height 4.25m (14ft)
Weight (estimated) Empty 6500kg (14,000lb); maximum take-off 10,000kg (22,000lb)
Powerplant Two 1500shp Isotov TV-2 turboshaft engines

Performance Maximum speed 320km/h (200mph); cruising speed 260km/h (160mph)
Ceiling 5500m (18,000ft)

Armament 12.7mm machine gun in nose (Hind-A and C); 14.5mm or 20mm four-barrel cannon in nose turret (Hind-D); 30mm cannon in nose turret (Hind-E); up to four underwing pylons for rocket pods (each containing 32 57mm rockets); up to four anti-tank guided missiles (Swatter or Spiral); wing-mounted 23mm cannon (Hind-A and C only)

Street fighting

The specialised tactics of urban warfare

Regular armies do not like fighting in built-up areas. They tend to be organised and equipped for campaigns of movement in open country, where observation is relatively good, space for manoeuvre is available and civilian populations are sparse. None of this exists once a city is entered. The army is forced down the narrow channels of roads or streets, attacked from all angles in a claustrophobic environment and split into small sub-units as individual buildings have to be cleared. Dependence upon vehicles may become a liability once anything on the streets is ambushed, and weapons designed for the comparatively longer ranges of open war may be rendered ineffective in close urban surroundings.

Civilians will get in the way and may even pose an additional threat if they actually take up arms. Soldiers will come under intense psychological pressure in circumstances of close combat for which they have probably not been specifically trained, and command and control will be difficult as communications break down. In short, what the British Army calls FIBUA

(Fighting in Built Up Areas) and the Americans term MOBA (Military Operations in Built-up Areas) has all the makings of a military nightmare.

Yet modern cities or urban sprawls cannot be ignored. They are centres of political, cultural and economic life in any state, often containing essential strategic targets, ranging from command headquarters to river crossings or road junctions. In addition, with the rapid process of urbanisation in recent years, cities are often too large to by-pass and are certainly too important to leave to the mercy of guerrillas or terrorists in an insurgency. Whether armies like it or not, urban operations have become a central feature of modern military life.

There are many possible approaches to the problems of urban fighting. Traditionally the idea has always been to by-pass such centres, cutting them off from outside support while pursuing the more important military goal of defeating the enemy army. If this can be achieved, the city will either 'wither on the vine' or surrender automatically once its military

An infantryman in South Vietnam mans a 0.3in Browning machine gun. Although seemingly exposed, the gunner is in fact commanding a wide arc of fire and thus giving cover to advancing troops.

support disappears. Such a ploy was effectively carried out by North Vietnamese troops in 1975 when the defeat of the South Vietnamese Army gave them a fairly effortless entry into Saigon.

Admittedly, if the city in question blocks the line of advance or contains a target of great strategic significance, more direct action may have to be taken, but even when a siege is organised it is often accepted that once the outer defences have been breached, surrender will ensue. The British entry into Port Stanley on East Falkland in June 1982 may be said to have followed this pattern. The strategy as a whole may be summed up as one of clear avoidance of urban fighting. Most armies prefer this approach.

But avoidance has become less feasible as cities have expanded and it is, of course, militarily unsound if the urban area is being assaulted from within by small groups of guerrillas. Such factors make military involvement inevitable, although it can vary dramatically in scale. As all regular armies contain an enormous potential for destruction, one of the easiest options open to them is to subject the city to an overwhelming weight of fire, forcing surrender through devastation. This was a favourite approach in the 'total war' conditions of World War II. On 7 July 1944, for example, as Anglo-Canadian troops approached Caen in northern France, 467 Lancaster and Halifax heavy bombers dropped 2560 tons of high explosive onto the town; nine months later, on 7 April 1945, the Russians did the same to Königsberg in eastern Germany, depositing 550 tons of bombs onto the city centre in just 45 minutes.

Artillery can achieve similar results. In the Berlin operation of April-May 1945 the Russians massed 41,600 guns and mortars, subjecting the city to a shattering barrage. In September 1980 the Iraqis used massed artillery fire against the Iranian city of Khorramshahr and in June 1982 the Israelis deployed both aircraft and artillery against Beirut. Indeed, it is not unknown for such methods to be used against urban insurgents. In February 1968 American artillery, aircraft and even naval units bombarded North Vietnamese and Viet Cong positions in the South Vietnamese city of Hue, pursuing a deliberate policy of destruction in an effort to minimise casualties among their own ground forces.

Such a strategy rarely works on its own, if only because, in the end, the urban centre has to be occupied and made secure. As complete destruction, even with today's sophisticated weapons, is virtually impossible to achieve, some defenders will survive and, if the city is not taken quickly, they will emerge and use the rubble to set up effective ambush positions. Even if the ultimate in destructive techniques – a nuclear explosion – was to be used, a follow-up assault would have to be carried out, in extremely difficult conditions. Chemical, biological or enhanced radiation ('neutron bomb') devices may provide new opportunities for the future, but the contamination involved could prove counter-productive while the mere threat of their use could generate civilian panic and produce a refugee problem that would delay a conventional advance. Add to this the political problems involved in such a policy of deliberate devastation and it may be seen that strategies of mass destruction are by no means straightforward.

There are more subtle approaches. The most attractive is to take the city in a sudden attack, occupying key features in a surprise move before the defenders

are properly organised. Soviet military doctrine favours this approach, advocating the use of airborne or special forces to operate in Nato rear areas and open the way for a conventional advance through towns and cities. Indeed, the Russians have used such methods on at least three occasions since 1945, with significant short-term results. In the early hours of 4 November 1956 for example, Russian tanks moved in to secure key buildings and bridges in Budapest, catching the Hungarian freedom-fighters by surprise; in August 1968 up to 500,000 Warsaw Pact troops suddenly seized the major cities of Czechoslovakia; and in December 1979 the cross-border invasion of Afghanistan was preceded by a seizure of important locations in Kabul.

Opposition is rarely silenced by such methods, however, leaving the occupying forces to face a guerrilla-style campaign that involves the commitment of troops to street-fighting. If the guerrillas, either in response to occupation or in pursuit of political change, choose to fight in the cities, they enjoy definite military advantages. Whether they are the Tupamaros in Montevideo or the Provisional IRA in Belfast, they operate from within the civilian population and are able to use their intimate know-

Running fast, splitting up as they go and keeping in constant radio contact with their commander, a unit of South Vietnamese marines move through the streets in a 'sweep and search' operation. They are carrying M16 assault rifles – high velocity weapons able to deliver accurate bursts of fire at comparatively long ranges which is invaluable in street fighting. Bottom: Government troops in Nicaragua come under fire from guerrillas.

ledge of the urban area to mount hit-and-run attacks upon security forces who find it almost impossible to locate and destroy them. The military options of avoidance or complete urban destruction are usually politically unacceptable, particularly if the campaign is being waged on home ground, and the use of such weapons as artillery or aircraft could be counter-productive, destroying valuable buildings and alienating the very civilian population the army is supposed to protect.

Security forces caught in such circumstances have to be subtle in the extreme and adopt a low-profile. It is an approach that the British Army has attempted to follow in Northern Ireland since 1969. Careful gathering of intelligence to isolate the guerrillas, constant military presence on the streets to prevent the creation of 'no-go' areas, selective counter-action against known targets and a constant search for a political solution which will 'defuse' the situation – all this adds up to a type of warfare for which few armies are trained and even fewer are psychologically prepared. In such circumstances command initiative has to be devolved to the lowest levels, special weapons have to be developed to cope with a strange environment and casualties have to be absorbed without the level of action escalating. Some armies have found this an extremely difficult task and have over-reacted: the use of institutionalised torture by elements of the French Army in Algiers in 1957 is a case in point, producing a political backlash in Paris which undoubtedly contributed to the eventual granting of Algerian independence.

But even this scale of involvement does not constitute the real nightmare of urban fighting – the full-scale military clearance of a city, street-by-street and house-by-house. The defenders hold many advantages, being able to fortify individual buildings, set up improvised road-blocks and force the attacking troops along narrow streets containing well-sited machine guns, booby-traps and snipers. They can also move quickly from place to place using the sewers or back streets. Even if the attackers use tanks in an effort to blast their way forward, the defenders can respond with Molotov cocktails or grenades dropped from the windows of surrounding buildings, as Soviet troops discovered to their cost in Budapest in 1956.

In the end the only effective method available to the attackers is to take out each building in turn, using individual tanks or artillery pieces for direct fire support. South Vietnamese and American Marines were forced to adopt such tactics in Hue in 1968, losing over 500 men in clearing the Citadel in the centre of the city despite a terrific preliminary bombardment. Israeli forces experienced similar problems in Jerusalem in June 1967, while the Iraqis probably suffered up to 5000 casualties in Khorramshahr in September 1980. It is one of the worst types of combat, requiring a depth of psychological tenacity and personal bravery that few armies naturally contain. It was graphically described in 1945 by BBC correspondent Denis Johnston, and the basic characteristics have not changed since:

'The old hands at the game go through a town keeping inside the houses and using bazookas to knock holes in the dividing walls as they go, and when they come to the end of the block and have to cross the street to the next block they throw out smoke first and cross over under cover of that. They say it's usually better to clear out a house from the top downwards if you can. Break a hole in the roof and get in by an upper floor if possible. . . . But of course a lot depends on the type of defence being met with; if it mainly consists of sniping, it's best to go slowly and very deliberately, and in small groups. Snipers very often won't fire at a group, when they'll shoot a single man; they're afraid of giving away their position to the men whom they can't hit with their first shots. But if the defence is heavy you've got to keep dispersed, move fast, and keep on moving whatever happens. . . . You feel inclined to drop down and bury your head, and the next shot gets you; you want to cluster together for mutual company, and in this way you may give them a real target, but all the old hands will tell you to keep your head up and your eyes open and your legs moving, and at all costs keep apart.'

Nor are the problems purely personal ones, for despite the growing importance of urban areas in both conventional and guerrilla campaigns, few regular armies appear to appreciate the procedures involved, making only token efforts to train specifically for them. The ones who are prepared tend to be those who have experienced the trauma of urban involvement in recent years – the Americans, Russians, British, Israelis and, probably, the Iraqis and Iranians. The attitude of the majority, reinforcing the traditional military predilection towards ignoring or avoiding urban fighting, is summed up by an anonymous West German general: 'My troops sit in vehicles, are trained to fight from vehicles and their weapons are specially suited to fighting a mobile enemy in open country. I don't have the manpower, the training, the equipment for city fighting.' **John Pimlott**

Below: A US M41 tank patrols the streets of a South Vietnamese town. Although it is supreme in open country, in built-up areas the tank is extemely vulnerable to determined infantry attacks.

Israel under siege

The young state struggles to survive

After the United Nations decided in November 1947 to partition Palestine, fighting broke out between the Arabs and the Jews. The Palestinian Arabs and the surrounding Arab states rejected partition out of hand and declared their intention to fight in order to prevent its implementation. Sporadic engagements followed the UN decision and as British withdrawal from the Mandate drew nearer, hostilities escalated.

For the Jewish forces the main problem was that they were still an underground army and in heavy weapons – tanks, artillery, aircraft – they were very inferior to the Arabs. In preparation for the British withdrawal, the Arabs attempted to coordinate their forces, but conflicting aims frustrated their hopes for a unified command; and, although the common hostility to Jewish nationalism provided a degree of unity, internal territorial struggles proved to be the Arabs' greatest weakness.

The Arab forces that attacked the infant state of Israel totalled approximately 37,000 troops in armies from Iraq, Syria, Lebanon, Egypt and Transjordan, two guerrilla forces who owed allegiance to the Grand Mufti of Jerusalem, and finally the Arab Liberation Army (ALA), which was formed by the kings and presidents of Arab countries (other than Transjordan) in the hope that such a force might contain King Abdullah's aims of a Palestinian-Jordanian kingdom. For, without a doubt, the strongest of the Arab armies was that of King Abdullah of Jordan. His Arab Legion, commanded by Lieutenant-General Sir John Bagot Glubb (popularly known as Glubb Pasha), numbered 10,000 troops with armoured and artillery sections and had the advantage of being trained by the British.

The confrontation between Arab and Jew became

open war upon the withdrawal of the British on 14 May 1948. The invading Arab armies – the Egyptians to the south, the Arab Legion and the Iraqi Army to the east, and the Syrians and Lebanese to the north – began full-scale military operations against the newly proclaimed state of Israel with what seemed to be a major strategic advantage, in that they were forcing the small Israeli Army to fight on three fronts. However, while the Israeli forces effectively numbered just 28,000, a high level of mobility and interior lines of communication gave them definite advantages over the dispersed and poorly coordinated Arab forces.

On 14 May Syrian and Lebanese formations moved against a single Jewish brigade in the upper Jordan Valley. The Syrian forces began the offensive with a concentrated artillery bombardment of the Ein Gev area and this was followed up with an armoured advance parallel to the Galilee coast, through Zemach and on towards the Degania villages.

At dawn on the 20th the Arabs opened the offensive on the Degania villages with a heavy artillery barrage. Following this was an advance by infantry with armoured support. However, although the advance reached the Israeli trenches, the defenders, using Molotov cocktails and PIAT anti-tank weapons, managed to repulse the Syrians – mainly due to the fact that the bulk of the Syrian infantry had not kept up with the armoured spearhead.

Later in the day a second Syrian advance proved to be no more successful, and it was at this point that the Israelis suddenly took the initiative. Artillery pieces that had only recently arrived in Tel Aviv were rushed to the north and, with no training whatsoever, the Israeli Army managed to get them into action. A few practice shots were used to zero the guns and it was not

Above: Jewish irregulars defend a position against Arab attack during the fighting in May 1948. Although only lightly armed, these forces put up a dogged resistance to their better-armed Arab opponents.

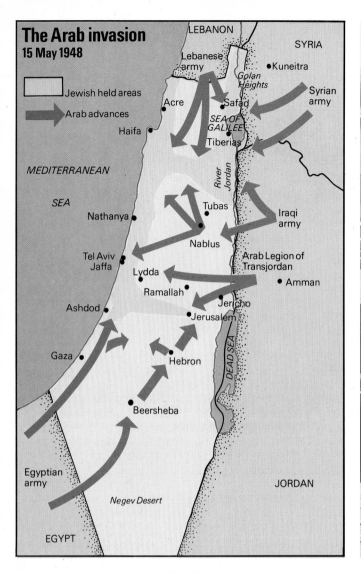

The Arab invasion
15 May 1948

☐ Jewish held areas
➡ Arab advances

Above right: Israeli troops of the Haganah await orders after occupying the Arab village of Kakoun. Just visible on the left is a US-built jeep, an invaluable vehicle in the rough terrain of Palestine. The ability to switch troops from one threatened sector to another was a central ingredient of Israeli success.

The Arab forces

The Arab League was formed with the aid and encouragement of the British on 22 March 1945. Its member states were Egypt, Iraq, Syria, Lebanon, Saudi Arabia, Transjordan and Yemen. The league had two major aims: opposition to French presence in the Levant, and opposition to the Jews in Palestine.

The Palestinian Arabs, some 1,200,000 strong, could raise less than 10,000 trained men so the other Arab powers created an Arab Liberation Army.

In May 1948 Arab ground forces committed to invading Israel were as follows:

Lebanese Army	1 battalion
Arab Liberation Army	6000 irregulars organised into 5 battalions
Syrian Army	2 Inf brigades + 1 armour battalion
Arab Legion	2 Inf brigades (motorised)
Iraqi Army	1 battalion + 1 armour regt
Egyptian Army	2 Inf brigades + 1 armour regt

The Arabs possessed 270 tanks, 300 combat aircraft, 150 guns and a total of 35,000 troops. By contrast the Israelis had 3 tanks, 35 combat aircraft, 5 guns and 28,000 troops.

long before Israeli shells were hitting Syrian targets. The sudden arrival of these artillery pieces caused panic among the Syrians who, until this point, had exploited the lack of Israeli artillery. As the Syrians withdrew, so the Israelis advanced and soon re-took all the territory that had previously fallen to the invaders. By 23 May the Israelis had effectively won the battle for the Jordan Valley.

On 6 June the Lebanese attacked Malkiya in the western sector of Galilee, while the Syrians, having reorganised, moved against Mishmar Hayarden in an attempt to sever the Israelis' north-south supply route in central Galilee. The Lebanese, with the help of some ALA units, quickly took Malkiya and followed up with the capture of Kadesh, thus opening a reinforcement route to the ALA in central Galilee. In the Mishmar Hayarden sector the Syrian attack, particularly well coordinated, advanced in two prongs and, although repulsed once, eventually took the town and headed towards the main road. Then, on 11 June, the first truce between the two sides came into operation.

In the east on 15 May an Iraqi force had forded the Jordan near Gesher. Repulsed by the Israelis, the Iraqis withdrew and moved south, crossing the river towards Nablus. In a concentrated spearhead they advanced through Israel – hoping to effectively cut the state in two – and successfully reached to within 12km (8 miles) of Nathanya. On the night of 31 May the Israelis, seeing the danger of the Iraqi advance, counter-attacked. However, the assault failed and the key town of Jenin fell to the Iraqis. And while this was happening, the Arab Legion advanced on Jerusalem, taking the Old City.

In a two-pronged attack on the southern front the Egyptian ground forces, some 7000 in all, had crossed into Israel on 14 May. A force of 2000 advanced towards Beersheba while the bulk of the troops moved along the coastal road. Despite the general superiority of the Egyptians in terms of arms and equipment, failure to coordinate artillery, armour and infantry led them into a series of stalemates. In one particular instance the village of Kfar Darom, defended by only 30 Israelis, managed to deny the Egyptians any territory. When the Egyptians finally took the village it had been evacuated. This and similar incidents convinced the invading forces that it would not be prudent to engage each and every settlement along the way.

On 20 May the Egyptian forces advanced on Yad Mordechai and after consolidating, moved northwards on the 29th. The Israelis, who had finally received some fighter planes from Europe, flew their first sorties against the advancing Arab columns. While their strafing was of little practical use, the appearance of Israeli fighters was enough to induce the Arabs to halt their advance and once more concentrate on consolidating their interior lines of communication with the aim of isolating the Negev sector. Just before the first truce came into effect on 11 June the Egyptians managed to gain command of the main Majdal-Faluja highway and effectively cut off the Negev.

It had been hoped at the UN that the truce agreement agreed for 11 June would help establish both peace and the state of Israel on a permanent basis. However, to both sides the truce was merely a breathing space in which to consolidate in preparation for the next round of hostilities. After the four-week truce the fighting resumed.

On the northern front on 9 July the Israeli Army – known as the IDF (Israeli Defence Force) since 28 May – launched an encircling offensive against the Syrian bridgehead (heavily reinforced during the truce) at a point very close to the north-south road in east Galilee. After nine days' fighting the positions of both sides remained virtually unchanged.

In western Galilee the Arab Liberation Army were mounting repeated attacks against the area around the village of Sejera, and on 14 July mounted eight attacks during this one day – but to no avail. The IDF, however, launched a counter-offensive and took Nazareth on the 16th.

To the Israelis the most potent Arab force was the Arab Legion which, after the end of the first truce, controlled Jerusalem, Lod and Ramle, including not only Israel's main railway junction but also its only international airport.

On 9 July the Israelis launched a major attack against the Arab forces in Lod. Glubb, realising that his forces could not hold the town, did not reinforce the garrison and the Israelis quickly established control. This advance was followed up with an attack against Ramle and on the 10th the Israelis controlled both towns. But Glubb, realising the strategic value of Latrun, had reinforced substantially in this area.

On the night of 15 July the Israelis mounted an offensive that successfully cleared the way for the IDF to bypass Latrun. Spotting the danger of encircle-

Tanks for Israel

One of Israel's first Cromwell tanks.

The Jewish forces were desperate for heavy armament as the open conflict with the Arabs approached. In the spring of 1948, a group of British soldiers – some genuinely sympathetic to the Jewish cause but others just interested in cash – contacted the Haganah and offered to 'supply' four Cromwell tanks that were parked in an ordnance depot adjacent to Haifa airport. As British drivers were available to deliver only two of the tanks, the Haganah decided to have Jewish truck drivers trained to drive the other two. The British drivers instructed their Jewish colleagues using a model made up of pieces of furniture moved around in a sitting-room; the position of the tank's controls was indicated on a rough sketch.

On the night of the snatch, the two British men entered the ordnance depot, waving their passes at the sentry on duty. At about the same time a small private aircraft carrying the two Jewish drivers landed on the nearby airfield and taxied to a corner. At midnight one of the British drivers, a sergeant, offered to relieve the guard on duty near the area where the

Cromwells were parked. His offer was readily accepted. Their entry into the depot thus assured, the Jewish drivers emerged from the aircraft where they had been hiding and joined the British men. Silently they made their way to the tanks, and climbed in.

The Jewish truck-drivers desperately tried to remember what they had been taught. Then there was a roar as the first tank, driven by one of the British, started up and smashed through the unguarded gate and headed for the rendezvous with the Haganah. Only two tanks turned up at the rendezvous – the ones with British drivers. A tank transporter failed to appear and so the British men fulfilled their promise to deliver the tanks to Tel Aviv by driving them all the way, thus founding the Armoured Corps of the Haganah.

As for the Jewish drivers, they had quickly found that a tank was more complicated than a truck. One could not find the ignition switch; the other, although he managed to locate the switch, did not get very far before he succeeded in breaking the gear box.

ment, the Arab Legion mounted a counter-attack which denied the IDF any hope of taking the key Latrun ridge. Once again, the results of the fighting were inconclusive. Although further offensives also failed to dislodge the Arabs, the IDF now held the airport at Lod and had removed the threat to Tel Aviv, and while a corridor to Jerusalem was being successfully widened the Arabs still controlled the Jerusalem road.

Before the end of the first truce the IDF in the south prepared plans for reopening the road to the Negev, forcing the Egyptians back from Ashdod, and destroying their east-west supply route. Conversely the Egyptians planned to widen their corridor in order to improve their interior lines of communication. Having watched IDF preparations for an offensive, the Arabs decided to launch a pre-emptive strike against the IDF, and on 8 July (a day before the truce officially

The new frontiers
Israel 1949-67

— Israeli border

▢ Arab territory seized by Israel 1948/49

LEBANON

SYRIA

Acre
Safad
SEA OF GALILEE
Haifa

Nablus

Tel Aviv
Jaffa
WEST BANK

Lydda

MEDITERRANEAN SEA

Jerusalem

DEAD SEA

GAZA STRIP

ISRAEL

JORDAN

Beersheba

EGYPT

The UN plan

▢ Jewish areas
▢ Arab areas

LEBANON

SYRIA

Haifa

Tel Aviv

Jerusalem

Gaza

Beersheba

PALESTINE

TRANSJORDAN

EGYPT

Below: Armed with British Vickers machine guns, an Arab Legion weapons section opens fire on an enemy position. Although an old design, the Vickers was a reliable gun capable of a high rate of accurate fire over long periods.

ended) attacked and captured Israeli positions at Kaukaba, Huleiqat and Hill 113. Severe fighting followed this offensive and for five days the Egyptians launched various unsuccessful offensives against Negba and Beerot Yitzhak. By the time the second truce came into effect on 18 July the IDF had managed to open a narrow corridor to the Negev.

Once again, UN pressure brought about a temporary lull in hostilities. Although both sides needed the respite the truces favoured the Jewish state, for they enabled the Israelis to add to their meagre stocks of heavy support weapons. When the truce ended the decision was taken by the IDF command to clear Galilee of all Arab forces using four infantry brigades and four batteries of artillery. This was Operation Hiram. On the night of 28 October a pincer-type offensive was launched against the Arabs in an attempt to encircle them; the two prongs were to meet at Sasa. The 7th Brigade IDF successfully pushed its way through to Sasa, completing the eastern arm of the pincer. Although the Oded Brigade in the west did not experience quite the same rapid advance, when news reached the Arabs that the IDF had taken Sasa in their rear they began to withdraw towards Lebanon. Continuous offensives by the IDF eventually forced the Arabs to withdraw completely – though the Syrians continued to retain their bridgehead at Mishmar

Hayarden. By 31 October the Israelis controlled the whole of Galilee.

In the south, Operation Yoav got under way on 15 October. By means of a large-scale attack, the IDF intended to force open a corridor to the Negev, cut Egyptian lines of communication and thus isolate and defeat the Egyptians. In the early stages the IDF were easily repulsed, suffering heavy casualties in their attempt to take the Egyptian fortified hilltop positions, especially Hill 113 and Hill 100. But after an initial retreat, and under cover of a heavy artillery barrage, the IDF attacked once more. A successful diversionary feint meant that Egyptian troops were totally surprised when the main attack was launched. By 18 October the Israelis controlled both hills, junction positions that commanded the east-west Majdal-Hebron road, and followed this offensive through with an attack that took Kaukaba to the south. Although efforts to take Huleiqat and open a corridor to the Negev met stiff resistance, further offensives along the coast in the Majdal area threatened the Egyptians with encirclement and they began to withdraw south using coastal routes.

This steady withdrawal was leading to inter-Arab disputes as it was felt that Egypt's retreat bordered on betrayal. The Israelis, recognising that it was unlikely that other Arab armies would come to the aid of the retreating Egyptians, decided to launch an allout attack against the Huleiqat stronghold. The offensive began on 19 October. The determination of the IDF to break the Egyptian stranglehold finally resulted in defeat for the Arab forces in the area.

Operation Horev, which was virtually a clearing operation aimed at removing the Egyptian forces from their footholds in Israel, was launched on 22 December. By the 27th Egypt's eastern front in the Negev had given way entirely and the Israelis crossed the border and took Abu Aweigila unopposed. The British government then stepped in and presented the Israelis with an ultimatum: unless Israel withdrew

from Egyptian territory Britain would come to Egypt's assistance. The Israelis acceded and switched their attention to Egyptian positions around Rafah in the Gaza area. Egypt, realising the hopelessness of her position, opened talks that led to the signing of an armistice with Israel on 24 February 1949.

A general ceasefire was agreed on 7 January. An armistice with the Lebanon was signed on 23 March and that with Jordan followed 11 days later – after the Israelis had asserted their control of the southern Negev by entering Um-Rashrash (Eilat) unopposed. Syria was the last to sign an armistice, on 20 July. Although she withdrew from Mishmar Hayarden, it was agreed that the bridgehead should be demilitarised. The state of Israel was finally established.

Simon Innes

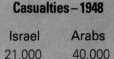

Casualties – 1948

Israel	Arabs
21,000	40,000

Above left: Firing a French Hotchkiss machine gun (dating back to 1914) an Arab detachment prepares to make an attack during the battle for Jerusalem.

Below: An Israeli military convoy sets out to reinforce the southern sector of the Israeli defences. The jeep leading the convoy has an MG34 machine gun at the ready, a weapon that was standard in the German Army during the early stages of World War II.

On a wing and a prayer

The early days of Israel's air force

At the time of the Arab invasion in May 1948, the Israeli Air Force totalled some three squadrons of light aeroplanes (mainly Piper Cubs) and approximately 40 pilots on active service. They had no fighter planes, only three transports and two bombers. Radio contact between ground forces and reconnaissance flights barely existed. Conversely, the combined Arab air forces enjoyed substantial quantitative advantages. The Egyptian Air Force was the most powerful. Egypt's active squadrons numbered approximately 40 Spitfires, two squadrons of transports, and about 30 bombers. The Syrian Air Force consisted mainly of Harvards, and the Iraqi Air Force a squadron of Furies.

Due to this severe imbalance the fledgling Israeli Air Force was virtually useless for daytime sorties. The only real function their light aircraft could perform during the day was reconnaissance for advancing ground forces. But even in this role, due to lack of radio facilities, messages concerning Arab forward positions had to be thrown in bottles to the troops below. Furthermore the Israeli ground forces had very few anti-aircraft weapons. Israeli airfields were therefore extremely vulnerable to attack from the air. For lack of any alternative, and desperate to launch aerial offensives against the Arabs, the Israelis were compelled to improvise. Supplies were parachuted to troops, and bombing runs against Arab airfields were carried out at night and in a similar manner – the bombs were simply thrown out of the aircraft door. Not surprisingly, the effect of these bombing runs on the Arabs was insignificant.

It was under these adverse conditions that, on 15 May, the Israeli Air Force was finally pushed into full-scale operations against the Arabs. On the morning of D-day Sde Dov, the main IAF base, was attacked by Egyptian Spitfires. The Egyptians destroyed three Israeli planes and inflicted casualties among ground-crew members. A second sortie later in the day by the same flight section was not so successful, and the Israelis actually managed to bring down one of the Spitfires.

Meanwhile the arms purchasing section of the Haganah had been hard at work in Europe and on 29

May the first delivery of fighter planes arrived at the newly occupied air base of Ekron. They were four Messerschmitts from Czechoslovakia. There was also a steady influx of volunteer pilots, most of whom had gained flying experience in World War II. On the maiden operation of the Messerschmitt section, the target chosen was an Egyptian column which had spearheaded as far as Ashdod, 50km (30 miles) south of Tel Aviv. As the Messerschmitts approached they broke formation and released their bombs

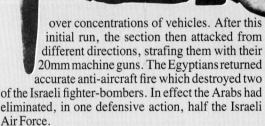

over concentrations of vehicles. After this initial run, the section then attacked from different directions, strafing them with their 20mm machine guns. The Egyptians returned accurate anti-aircraft fire which destroyed two of the Israeli fighter-bombers. In effect the Arabs had eliminated, in one defensive action, half the Israeli Air Force.

Despite this setback buying efforts abroad were beginning to reap dividends. In one instance two Egyptian C-47 Dakotas approached Tel Aviv late one evening. As they began to release their bombs an Israeli Messerschmitt returning from patrol spotted them and moved in to attack. Although the Egyptian aircraft desperately attempted to avoid the oncoming fighter the Israeli pilot managed to shoot both the Dakotas out of the sky. In another incident Egyptian naval vessels approached the Tel Aviv coast with the obvious intention of shelling the city. The IAF scrambled all available aircraft and a Bonanza, a Fairchild and a Rapide headed for one of the ships. Without so

Above: A battered Israeli Air Force Mosquito taking off. In the desperate search for aircraft the IAF were prepared to use almost any aircraft that they could get hold of.

Above: A flight of US B-17 Flying Fortresses over Israel. In some instances these planes were flown out of America under the very noses of the FBI.

much as a bombsight between them this motley force created such panic among the Egyptian commanders that the three ships actually turned and fled.

After 3 June Arab air attacks against Tel Aviv were few: the first truce was not far distant. And it was during the period of this truce, which lasted for a month, that the IAF really began to take shape. Volunteers from America, Canada and even Britain had joined the IAF as radio operators, navigators, ground crew, instructors, pilots and gunners. No real command structure existed but objectives were quite clear to each and every member of the IAF. During the truce aircraft arrived regularly from Czechoslovakia and the arrival of war surplus B-17 Flying Fortress bombers from the US greatly increased the number of sorties the IAF could fly once fighting resumed in July. After the acquisition of these bombers the complexion of the air war changed in favour of Israel.

One of the Israelis' greatest coups was the 'borrowing' from the British Air Ministry of four Bristol Beaufighters, one of Britain's finest fighter-bomber designs. Emmanuel Zur, the Israeli agent for aero-

plane acquisition in Britain, decided that a few Beaufighters would make a useful addition to the IAF. Under the guise of making a film about Beaufighters, Zur persuaded the authorities to issue permits allowing five of the aircraft to be flown to a remote airfield in Scotland. With an assembled aircrew sympathetic to the Israeli cause, Zur filmed the ground scenes in front of an audience of rather smug officials. The aircrews then climbed into the planes, took off, made a pass over the 'base', promptly disappeared over a hill and headed for Israel, refuelling in Corsica. The problem of parts was solved by the extraordinary acquisitional powers of a former RAF pilot, John Harvey. Having obtained a war-surplus Handley Page Halifax bomber, Harvey filled it with Beaufighter parts, guns, ammunition, and even a complete engine and flew it to Israel.

By utilising many different sources of supply the IAF had, by early 1949, an air force of some 150 planes – though widely assorted – and pilots to match. Such was the spectrum of Israeli aircraft that many of the pilots were required to be proficient in flying up to 10 different types. Squadron 101, the IAF's only operational fighter squadron, was still desperately

short of fighters, but in early 1949 the Czechs offered Israel 50 reconditioned Spitfire LF Mk IX fighters.

At this time the Suez Canal zone remained under British military occupation and an RAF base was maintained at Fayid to protect shipping rights. But this non-aggressive RAF presence was no more acceptable to the IAF than that of the Arabs. Although the RAF's Mk 18 Spitfires outclassed the Mk IXs of the IAF, the pilots of 208 Squadron RAF had little battle experience, if any, while the bulk of the IAF pilots were veterans of World War II.

An incident that occurred on 7 January 1949 illustrates the point that the skill of their pilots was the hidden strength of the Israelis. On the day in question, four RAF Spitfire Mk 18s took off from their base in the canal zone for a reconnaissance flight. Approximately half an hour later two IAF Mk IXs left from Hatzor on an armed combat patrol. Because the IAF had not developed any form of aerial early warning system, most patrol routes were based on pilots' hunches. By pure chance they made visual contact with the RAF flight and engaged. Despite the superior power and manoeuvrability of the Mk 18s the final result was the destruction of all four RAF planes.

Alexander McNair-Wilson

Top: Israeli Air Force Harvards on an operational flight. The IAF acquired their first Harvards in late 1948. Though Harvards were originally designed for reconnaissance purposes, the Israelis adapted the aircraft, adding machine guns and bomb racks which could carry light bombs of up to 110lb (50kg).

Assault on the Holy City

House-to-house battles in the streets of Jerusalem

'A pink bromeliad bloomed in an old gasoline can on the window ledge. From behind it two Arab irregulars fired away. A third jammed a fresh clip into his rifle. A fourth was slumped on a chair, sound asleep. I had no idea where I was. The British deserter, whom I had met at the *rauda* . . . , had led me here via a zigzag course from legion headquarters. Hurrying down narrow streets, we had passed barbwire entanglements at intersections guarded by tense, brooding irregulars. We had crawled over the rubble of houses, which had collapsed into the streets, and trudged through mounds of debris – ankle deep in broken furniture, piles of newspaper, rags and smashed crockery. We had ducked beneath low archways and sneaked from one building to another through gaping holes in the walls. Whenever we paused to catch our breath, all I seemed to see were damaged synagogues. ''They must have at least fifty, and every one is a fortress,'' the deserter had said in disgust.'

John Phillips, who witnessed the fighting in Jerusalem in 1948 and took the photograph that appears on this page.

On 14 May 1948 the British Mandate in Palestine officially ended. By nightfall on the 15th the sole remaining British military presence consisted of a small garrison in Haifa. Full-scale war between the Arabs and the Jews was imminent, and the key city of Jerusalem lay open to invasion.

Despite various attempts by the Arab League to form a high command that could effectively coordinate the offensives of the five Arab armies, the conflicting aims of the Arab leaders meant that only one major decision had been arrived at on which all Arabs were agreed: when the British withdrew there should be an immediate invasion of Palestine. As the British prepared to withdraw from the Mandate, the forces from Lebanon, Syria, Iraq, Transjordan and Egypt gathered on the borders of Palestine. Of these armies by far the strongest was King Abdullah of Transjordan's British-trained Arab Legion.

It was the Arab Legion, under the command of General Glubb Pasha, who moved against the Jewish positions in Jerusalem. On 13 May the order to advance into Palestine had been given, and on the morning of the 14th the Arab Legion crossed the Jordan. News reached the Israelis occupying Jerusalem that the Arabs were advancing from the north and east and they prepared for the inevitable Arab offensives. By the 17th the Arabs had effectively isolated the city, occupying the Latrun area and blocking the main approach road. Having shelled and mortared Jewish positions since 15 May, the Arab Legion took up positions in Sheikh Jarrah and attempted entry into Jerusalem through the Mandelbaum Gate in the north, while in the southern part an armoured column advanced through the Damascus Gate, parallel with the Old City walls, and headed towards the Jewish sector. Practically the whole of Jerusalem outside the Old City walls was in the hands of the Israelis who, upon the British withdrawal, had quickly occupied all areas except those held by the Arabs in the Old City.

The Arab advance through the Old City progressed rapidly towards the Notre Dame monastery, a key building that dominated a large part of the city. Although the narrow streets made it difficult to launch an armoured offensive, the Jews, in their haste to occupy key locations, had not had time to erect substantial anti-tank barriers or dig ditches. As the Arab armour approached the Israeli positions, hoping to push through to the Jaffa road, the leading armoured car was hit by a Molotov cocktail. The remaining vehicles were forced to retreat.

After this initial repulse, the Arab armour was used simply to bombard Israeli positions. Despite successive attempts on the 23rd, 24th and 25th to dislodge the Israelis, the monastery could not be taken. Eventually the Arab Legion brought in their artillery, 25-pounders, and contented themselves with a continuous bombardment of Israeli positions. A form of stalemate developed, the Jews occupying and holding the New City (west of the Mandelbaum Gate) and the Arabs holding the eastern sectors.

While this stalemate was continuing, another battle was taking place. Despite the overwhelming Arab forces in the eastern sector, defeats in the south had galvanised the Arabs into direct action against the final Israeli stronghold – the Jewish quarter in the Old City. Although the Jewish garrison numbered just 300, the narrow, winding alleyways of the quarter were in themselves an effective defence against any

Above: Soldiers of the Arab Legion advance, bayonets at the ready; in the narrow lanes of the Old City the Jewish defenders were extremely difficult to dislodge.

assault by ground troops. Although the Arabs had not been able to occupy the area they could at least claim success in isolating it.

For the Jewish defenders the situation was becoming increasingly difficult. Lack of supplies, ammunition and men was gradually weakening their resolve. Several attempts were made by Israeli 'troops' in the New City to reach and resupply the Jews in the Old City. In one attempt, two platoons of the Palmach secured and blew open the Zion Gate in the south of the Jewish quarter. While a section held the gate against possible Arab attack, reinforcements (some 80 men) and ammunition passed to the beleaguered defenders. While this supply route could well have meant the continued successful defence of the Jewish quarter, the immediate counter-attack launched by the Arabs dislodged the Palmach and once more sealed off the Jewish quarter.

Following this attempt at resupply, the Arabs changed their tactics in the old quarter. In a systematic operation, an artillery barrage was combined with concentrated mortar fire. This barrage was closely backed by infantry who took advantage of the artillery cover, moving from house to house, relentlessly pushing the Israelis back. Completely isolated and crammed into a tiny area, the Israelis had no alternative but to surrender. The result had long seemed inevitable, simply because it was not tactically sound to attempt to defend an area so far removed from the main defensive positions.

In early June the Israelis launched a number of offensives, the first concerted one being an attempt to retake Sheikh Jarrah from the Arab Legion. In its early stages the attack was quite successful, due mainly to the fact that the Arabs were taken by surprise. There was no follow through, however, and the Israelis were soon pushed back. Similar attacks were mounted against Arab forces in the Musrara quarter, and these were also defeated; but on 8 June two Palmach columns, supported by concentrated mortar fire, advanced once more. Within a day, and after furious close-quarter combat, the Israelis had occupied most of the quarter. Following this success, the Palmach moved against Sheikh Jarrah, hoping that a successful offensive would link them with their troops on Mount Scopus, but a swift counter-attack by the Arabs drove the Israelis back.

The result of this failed offensive was that military operations virtually ceased in that area. The Jewish quarter of the Old City had fallen, and the Arabs controlled the Latrun sector through which the main Tel Aviv-Jerusalem road passed. It was to this sector that the main military operations now transferred.

Simon Innes

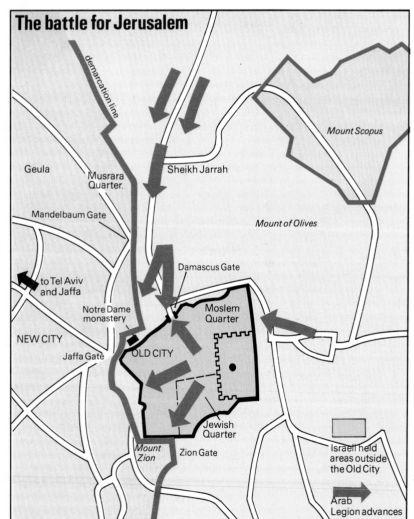

The battle for Jerusalem

Geula
demarcation line
Musrara Quarter.
Sheikh Jarrah
Mandelbaum Gate
Mount Scopus
Mount of Olives
to Tel Aviv and Jaffa
Damascus Gate
Notre Dame monastery
Moslem Quarter
NEW CITY
OLD CITY
Jaffa Gate
Jewish Quarter
Mount Zion
Zion Gate
Israeli held areas outside the Old City
Arab Legion advances

Key Weapons

The CENTURION
part 1

Developing the Centurion

In over three decades of active service the British Centurion main battle tank (MBT) has proved itself one of the finest and most durable armoured fighting vehicles produced since 1945. Combining reliability with a powerful main armament and effective armour protection, the Centurion has been engaged in wars fought throughout the globe – in Korea, India, the Middle East and Vietnam – and has gained the respect of both friend and foe alike. The great strength of the Centurion – like many other successful weapons and vehicles – has been its ability to be upgraded to incorporate new developments in weapon technology and thus remain one step ahead of obsolescence. The developmental range of the Centurion was demonstrated by the 25 separate variants that were produced in a production run of over 4000 tanks that spanned the period from the end of World War II to 1961.

Plans for the Centurion first took shape in 1943 when the existing British cruiser tanks, the Cromwell and its successor the Comet, had reached the limit of their design potential. Mounting 75mm and 77mm guns respectively, they were inferior in terms of armament and armour to the more powerful German tanks then entering service. To counter this threat, design work began in mid-1943 on the Heavy Cruiser A41, later to be known as Centurion. The British Army considered the following characteristics to be of the greatest importance: reliability; gun and armour configuration combat ability; cross-country performance; ease of maintenance.

The earlier British cruisers had suffered a depressing record of mechanical unreliability. Many had been lost in the Western Desert due to trivial breakdowns that strained recovery facilities. The adoption of the Meteor engine and the Merritt-Brown gearbox in the Cromwell and Comet overcame many of these earlier deficiencies; consequently, this successful combination was installed in the A41.

Though consideration had been given to the 77mm gun because of its superior high-explosive capability, a main armament capable of defeating the German Tiger and Panther tanks was deemed essential, and so the 17-pounder, which had proved its worth in anti-tank roles, was adopted. Various combinations of auxiliary weapons were considered, including a quick firing 20mm Polsten gun or two 7.92mm Besas in a ball mounting alongside the main gun, together with a machine gun in the turret rear. The 20mm Polsten, used in the first prototypes, was replaced by a single 7.92mm Besa in later prototype vehicles. The weight of armour was determined by the need to withstand the formidable 88mm anti-tank gun employed by the Germans in heavy tanks and in ground roles. In view of the increased protection afforded by a sloping glacis plate, the hull machine gunner, characteristic of earlier British designs, was dispensed with and his space used for ammunition stowage.

Performance was regarded as secondary to both reliability and effective combat characteristics. Good cross-country ability, comparable to that of the Comet, was, however, deemed necessary – even at the expense of high road speed. Experience having shown the necessity of a high reverse gear, the gearbox was modified accordingly. The hull, built with sloping sides to minimise the effects of mine damage, as well as the vehicle's increased weight, precluded the use of the Christie-type suspension of the earlier cruisers; a modified Horstman type was therefore adopted. Skirting plates were added to protect the suspension against the effects of hollow charge anti-tank weapons, common during the closing stages of the war.

One of the great virtues of the American-built Sherman tank was its ease of maintenance under field conditions; this meant that it could be repaired and

Previous page: Centurions of the Israeli Defence Force rumble forward to the front in Sinai. Top: The first prototype of the A41; developed early in 1945 this tank was to evolve into the Centurion. Alongside the 17pdr main armament is the 20mm Polsten gun, though this secondary armament was not used in subsequent prototypes and was replaced by a co-axial machine gun.

Top: A Centurion Mark 5 of the 14/20th Hussars thunders across desert at high speed. Based on the Mark 3 design, the Mark 5 was armed with a 20pdr main gun. Above: A Centurion Mark 3 of the 8th Hussars lurks in a defensive position overlooking Seoul on the Han River. The Korean War marked the combat debut of the Centurion, where it gained a reputation as a reliable tank with a gun of deadly accuracy.

returned to the battlefield with a minimum of delay. Thus, attempts were made to ensure the accessibility of major components within the Centurion. An interesting innovation was the provision of an auxiliary charging engine to give reserve electrical power for the radios and gun-control equipment.

In May 1944 the mock-up of A41 was viewed at AEC Ltd and an order placed for 20 prototype models. Extensive running trials of test rigs began in September and by the following January production of the prototypes was under way. The first six prototypes, sent to Germany in May 1945, were intended to go into action with the Guards Armoured Division, but the war ended before this could be achieved.

Once the basic design was set, a limited contract was placed in 1946 for 100 vehicles designated

Centurion Mark 1. Development continued, however, resulting in a number of modifications which could not be readily embodied in the production of the Mark 1. Under the design parentage of Vickers Armstrong, the Centurion Mark 2 was introduced in the summer of 1946. The new model incorporated a fully cast turret, replacing the earlier fabricated one, and a coaxial machine gun integral with the main armament as well as stabilised gun-control equipment in both elevation and azimuth. A number of other important features included a commander's vision cupola, increased hull armour and a periscopic gunner's sight in the turret roof.

However, the army did not consider that the Centurion could satisfy the current requirements for a 'universal' tank suitable for both independent armoured operations and infantry support. Such a concept, proposed by Field-Marshal Montgomery, led to the development of the A45, intended to supersede the Centurion. As the specifications called for a tank capable of a number of roles such as bridge-laying, dozing, mine flailing and swimming, it was thought that the Centurion could not fulfil this requirement without extensive redesign. The prototype – now designated FV201 – which appeared in 1948 was based on a more heavily armoured version of the Centurion, with which it shared a number of common features, including the turret and main armament.

As it happened, it was decided not to abandon the Centurion. Accordingly, in 1948, the Mark 3 – mounting a new 20-pounder gun – was introduced. This version, similar to the Mark 2, featured a hull shortened by 10cm (4½in) and redesigned transmission covers. Other improvements, including more advanced gun-control equipment and minor engine modifications, increased power output and improved reliability.

The Centurion Mark 4 was to have been a close-support version mounting a 95mm howitzer as its main armament. But in early 1949 – before production could begin – it was realised that the Mark 3 could fulfil the role with the introduction of the new 20-pounder high explosive and smoke ammunition. The

Mark 4 was then cancelled.

By 1951, production of the Mark 3 had reached the rate of 20 a month. During this period approximately 250 modifications were approved, consistent with experience gained from conditions in the field. These, though of a minor nature in themselves, combined to achieve considerable overall improvement. They included an additional guide roller, removal of the two-inch bombthrower, relocation of the loader's hatches and episcope, and elimination of the turret rear escape hatch. Earlier vehicles were constantly updated to current standards including the Mark 2s, which were upgunned with the 20-pounder to become Mark 3s.

The most pressing requirement, however, was for an increase in the Centurion's radius of action. This had dropped to barely 100km (60 miles) as the vehicle's weight rose from the A41's original 45 tons to the 50 tons of the Mark 3. To remedy this shortcoming, jettisonable fuel drums, similar to those carried by Soviet tanks, were fitted to the rear of the hull. An armoured mono-wheel trailer with 200 gallons of fuel, developed in 1952, proved unpopular with tank crews, as the increased length made manoeuvring difficult. A satisfactory compromise was found in a 100-gallon armoured fuel tank bolted to the hull rear; this was subsequently fitted to many early Centurions.

In the interests of Nato standardisation, the co-axially mounted Besa machine gun was replaced with the .3in Browning; vehicles so fitted were designated Centurion Mark 5s. Apart from an adaptation to the gun mounting, they were identical to the Mark 3s, which were retrospectively modified in 1955.

The Centurion made its combat debut during the Korean War and the first armoured engagement took place in February 1951 when a Centurion Mark 3, supporting an American patrol along the Han River, knocked out a Chinese tank at a range of 2750m (3000yds) with its second shot. In the rugged mountainous terrain of Korea the good hill-climbing performance of the Centurion was a decided asset; it could climb seemingly impossible hills to bring direct fire to bear against the enemy – an ability much envied by the crews of the US Patton and Sherman tanks.

As the conflict bogged down into positional warfare, the Centurion assumed an important infantry-support role. As the Centurion's direct fire was more accurate than that of conventional artillery, valuable support could be given to infantry attacks against the enemy's hillside positions. The accuracy of the Centurion's 20-pounder gun allowed long-range destruction of enemy bunkers and observation posts, a process known as 'posting letters'. Centurion tank crews claimed to be able to put a high explosive round through an opening two feet by one at a range in excess of 1800m (2000yds).

When the Korean War ended, overseas sales orders increased remarkably: the Centurion has seen service with the armies of Australia, Canada, Denmark, Egypt, Holland, India, Iraq, Israel, Jordan, Kuwait, New Zealand, South Africa, Sweden and Switzerland.

In January 1952, an extensive redesign programme was authorised under the auspices of Leyland Motors. The resulting Mark 7 embodied a new hull with increased fuel capacity which, sited internally within the tank, effectively doubled its range. Other principal features were lighter cover louvres for the engine

and transmission, improved ammunition stowage with more 'ready' rounds and a loading port in the hull, an integral turret floor, unified screw threads, revised drive controls and larger headlights. A mock-up of the new vehicle was inspected in November 1952; production began in late 1953.

The Centurion Mark 8, introduced in September 1955, featured a revised turret design incorporating a resilient gun mounting to lessen the likelihood of the trunnion pins shearing under impact from armour-piercing projectiles. A new fire-control system, with elevation by chain drive instead of gears, was fitted, as well as an automatic sensor which engaged the stabilisation system when the tank exceeded a speed of 3.2km (2mph). Better protection was provided for the commander by means of a new cupola with a split hatch which could be elevated in an umbrella position to give overhead cover while retaining the advantages of direct vision. The cupola also enabled contra-

Top: Supported by armoured personnel carriers a Centurion Mark 13 pushes forward on a training manoeuvre. The Mark 13, like other later Marks of the Centurion, was armed with the L7 series gun, a highly successful design that has been used by the Americans in their M48 and M60 tanks and by the Israelis in the Merkava MBT.

Centurion Tank Series Main Variants

Mark	Main Armament	Remarks
A41	17pdr (76.2mm)	
Mark 1 (A41*)	17pdr	
Mark 2 (A41A)	17pdr	
Mark 3	20pdr (83.4mm)	Saw service in Korea; Most later modified to Mk5 standards.
Mark 4	95mm howitzer	Proposed model; later cancelled
Mark 5	20pdr	Based on Mk3 but with a new machine gun mounted on commander's cupola plus modified gun and fire-control equipment
Mark 5/1 (FV4011)	20pdr	Increased glacis-plate armour
Mark 5/2	105mm	Upgunned Mk5
Mark 6	105mm	Upgunned and uparmoured Mk5, some models with an extra armoured fuel tank on hull rear plate
Mark 6/1	105mm	Mk6 with infra-red driving and fighting equipment; stowage basket on turret rear
Mark 6/2	105mm	Mk6 with .5in ranging machine gun
Mark 7 (FV4007)	20pdr	Increased fuel and ammunition stowage
Mark 7/1 (FV4012)	20pdr	Uparmoured Mk7
Mark 7/2	105mm	Upgunned Mk7
Mark 8	20pdr	Resilient mantlet mounting for main gun (fitted with fume extractor on barrel); new commander's cupola and fire-control equipment
Mark 8/1	20pdr	Uparmoured Mk8
Mark 8/2	105mm	Upgunned Mk8
Mark 9 (FV4015)	105mm	Upgunned and uparmoured Mk7
Mark 9/1	105mm	Mk9 with infra-red driving and fighting equipment; stowage basket on turret rear
Mark 9/2	105mm	Mk9 with .5in ranging machine gun
Mark 10 (FV4017)	105mm	Upgunned and uparmoured Mk8 with automatic stabilising system
Mark 10/1	105mm	Mk10 with infra-red driving and fighting equipment; stowage basket on turret rear
Mark 10/2	105mm	Mk10 with .5in ranging machine gun
Mark 11	105mm	Mk6 with .5in ranging machine gun; infra-red driving and fighting equipment; stowage basket on turret rear
Mark 12	105mm	Mk9 with .5in ranging machine gun; infra-red driving and fighting equipment; stowage basket on turret rear
Mark 13	105mm	Mk10 with .5in ranging machine gun; infra-red driving and fighting equipment

Other Variants

Vickers Modified Centurion In 1973 Vickers introduced a refitted Centurion complete with a new General Motors 720bhp diesel engine, semi-automatic transmission and improved gun-control equipment

ARV Centurion Mk2 (FV4006) Armoured Recovery Vehicle, a Mk3 fitted with a winch of a capacity of 91,445kg (90 tons) and armed with a 7.62mm machine gun

BARV Centurion (FV4018) Beach Armoured Recovery Vehicle, turretless and able to operate in water to a depth of 2.90m (9ft 6in)

AVRE Mk5 (FV4003) Armoured Vehicle Royal Engineers, armed with a 165mm demolition gun and equipped with a hydraulically-operated dozer blade mounted on the hull front

Bridgelayer Mk5 (FV4002) Utilises a Mk5 hull and can lay a 13.72m (45ft) single track bridge in two minutes

Above: A Centurion Mark 12, complete with infra-red searchlight and smoke launchers. The penultimate Mark in the Centurion series, the Mark 12 embodied the improvements that had taken place in over a decade of research and development.

rotation to assist in target acquisition.

Meanwhile, developments in tank gunnery had proceeded apace. The L7 105mm gun, designed by the Royal Armament Research and Development Establishment, was introduced in 1959. The new gun, together with appliqué armour for increased protection of the glacis plate, was retrospectively fitted to the majority of Centurions in the British Army. By further limitation of operating space, a total stowage of 70 rounds was achieved – compared with 63 rounds on the Centurion Mark 7 and 65 on the Centurion Marks 3 and 5 – despite the L7's larger rounds.

To increase the effectiveness of the 105mm gun even further, a .5in ranging machine gun was mounted in the mantlet and aligned with the main armament. This made for a simple and accurate method of range-finding and eliminated the need for corrections due to factors such as trunnion tilt and crosswinds. In addition, a thermal sleeve was fitted to the main armament, reducing distortion of the hot gun barrel due to the uneven cooling effects of wind or rain. Infra-red equipment for night fighting and driving was also installed on later models including the Mark 13, the last production Mark of the Centurion series.

Centurion production ended in 1961 but the tank remained in service with the British Army until 1967, when it began to be replaced by the Chieftain MBT. Overseas, the Centurion's life has been extended further still. A mainstay of the Indian Army, the Centurion proved more than a match for the US-built Pakistan M47 and M48 tanks during the border conflicts of 1956, and in the war of 1971 the Centurion again outfought the Pakistani's tank force – this time comprising the T59, the Chinese version of the Soviet T54.

The Australian Army sent a squadron of Centurions to Vietnam in 1968 where, in spite of the difficult terrain for tank warfare, they proved useful in an infantry support role; the tank's thick armour was able to survive the effects of North Vietnamese RPG rocket launchers and its canister rounds were very effective against unprotected infantry, as well as for clearing jungle and vegetation covering enemy bunkers. In the wars of the Middle East between Israel and the Arab states the Centurion achieved further renown when, in the hands of the Israeli Defence Force, it was acknowledged as one of the outstanding battlefield weapons of the 1967 Six-Day War and the Yom Kippur War of 1973. From a medium cruiser tank of the World War II period, the Centurion had come a long way.

Below: The .5in ranging gun and the .3in co-axial machine gun are situated within the turret mantlet on the right of the 105mm main gun. Above the mantlet is the infra-red search light, an invaluable aid to night-fighting.

A Centurion Mark 13 – the final model to see service with the British Army. The tank commander stands by his .3in Browning which replaced the old 7.92mm Besa model in order to ensure ammunition compatibility with the rest of Nato.

Centurion Mark 13 MBT

Crew 4
Dimensions: Length (gun included) 9.85m (32ft 4in); width 3.39m (11ft 1½in); height 3.01m (9ft 10½in)
Weight Combat loaded 51,820kg (114,250lb)
Ground pressure 0.95kg/cm² (13.2lb/in²)
Engine Rolls-Royce Meteor Mk IVB 12-cylinder, liquid-cooled petrol engine developing 650bhp at 2,550rpm

Performance Maximum road speed 34.6km/h (21.5mph); range (road) 190km (118 miles); vertical obstacle 0.91m (3ft); trench 3.55m (11ft); gradient 60 per cent; fording 1.45m (4ft 10in), with kit 2.74m (9ft)

Armour Min-max 17-152mm (0.67-6.08in)
Armament One 105mm L7A2 gun; one .5in ranging machine gun; two .3in machine guns – one co-axial with main armament, the other mounted on the commander's cupola; two six-barrelled smoke dischargers, one on each side of the turret

Communist takeover

The Iron Curtain descends on Europe

From 4 to 11 February 1945 an Allied summit conference was held at Yalta. The name of this pleasant resort on the Crimean peninsula has, to many ears, particularly in eastern Europe, as infamous a ring of appeasement and sell-out as has Munich. But at the time, to the peoples of Europe, weary of the war against Nazism and kept in ignorance of Josef Stalin's deep suspicions of his capitalist allies, Yalta was a beacon of hope.

Stalin's main objective at the Yalta conference was to obtain British and United States approval for the postwar dismemberment of Germany and Russia's territorial acquisitions in eastern and central Europe. Much time was taken up by the question of the future of Poland, which was by then occupied by the Red Army and had a Soviet puppet government issuing decrees from the town of Lublin. Stalin wanted this so-called Lublin committee to be recognised as the

provisional government pending free elections in Poland. Churchill and Roosevelt argued for the formation of a new provisional government, to be composed of the Lublin committee along with other Poles from inside and outside Poland. But Stalin would agree only to the enlargement of the committee by the addition of 'one or two democratic leaders' from Polish 'émigré circles'. Roosevelt and Churchill agreed on a slightly revised Soviet plan for Poland, in effect accepting the Lublin committee as the provisional government but enjoining it to hold 'free and unfettered' elections as soon as possible, with the participation of 'democratic and anti-Nazi parties'.

Stalin's long-term strategy for Poland extended beyond making sure of a subservient government, which he insisted must collaborate with Moscow against a rebirth of German militarism. He demanded that Roosevelt and Churchill recognise the old frontiers of the Russian empire in Romania, Finland and the Baltic states. In the case of Poland he had already obtained the support of Churchill and Roosevelt for the 1920 Curzon frontier between Russia and Poland, restoring to the Soviet Union the Polish territory acquired under the Nazi-Soviet pact in 1939.

The Yalta conference produced a 'Declaration on Liberated Europe', which affirmed the desire of the Big Three to see democratic institutions installed in the countries that had been occupied by Germany. During the Yalta negotiations, however, Stalin had not disguised his very different beliefs about the rights of small nations. Large powers, he said, must dictate to the small. When Churchill countered with the responsibility of large nations to respect the rights of the smaller, Stalin disagreed.

The Yalta agreements did not grant Stalin specific rights in eastern Europe. The notorious percentages scribbled half-seriously by Churchill on a piece of paper, dividing Europe into spheres of influence at an earlier meeting with Stalin, were not even mentioned at Yalta. But the obvious divisions and lack of coordination in the presentation of Western proposals and policies convinced Stalin that he had a free hand in east Europe.

At the end of June a provisional coalition government was formed in Warsaw and recognised by the Western powers. It consisted mainly of members of the former Lublin committee. Elections were finally held in January 1947 in conditions of terror and fraud. Many supporters of Stanislaw Mikolajczyk, the former prime minister, were murdered and attempts were made on his life after his large Peasant Party had refused to merge with the communist-dominated 'government bloc'. The United States and Britain declared that the elections were not free. In October that year Mikolajczyk received information that he was about to be put on trial, and he fled to the West.

A similar pattern of events unfolded in the rest of eastern Europe as Stalin imposed communist rule, disregarding the provisions of the Yalta agreement. By that time America and Britain had withdrawn from those parts of Germany which it had been agreed at Yalta would go to make up the Soviet zone; and their wartime armies had been demobilised. Although there was a steady demobilisation of Soviet forces in subsequent years, a huge standing army and air force was maintained, several divisions remaining in occupation of eastern Europe.

Communism was imposed mainly by the Soviet armed forces. Except in the case of Yugoslavia and Albania it was not a natural outcome of the political situation of any of the countries of east and central Europe. In the eyes of Moscow, communism in eastern Europe was not an end in itself but rather an instrument for the establishment of complete Soviet control over the whole of that area principally for the purpose of creating a 'buffer zone' between the Soviet Union and a resurgent Germany or aggressive Western Europe. Control meant seizing and keeping an exclusive hold on the two main levers of power, the secret police and the sole political party in a single-party state.

The rather general military agreements made by the Big Three at Yalta were too generously interpreted by the Western allies. Western troops were prevented from advancing not only on Berlin but Prague also, thus allowing the Soviet armies to reach these capitals first. Whether, under a different strategy, Berlin could have been reached before the Russians remains

Previous page: Churchill, Roosevelt and Stalin, the 'Big Three', decide upon the future of Europe at the Yalta conference in 1945. Inset: A cover of *Newsweek* expresses fears of Soviet expansionism in 1948.

Europe in 1936

Left: The Russian presence in Europe in 1945. Soviet infantry advance through the Polish town of Breslau against German units.
Right: Outside the Vienna Opera House in 1945, an American soldier (to the left) and a group of Russian soldiers illustrate the spirit of alliance that existed before the Iron Curtain descended upon Europe.

an open question, but Prague certainly could have been.

By May 1945, Soviet troops were in control of what, before the war, had been eight independent states: Estonia, Latvia, Lithuania, Poland, Czechoslovakia, Hungary, Romania and Bulgaria. During the war Soviet leaders had given public pledges that Russia did not seek territorial gains or the subjugation of peoples. Yet after the war the Soviet Union acquired in Europe 470,850 square km (181,800 square miles) of territory with a pre-war population of over 22.3 million. Estonia, Latvia and Lithuania had been covered by two secret protocols to the Nazi-Soviet pact of August 1939 and were simply re-annexed during the Soviet Army advances in the autumn of 1944. The eastern territories of Poland, covered by another secret protocol, were re-occupied in similar fashion.

The other country affected by the secret protocols of the Nazi-Soviet pact was Romania, which was forced to cede Bessarabia to Russia. This was confirmed by the Paris Peace Treaty of February 1947, which also awarded the adjacent territory of northern Bukovina to Russia. Under the same treaty Russia regained from Finland the Karelian Isthmus and other Finnish provinces. From Germany the Soviet Union obtained East Prussia. Unlike the other annexations which had been 'awarded' to the Soviet Union by the Nazi-Soviet pact of 1939, East Prussia was, as it were, a postwar bonus.

In the same category was an area taken this time from an allied country. On 15 May 1945 the pro-Soviet Prime Minister of Czechoslovakia, Zdeněk Fierlinger, declared that his government would not oppose the desire of the predominantly Ukrainian-speaking people of Ruthenia for incorporation into

Communist expansion in Europe 1939-49

- Soviet Union and territory acquired from 1939 to 1945
- postwar satellite states
- independent communist state
- — limit of Soviet expansion

The KGB in Latvia

Georgi Martynov was a long-serving member of the KGB who defected to the West in the 1960s. He took part in several actions against Ukrainian nationalists such as the Provoda group and the followers of Stephen Bandera, against anti-communist partisans in Russia proper and, as he relates here, against nationalists in the Baltic states in 1945 and 1946.

" I was at the time a commando officer in the KGB and had taken part, not only in battles with German troops, but also in the extermination of saboteurs dropped behind our lines and of collaborators operating in the liberated territories. The scale of the operation depended, of course, on the size and armament of the nationalist group we had to liquidate. For example, two divisions of KGB troops were used in the Ukraine to liquidate a large detachment of Banderites who had gone into hiding in an area close to the frontier of the Lvov region. The whole area was encircled by three ranks of soldiers, each within sight of the other. The circle was then gradually reduced in size to the point when we came face to face with the enemy and the fighting started. It was the most desperate and brutal fighting, in which there was no surrendering and no prisoners taken.

We continued with these operations in district after district, wherever our commanders had information that there were still 'left-overs', as we called them. In central Russia and in the Ukraine it was relatively easy to uncover these bands. But in Latvia we were amazed at the situation we stumbled on. On one occasion we had very precise information about a detachment of nationalists said to be hiding in a forest not far from a small farm from which they obtained food and water. We surrounded the area and then gradually moved in towards the centre where the Latvian nationalists were supposed to be. But, instead of coming face to face with the nationalists, we came up against each other. They seemed to have vanished into thin air. We began to go over the area inch by inch, looking into every bush and tree, but could still find nothing to arouse our suspicions.

Finally somebody noticed that there was a barn near the farm, rather tumbledown but, for some reason or other, full of hay. This was rather suspicious, because, at a time when the cattle were dying for lack of fodder, it was odd to come across so much apparently neglected hay. We threw it to one side and revealed a carefully disguised trap-door. It was obviously the entrance to an underground bunker.

We had already come across such bunkers in Russia and the Ukraine, but what we experienced now was beyond anything we could have imagined. And the action that followed was, I believe, the most frightful of all those I took part in, not so much in its intensity as in its savagery and cruelty and its inhuman end.

One of our number who spoke Latvian called out through the trap-door and proposed that they should leave the bunker and lay down their arms. He warned them that unless they complied we should attack the bunker with grenades. The reply came that they agreed, but on condition that we moved back not less than two hundred metres from the barn to wait for them to come out.

We knew about the desperate courage of the Latvians and their strong nationalist feelings, but our commanders accepted their proposal and we moved back two hundred metres without taking some elementary precautions to defend ourselves in the event of an attack. We paid dearly for this. The time passed very slowly. It was probably half an hour before anybody appeared. But hardly had our Latvian shouted out to find out when they were going to start surrendering when suddenly they opened furious fire on us from automatics, machine guns and even mortars mounted in the loft. Many of our men were hit by the Latvian fire, although there was no panic, because troops of the task force were well trained and ready to deal with surprise attacks.

After a couple of minutes' confusion our men took cover and fierce fighting began. Nobody wanted to surrender and no one wanted to die, but in that duel death was inescapable. Suddenly the Latvians ceased firing. The door of the barn opened and we were horrified to see women and children coming out. The colonel in charge of the operation gave the order not to fire and to let the women pass through the ring of armed men. It is difficult to convey the state of tension and of total immobility that took hold of us when we saw the Latvian men coming out behind the women and children. There were 30 or 40 women and children and perhaps as many men, who had gone into hiding and sworn never to surrender to the Russians.

We had somehow or other to separate the male Latvians from the women and children, so we opened fire from the right and left flanks, but the women and children not only failed to run ahead, as we expected, but rushed back into the barn with the men. An attempt at negotiations proved fruitless. Their reply was quite explicit: either we are allowed to leave with our families or you can shoot us all together. None of us had come up against such a situation before, and even our heartless commanders could not apparently bring themselves to shoot the lot of them in the hope that all would be forgotten because of the war.

The ring around the Latvians was drawn still tighter, until we were no more than 25 or 30 metres from the barn, so that no one could leave it and they could not count on darkness to help them. Then came the night and total darkness. We had no means of lighting up the area and had to strain our eyes lest we missed something in the darkness.

Suddenly the Latvians opened fire, powerful but disordered, in our direction. One of our men could not restrain himself and fired in reply, and others did the same. Can one now blame those who opened fire on the women and children? There may be some who can, but I cannot, for it took place when Hitler's Germany had already been routed, and yet we were still fighting, nerves were strained to the limit, and no one wanted to die in peacetime.

There was an unbelievable noise, the trunks and branches of the trees crackled as the bullets hit them, and then suddenly there was an explosion and in a moment a huge flame turned the barn into one big torch, which lit up everything in the neighbourhood, including our pallid faces. There were no cries or groans to be heard, although there were living people burning within. Without any word of command we ceased firing and looked silently at the destruction in the fire of people who, even if they were enemies, were strong and courageous.

Suddenly a dark figure came staggering out of the fire. It was someone who was out to save his life but who was blinded by the darkness and rushed straight into the arms of our soldiers. Seriously burned but still living he was the only person who survived to tell the tale of what happened in the barn. He was not executed because he was a much-needed witness to the affair. All the others perished – more than 150 people. Like them, the survivor hated us and did not conceal it, but he had been afraid to die along with them. There was nothing special about his hatred, because in war people kill each other because they hate each other, and it is difficult to kill without hatred.

The 'unfinished war' continued well into 1946, and the nationalists and supporters of fascism who managed to survive and realised the futility of armed resistance went into the deep underground in the hope of concealing their past. But many of them were not successful and met their ends twenty or thirty years later from a bullet delivered by a soldier of the KGB's internal security troops. "

the USSR. Six days later, without any plebiscite to determine the real wishes of the people, it was announced that an autonomous Ruthenian government had been formed. In June Fierlinger signed a treaty in Moscow handing over this area to Russia.

The key to the takeover of the five independent states of east Europe, with 80 million people living in them, was the secret police. In the Soviet system they played a far more important role than had been the case even in Hitler's Germany.

After the military occupation of a country by the Soviet Army the first step was to put the secret police into communist hands by installing Moscow-trained communists in the Ministry of the Interior. In Poland and Bulgaria these departments had been in communist control since mid-1944; the communists secured control of the Interior Ministry in Romania in March 1945, a month before they did so in Czechoslovakia. Success in Hungary followed in November. In Yugoslavia, as in Albania, communist control over the secret police had been established in the course of the war as the communist resistance forces took over civil government in liberated areas. Only Finland managed, in 1948, to get rid of its communist Interior Minister, who had been appointed in March 1945 by a pro-Soviet prime minister.

The appointment of communists to these positions opened the door to Soviet 'advisers' who rapidly took control of all secret police operations. All these men were officers of the Soviet secret police. They arranged for the strategic placing of more Soviet 'advisers' throughout all the ministries and departments. This meant that even when the occupation armies had withdrawn, Moscow was able to keep every department of government in the satellite countries under direct supervision.

With the levers of power throughout eastern Europe already in their control, the Soviet leaders proceeded to impose communist regimes – a process that involved the intimidation of entire populations and the physical extermination of thousands of political opponents. Once the communist regimes were installed, control remained in Moscow's hands – except in Yugoslavia and Albania, where the regimes had installed themselves and the countries had not come under Soviet occupation.

Broadly the political operation was carried out in four stages. First, a 'front' was formed – a new and more efficient form of the pre-war 'popular fronts' of the 1930s. The second stage in the postwar communist takeover consisted of forming coalition governments with left-wing parties and sometimes with right-wing politicians. In the third stage the non-communist parties in the coalition, while nominally sharing power, were effectively emasculated, their leaders being chosen by the communists. Political opposition, though risky, was still tolerated. In the final phase, when the coalitions were transformed into 'governing blocs' the non-communist parties were absorbed or simply suppressed. Socialist parties were forced, with the help of turncoat members, to fuse with the communists. Political opposition was no longer tolerated in parliament or anywhere else. Mátyás Rákosi gave a classic description of the methods used to fragment the opposition in Hungary – 'demanding a little more each day, like cutting up salami, slice after thin slice'. Strict censorship was imposed. Political opponents were destroyed through political trials on charges of collaboration, treason, espionage or sabotage. The church was infiltrated by the secret police. The operation was then rounded off by the adoption of written constitutions closely modelled on that of the Soviet Union, guaranteeing human rights that were now honoured only in the breach. General elections would then take place, sometimes preceded by campaigns of intimidation and violence.

Following the virtual neutralisation of the other parties it was a simple matter to take over the civil service bureaucracies, to unify and bring trade unions, agricultural organisations, cultural, youth, sports and other institutions under communist control. The remnants of private industry, banks, farms and insurance companies would then be nationalised. The process would often be ushered in by fraudulent elections. In the last stage, secret police activity would come to permeate every facet of life.

Finally, the economies of eastern European countries were made increasingly dependent upon the Soviet Union. But by then the safeguards enshrined in the Yalta agreements to protect human rights and democratic freedoms no longer had any relevance in that part of Europe. It was a state of affairs which led the West to question Soviet motives in the postwar world, and this was a central feature of the decline in relations between East and West which is usually and aptly termed the Cold War.

Hugh Lunghi

The Red Army

Stalin's most fearsome weapon

At the end of World War II international politics were dominated by two powers whose full potential had not previously been fully realised. The United States' pre-eminence rested on the strength of its economy, the range of forces and weapons it could deploy and, in particular, its possession of the atomic bomb. By contrast the Soviet Union's position derived almost entirely from the strength of the Red Army. Observers were impressed by its size, its achievement in defeating the German Army and the price it had paid in casualties for victory. There was, however, little understanding of the true nature of the Red Army; much of the 'Russian steamroller's' menace lay in this ignorance. It is still difficult to analyse the Russian war machine in conventional Western terms. It is necessary to emphasise its uniqueness.

The Red Army was undoubtedly vast. In 1945, although it had passed its peak strength, it still numbered more than 11 million. It deployed over 600 divisions and independent formations. But the reality behind these figures was complex. Very few Soviet divisions were as strong as 8000 men, most were 5000 to 7000 strong, and some were only cadres of 3000. About 500 of these divisions and brigades were infantry formations that would not have been out of place on any World War I battlefield. The divisions marched into battle on their feet and relied on horse-drawn transport for their supplies.

The striking power of the Red Army was concentrated in its 40 artillery divisions and its armoured forces. It possessed 25 tank corps and 13 mechanised corps (equivalent to divisions in size). In these and a variety of independent units the Soviets fielded 14,000 modern tanks. The importance of these formations was out of all proportion to their numbers.

Numbers also tell us little about the quality of Soviet manpower. The overwhelming majority of Soviet soldiers came from a peasant background. They were renowned for their endurance under appalling conditions and their passive acceptance of casualties. They did not lack tactical cunning, excelling at camouflage and deception; but the educational standard, even of Soviet officers, was low and the

The two faces of the Russian Army. Below left: Cossack cavalry in the Don Valley attack an enemy position. The spearhead of the Soviet forces was, however, the armoured formations (left). Here T34/85 tanks and SU-100 self-propelled guns take part in a victory parade through Moscow in 1945.

army was forced to rely on simply battle drills which were easily taught but were often applied too rigidly. Discipline was exceptionally harsh and was enforced by officers who knew that laxness on their part would be severely punished. The Red Army's behaviour in occupied territory suggests that this discipline was deliberately relaxed at the end of the war. Widespread reports of looting and rape gave the army an evil reputation and spurred millions of refugees to flee westwards. Among them after the war were unknown thousands of deserters, disillusioned with Soviet life, who joined the mass of displaced persons in western Europe.

Despite the size of the Russian war machine it was rigidly controlled from the centre. Josef Stalin in Moscow, as commander-in-chief as well as political leader, kept a very tight grip on operations. He worked through the Stavka (General Headquarters of the Supreme Command), which was a small group of senior officers supported by the General Staff. All major operations were planned in Moscow, leaving field commanders much less freedom than in other armies. Members of the Stavka, such as Marshal Georgi Zhukhov, were then sent to the front to supervise these plans in action. Stalin was briefed three times a day about operations and was in constant touch with his commanders by teleprinter and radio, which enabled him to intervene even at the lowest tactical level. In addition, every commander down to company level had a Communist Party official as deputy commander for political affairs. Both Stalin's successors, Nikita Khrushchev and Leonid Brezhnev, served as political deputies (commissars) at the front.

All these elements – the superfluity of manpower, combined with a limited mechanised element, a largely uneducated army and strict central control – were reflected in the operations of the Red Army. Western observers have tended to discuss the Red Army's tactics purely in terms of the 'Russian steamroller' overwhelming the enemy by sheer weight of numbers regardless of casualties. Anything more sophisticated in Soviet tactics has been ascribed to

copying the German blitzkrieg. This is a misconception of what the Russians were trying to do.

Before World War II the Red Army had paid as much attention to new weapons such as the aeroplane and the tank as any of its rivals. It was not ignorant of Western concepts but whereas Western armies tended to believe that the revolution in warfare favoured smaller, more professional armies, the Russians retained their traditional belief in the virtues of a mass army. However, the state of the Soviet economy, even after the forced industrialisation of the 1930s, did not permit the creation of a totally mechanised

Above: Russian soldiers advance during the battle for the Emperor Bridge in Vienna during World War II.

Soviet 'new type' rifle division – 1948
Strength 11,000

DIVISION

- reconnaissance battalion
- signals unit
- medical unit
- engineer battalion

armoured regiment
50-55 T54s
15-20 SP
100mm guns

artillery brigade
24 x 76mm guns
36 x 122mm howitzers
12 x 160mm mortars

anti-tank battalion

anti-aircraft battalion
37mm A/A guns

rifle regiment | rifle regiment | rifle regiment

miscellaneous small units | rifle battalion | rifle battalion | rifle battalion | regimental artillery
76mm SP guns
120mm mortars
57mm A/T guns

miscellaneous small units | rifle company | rifle company | rifle company | heavy weapons company
8-12 HMGs
8-12 82mm mortars

heavy weapons company

rifle company
200-250 rifles
27 LMGs
9 HMGs

mass army. Despite this, an able generation of Soviet military writers did develop a doctrine for modern armoured offensive operations. Unfortunately many of these officers disappeared during Stalin's purges, which generally had a stultifying effect on Soviet military thought. Then Germany's surprise attack in June 1941 forced the Russians into a defensive war for which they were totally unprepared in doctrine and *matériel*. By the middle of 1943 the defensive phase was over and the Red Army was poised to recover its lost territory and carry the war onto German soil.

It is important to understand the problems faced by the Red Army in this offensive phase. The Eastern Front was thousands of miles long, and most of the army consisted of foot-slogging troops incapable of sustained offensive action. But it is equally true that infantry divisions comprised most of the German Army, and by 1944 the Red Army was capable of concentrating the forces required, according to its doctrine, for a successful attack on certain narrow sectors of the front. However, there is no doubt that, right to the end of the war, the German Army maintained its advantage in the individual standard of its troops, who were better trained and showed greater initiative. German commanders and staffs were also on the whole more capable of fighting a mobile war, when Hitler allowed them the opportunity, although some Soviet leaders were the equal of any as armoured commanders. Lastly the Red Army lacked the logistic support to fight a continuously mobile battle. Only the arrival of American Lend-Lease trucks – 440,000 out of a total Soviet vehicle strength of 500,000 – made a rapid offensive possible.

Soviet policy was therefore to hold the front line with lower quality infantry units. Stavka then selected the sector on which an offensive was to be launched and concentrated its reserves there. These reserves included divisions of artillery and especially multi-barrelled rocket launchers, tank armies and the so-called 'shock armies' that were composed of high quality troops backed by concentrations of artillery and tanks. Support elements such as engineers and transport were also assembled. As far as possible this concentration was carried out in secret, using the night for movement and paying great attention to camouflage. Deception measures included dummy concentrations elsewhere along the front.

The offensive was controlled by at least one *front* headquarters. *Front* was the Soviet term for an army group and its size and composition depended on its task; it was often commanded by a member of Stavka. The basic principles of the offensive were concentration, momentum and mobility. Concentration was achieved by dividing the front into a breakthrough sector and a passive sector. The breakthrough sector was no more than 5 to 15 per cent of the whole, but it would be allocated 50 to 80 per cent of the infantry and artillery and 90 to 100 per cent of the tanks and aircraft. The size of the breakthrough sector varied: it was 14 to 25km (8 to 15 miles) for a *front*, 7 to 12km (4 to 7.5 miles) for an army and 1 to 2km (0.6 to 1.2 miles) for a division.

The aim was to achieve the 'correlation of forces' stated in Soviet doctrine, which required superiorities of 4 or 6 to 1 in manpower and up to 10 to 1 in artillery and tanks on the breakthrough sector. As an additional guide Soviet doctrine expressed the requirements for success in density norms, which by 1945 had reached at least 250 guns and mortars and 70 tanks per kilometre of front. Forces on the passive sector were obviously much less well supported but they were expected to attack the enemy just as fiercely in order to disguise the direction of the main blow and prevent the enemy from manoeuvring his reserves to meet it.

Momentum was achieved by echelonning forces. German defensive positions were generally constructed in depth, with an outpost line, a main defensive zone with probably three lines of trenches, and a rear defensive zone. The Red Army faced basically the same problem as commanders of World War I – that is how to maintain the offensive once it passed the initial range of artillery. Each formation or unit down to regiment was organised in at least two echelons, the first echelon being roughly twice as strong as the second. The formation was allocated a primary and a secondary objective, to be taken by the first and

Below: Soviet tanks and armoured personnel carriers move at speed over rough terrain. The emphasis on overwhelming massed offensives in Soviet training greatly increased Western fears about Russian intentions.

Russia's penal battalions

'The penal battalions [of the Soviet Army in the early 1940s] contained individuals who had shown reluctance to fight and others who were suspected of cowardice. With them were officers and soldiers who had been sentenced for various crimes and offences. The officers who were sent to the battalions lost any decorations they had been awarded, together with their ranks, and joined the battalion as privates. During periods of calm the penal battalions were kept in the rear. At the last moment before an offensive, they were brought up, under guard, and positioned at the forward edge of the battle area. As the artillery preparation began, the guard company, armed with machine guns, would take their place behind the penal companies, who were then issued with weapons. Then, on the command "Advance to attack!" the guard company's machine guns would force the reluctant penal companies to get to their feet and to advance. Being unable to move in any other direction, they attacked, frenziedly. The most brilliant victories achieved by the Soviet Army were bought with the blood of the penal battalions.'

From Inside the Soviet Army *by Viktor Suvorov.*

Above: A Soviet armoured spearhead of T34/85 tanks supported by infantry push forward through a Polish wood during a winter offensive in January 1945. Although interarms cooperation in the Red Army was less sophisticated than in Western forces, the Soviet Army had an enviable ability to maintain an offensive in the most adverse conditions.

second echelons respectively. For example, a division's first echelon would normally be expected to penetrate 4 to 5km (2.5 to 3 miles) into the defences and its second echelon to advance to a depth of 8 to 10km (5 to 6 miles), probably breaking through the German main defence zone in the process.

The assault would normally start with a paralysing heavy artillery bombardment. For the Berlin operation in April 1945, for example, the Red Army assembled more artillery than was available to all the armies in World War I. Because of the comparatively low level of training in the Red Army a high proportion of the artillery would be used for direct fire – that is, the gunners could actually see their target rather than relying on observers to control their shooting as in the indirect fire which most armies used.

Following closely on the heels of the rolling barrages of the artillery would come the infantry with their close support tanks. A battalion attacked in one echelon with three companies in line, each company formed in lines of platoons. The regiments' second echelon battalions would follow, and the divisions' second echelon regiments would be at hand. Thus the German defenders would see apparently unending waves of troops and tanks moving towards them. Seasoned troops who kept their nerve could inflict terrible casualties on the attackers, and some Soviet offensives did come to a juddering halt. However, more often the artillery barrage had done its work and the Soviet infantry would ignore their casualties and breach the defences. They were encouraged not only by the intensive political work which preceded any attack, encouraging patriotic and communist fervour and hatred of the enemy, but also by the knowledge that behind each assaulting division would come a battalion of NKVD (secret police) troops, with orders to shoot anyone who turned back.

Once a breach had been created, mobility became more important. A 'mobile group' would be passed through the 'cannon fodder' infantry divisions to penetrate rapidly into the enemy's deep rear. An army would normally use a tank corps in this role and a *front* would send an entire tank army. The aim of the mobile group was to prevent the enemy stabilising his position by occupying new defence lines to the rear. The mobile group would press on, bypassing strongpoints, until it reached the limits of its logistic support or reached an obstacle, such as a major river, which required full-scale preparation to surmount. The offensive would then die down, and a pause would follow in which Stavka might shift the emphasis to another part of the front and the whole process of assembling forces and stockpiling supplies would begin again.

Thus the 'breakthrough operation' relied for its success on very simple ingredients. It was designed to exploit Soviet strengths and German weaknesses. The Germans did not have the resources to endure battles of attrition. The Red Army did but would have been at a disadvantage in a war of manoeuvre. As long as the leadership was prepared to pay the price (and 13 million servicemen were killed during the war) then this was a successful policy.

The Red Army finished the war with its prestige at a peak. It had done everything asked of it, and wherever it stood a communist regime was soon established. The Red Army had in fact played a major part in creating the new world it faced in 1945. The new situation was characterised by the Cold War, but it was also clear that a revolution in military technology was beginning which would change the whole face of warfare. There followed superficial changes, such as renaming the Red Army of Workers and Peasants as the Soviet Army in 1946. The army was reduced in size from 11,365,000 in May 1945 to 2,874,000 in 1948. New tank and mechanised infantry divisions were created gradually, replacing the traditional rifle division. However, progress was delayed by the intervention of Stalin.

Concerned by the status and popularity of the army, which rivalled those of the Communist Party itself, Stalin reasserted his personal control. Marshal Zhukhov, Russia's most successful commander, was demoted to command the obscure Odessa Military District. Senior naval and air force officers were arrested. Analysis of the lessons of the war was completely unbalanced by insistence on Stalin's personal contribution and military genius. His five 'permanently operating factors' – stability of the rear, morale, quantity and quality of divisions, armament of the forces, and abilities of the commanders – were held to be the whole secret of success. Factors such as surprise were said to be only transitory in their effect. Furthermore, although he gave secret orders for the development of atomic weapons, Stalin publicly refused to admit that they could decide the outcome of a war.

And so, until Stalin's death in 1953, the Soviet Army made little progress in adjusting to the new realities of warfare. Its roles were to secure Russia's hold on eastern Europe and, in the event of war, to seize western Europe as rapidly as possible to counter the American nuclear threat. It remained potentially a most formidable force and undoubtedly capable of its peacetime role; but a question mark remained about its capabilities and relevance on a nuclear battlefield.

Michael Orr

Private Ivan
The Russian fighting man

In most Western countries the army is apolitical: it does what is commanded of it by the government of the day. This is true in the Soviet Union too; but as there is only one party, permanently in power, the Soviet Army is a political army. In this, it reflects Soviet society, where every aspect of human life is directed by the Communist Party. Military training is carried out with a political goal in mind and this political goal is defined early in a person's life.

Before Soviet children start their formal education they will have been exposed to the ideas of Marx and Lenin, and the role the Soviet military plays in helping to fulfil them. Books such as *A Soldier was walking along the street* are accepted early readers for children of pre-school age. When they are 7 years old, children are eligible to join the Octobrists, the first rung on the ladder to party membership. The more overtly military part of their education begins on the next rung when, aged 10, they join the Pioneers. As well as being taught of the glorious victories of the Soviet Army in the Russian Revolution and the Great Patriotic War, the Pioneer experiences his first military training, mainly at summer camp. Here girls and boys are introduced to the rudiments of military discipline and regulations, guard duty, tactics and civil defence. When the child moves up to the Komsomol, the Young Communist League for 15 to 28 year olds, these skills will be further developed with the addition of map reading, weapons use and grenade-throwing. The ability to throw a grenade is tested in the school-leaving examination.

From the age of 14 the Soviet citizen may well have been a member of the Voluntary Society for Cooperation with the Army, Air Force and Navy (DOSAAF). On top of attending camp he or she will take part in a 140-hour training programme spread over two academic years in which general military skills are enhanced and basic training is given in a military technical speciality such as driving, radiotelephone operation or electrical tasks. This training has taken on an added significance since the Universal Military Service law of 1967 reduced the period of conscription from three years to two in the army and four to three in the navy.

The soldier's day

Reveille	0600-0605
Physical training, cleaning barracks	0605-0630
Washing, bed-making	0630-0650
Political information	0650-0720
Breakfast	0725-0755
Lessons	0800-1350
Lunch	1400-1440
Break	1440-1520
Weapons and equipment maintenance	1520-1530
Political education (Mon, Thu) Technical maintenance (Tue, Fri) Sport (Wed, Sat)	1530-1830
Study	1830-1940
Supper	1940-2010
Free time	2010-2140
Evening walk, roll call	2140-2155
Lights out	2200

Above: Military cadets parade in Red Square during the 1979 celebrations of the anniversary of the 1917 revolution. Opposite: Soviet Marines train for many hours each day. Here they are put through their first parachute jumps from a static descent tower.

Below: A short-range tactical missile, lying in its launching slide, during exercises near Leningrad.

Despite 'universal' military service in the Soviet Union, not all Soviet youths aged 18 are conscripted. Some are omitted for health or family reasons; some in order that they may continue their education; others are merely lucky. Nevertheless, the majority are called-up and for them the two (or three) years ahead are tough. The policy of two call-up periods a year has led to the development of a four tier society in the barrack block. Treatment of the juniors by the seniors is harsh – as are the rates of 'pay', between 3 and 5 roubles a month. A conscript is not allowed to wear civilian clothes, nor will he normally be granted leave. As far as his superiors are concerned, the Soviet soldier has no cravings for such pleasures as alcohol or women. In practice, of course, he does. On occasions girlfriends are smuggled into barrack blocks; but if this is discovered the guilty soldier is severely punished.

Every minute of the conscript's day is carefully accounted for, from reveille at 0600 hours to lights out at 2200. As in any army, great stress is laid upon physical fitness and discipline. On 1 November 1973, a gruelling fitness test was introduced, setting minimum standards for running, swimming, and either skiing or long marches, which all military personnel are required to attain in their first year of service. Discipline is often enforced by 'collective responsibility'. If one soldier steps out of line the whole of his section is likely to be punished.

Training is kept simple. If a soldier's speciality is driving a tank, this is all he will do. He will practice his tasks again and again until they become second nature. Simplicity is the key in Soviet weapon design, too. This ensures that the conscript is able to perform effectively if recalled as a reservist in later life, as all medically fit Soviet males are on the reserve list from the age of 17 until they are 50. An important consideration, too, is the thought that in the heat of battle the less complicated the weapon the more reliable it will be in the hands of a possibly frightened man. The Soviet Army does its best to acquaint its soldiers with the fear of battle. Combat realism is emphasised in exercises. An infantryman in training is made to lie in a shallow ditch, or directly between the tracks of a tank, as it rumbles over him.

The Soviet leadership believes that it has a secret weapon: ideology. Marxism-Leninism is the whole raison d'être, not only of the Soviet armed forces but of the structure of Soviet society itself. There is a greater concentration of party members in the armed forces than in any other area of society, since it is virtually essential for an officer to be a member of the party if he is to succeed in his career. Military personnel are exposed to a higher level of political indoctrination than anyone else, not only in the periods set aside for it in the daily routine, but also by means of films on Saturday evenings, and often in 'free time'.

Unquestionably, Soviet conscript soldiers are fit and well disciplined. It is not so easy to say, though, to what extent they are convinced of their ideology. The Communist slogans with which they have been brought up become hackneyed and meaningless for many. Nevertheless, Soviet doctrine prefers a politically sound soldier who has only limited ability with a rifle to a crackshot who does not respect the pronouncements of Lenin. And despite the emphasis on combat realism, self-imposed economies mean that not only are rounds limited for rifles, but tank crews often carry out 'attacks' on foot!   **S.P.C. Dalziel**

Atomic dawn

The new weapons
and their strategic impact

At 5.30 am on 16 July 1945 at Alamogordo in the New Mexico desert, the first atomic bomb was exploded to the satisfaction, wonderment and dismay of the scientists and engineers who had designed it. It was the culmination of the efforts of an international team of physicists who had worked on the project in the United States since 1942.

Three weeks after the successful test of that first atomic bomb, a similar weapon was dropped from an aircraft on the Japanese city of Hiroshima, devastating the city, killing some 75,000 people and ushering in the nuclear age. So complete was the destruction that military strategists were compelled to re-assess all previous concepts of military power and its role in politics. Clausewitz's famous dictum that war is the continuation of policy by other means took on a new meaning when the full impact of the destructive power of just one nuclear warhead was pondered by politicians and military strategists alike. The debate on future military strategy, doctrine and tactics, begun in 1945, has continued unresolved to the present day.

Having discovered that the atom could be made to release its energy by 'fission' or splitting atoms of a heavy element such as uranium or plutonium, it was only a question of time before the nuclear physicists devised a process by which atoms of the lightest element, hydrogen, could be fused together to form a heavier element, helium, with an accompanying release of energy far greater than that released by the fission process. The thermonuclear, or hydrogen, bomb appears to have no limit to the explosive power which may be derived from it; conversely it was to provide the basis on which weapons of very small yield with controllable effects were to be designed in later years.

The yield of the atomic weapon that destroyed Hiroshima was about 13 kilotons (13,000 tons of TNT equivalent). The largest yield thermonuclear weapon tested so far has been a Soviet warhead of 58 megatons (58,000,000 tons of TNT equivalent). In between, a whole range of nuclear warheads varying in yield from less than 1 kiloton to several megatons has been added to the stockpiles of both the superpowers.

The reaction of military strategists to the new weapons in the immediate postwar years was one of confusion and anguished disbelief at what the scientists had produced. How, they asked, could such destructive weapons be used in a future war; and, if they were used, what would be the likely consequences for both sides in the conflict? It did not at first appear that political aims could be achieved by resort to war in which, if nuclear weapons were used, the results would negate the political or territorial advantages which resort to war had sought to achieve. The visible destruction of Germany and Japan which conventional weapons had inflicted in World War II was a stark reminder of the consequences of modern war even without nuclear weapons.

Nevertheless, the concept of deterrence, by no

Right: The magnitude of the devastation that could be wrought by an atom bomb. Hiroshima one year after the atomic attack in 1945. Far left below: In 1953 the US fired the first atomic artillery shell, from a new 208mm artillery piece. Left: A mushroom cloud hangs over the Pacific after a successful detonation of a French nuclear bomb in 1968.

The hell of Hiroshima

'It was just after eight o'clock in the morning, a moment I shall never forget. There was a reverberant boom like an exploding shell and at the same moment a flash of orangeish-yellow light came through the bullet-proof glass in the ceiling. It became as dark as night. A blast of wind threw me into the air and smashed me down on the flat stones. The pain of this was still shooting through me as the building began to collapse around me.

'Gradually the air cleared and I climbed out from the wreckage. As I made my way to an emergency centre there was such confusion. The streets were so hot they burnt my feet, houses were on fire, the street-car rails radiated an eerie light and in the grounds of a shrine people were lying all over each other – some breathed, most had stopped. At the first-aid station people came running in stripped of their clothing and crying, some had puffed-up bloody faces, some had burned skin hanging from their arms and legs. In a street-car outside there were rows of white skeletons. There were the bones of the legs of people who had tried to escape. Hiroshima had become nothing other than hell.'

Sumie Kuramoto, 16 years old when the atomic bomb was dropped on Hiroshima.

means a new theory, was revived with particular emphasis to nuclear war. The United States had undisputed superiority in nuclear weapons and the means of delivering them, so a strategy of 'massive retaliation' was adopted in the late 1940s as a means of deterring war of any kind, not only against the United States but also against members of the Nato alliance. But when the Soviet Union tested its first atomic bomb in 1949 and began to build up a nuclear stockpile in the early 1950s the situation was radically altered.

In 1952 America introduced what were called 'tactical' nuclear weapons into the European theatre, but there was no clearly defined doctrine or strategy for their use. The yields of most of these weapons were high and the delivery systems inaccurate by today's standards. Meanwhile, both the superpowers continued to expand and diversify their strategic nuclear forces, with the United States maintaining a clear lead in warhead and delivery systems technology, as demonstrated dramatically in the Cuban missile crisis of 1962, when Premier Khrushchev was forced to back down and remove Soviet nuclear missiles from Cuba in the face of determined American opposition to their deployment so close to the United States.

Britain became a nuclear power in 1952 and France in 1960, but with nothing approaching the capability of the United States or the Soviet Union in numbers or variety of nuclear warheads and delivery systems. China followed in 1964, but has been slow to develop its strategic nuclear force, mainly because of the lack of an appropriate technological and industrial base. These five are still the main nuclear powers; others lay claim to having nuclear warheads but do not possess credible delivery systems. The technology and the fissile material necessary to produce nuclear weapons are available to a number of countries who have not signed the Non-Proliferation Treaty of 1968, so the possibility of others joining the nuclear club cannot be ruled out.

In 1977 the United States announced that its scientists had produced a new nuclear weapon in which blast damage could be drastically reduced and the effects from deadly radiation greatly increased. The weapon became known as the neutron bomb, though its proper designation is enhanced radiation warhead.

The United States in fact possesses something like 30 varieties of nuclear warheads. Yields range from 5 megatons in the W-53 fitted to the Titan intercontinental ballistic missile to 40 kilotons in the W-68

Effects of a nuclear 'airburst'

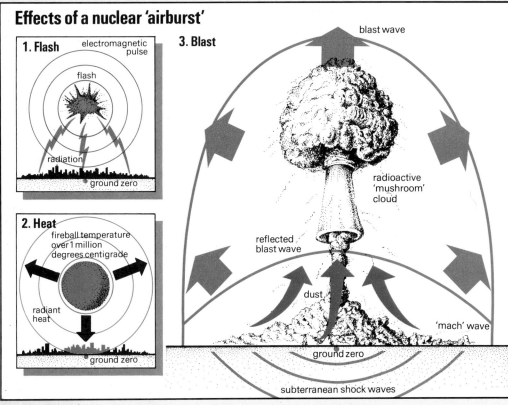

1. Flash
electromagnetic pulse
flash
radiation
ground zero

2. Heat
fireball temperature over 1 million degrees centigrade
radiant heat
ground zero

3. Blast
blast wave
radioactive 'mushroom' cloud
reflected blast wave
dust
'mach' wave
ground zero
subterranean shock waves

4. Wind
prevailing wind
cloud disperses
radioactive fallout
960km/h (600mph) ground winds
ground zero

An airburst detonated above ground level produces a blinding flash, an electromagnetic pulse and radiation (**1**). The resulting fireball and heat wave (**2**) are followed by a devastating blast wave with a doubled 'mach' wave at ground level where reflected blast merges with the original wave (**3**). Outward pressure of the blast creates a low pressure area at the centre, drawing in 960km/h (600mph) winds and sucking up dust to form the mushroom cloud which disperses as radioactive fallout (**4**).

fitted to Poseidon submarine-launched missiles. Variable yields of 60, 200 or 400 kilotons are available in the W-50 warhead fitted to the Pershing 1a mobile ballistic missile deployed in Europe. Atomic shells armed with the W-33 or W-48 have yields varying from less than 1 kiloton to 10 kilotons, and a whole range of nuclear bombs for delivery by manned aircraft possess yields up to several megatons.

As the means of delivery has improved, the yield of warhead required to achieve a given level of destruction on a target is reduced. A delivery system such as the proposed Pershing 2 equipped with a radar terminal guidance system gives an accuracy that is measured in feet instead of miles and will have a warhead in the 10-20 kiloton yield range.

With weapons such as those now in development or about to be deployed the possibility of limited nuclear war in Europe which would not devastate the countryside or destroy entire cities has become a reality. It is equally possible that the use of highly efficient, small yield nuclear warheads would not escalate to strategic nuclear exchange between the two superpowers and lead to nuclear holocaust. These are scenarios that professional military strategists cannot ignore.

Air Vice-Marshal Stewart Menaul

Below: A Thor missile is launched from its silo during tests in 1960.

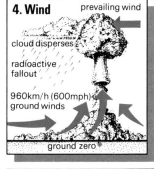

'It was a sunrise such as the world had never seen, a great green super-sun climbing in a fraction of a second to a height of more than 8000 feet, rising ever higher until it touched the clouds, lighting up earth and sky all around with a dazzling luminosity. Up it went, a great ball of fire about a mile in diameter, changing colours as it kept shooting upward, from deep purple to orange, expanding, growing bigger, rising as it was expanding, an elemental force freed from its bonds after being chained for billions of years. For a fleeting instant the colour was unearthly green, such as one only sees in the corona of the sun during a total eclipse. It was as though the earth had opened and the skies had split. One felt as though he had been privileged to witness the Birth of the World – to be present at the moment of Creation when the Lord said: Let There Be Light.'

William L. Laurence writing on the Alamogordo atomic test in the New York Times, *26 September 1945.*

Key Weapons
The CENTURION
part 2

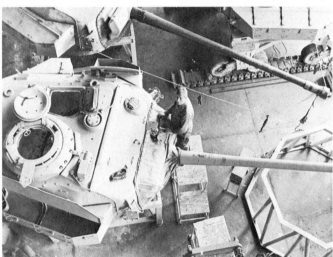

Centurions in Action

Although the Centurion tank had gained an impressive service record during the war in Korea, it came into its own in the wars in the Middle East between Israel and the Arabs. As the spearhead and mainstay of the Israeli Armoured Corps, the Centurion was to prove itself as a weapon system second to none.

Centurions entered service with the Israeli Defence Force (IDF) in 1960, but despite their reputation they took a long time to become accepted by Israeli tank crews. The Israelis had long been used to the relatively simple Sherman tanks, which ran under almost any conditions – especially after having been modified with the Cumming diesel engine – and which, after being upgunned with the high-velocity, French-made 75mm AMX-13 gun, could out-shoot the Soviet-built T54 tanks employed by the Arabs.

The first results with the newly acquired British

tanks were disappointing. In the barren Negev Desert, where the Israelis trained their armoured units, the Centurions performed badly. Their radiators clogged up either with dust or mud, causing the engines to overheat and seize up. The detailed pre-march maintenance and closing-down checks were too complex for the inexperienced Israeli tank crews, and this resulted in many mechanical breakdowns which were blamed on the tank.

The Israeli General Staff realised a radical solution was required to overcome these problems. Accordingly, a team of Ordnance Corps experts, who had gathered useful experience in modifying the Sherman, were ordered to put forward a plan to modify the tank to meet Israeli requirements.

A significant factor in the rehabilitation of the Centurion in the IDF was the appointment of General

Israel Tal as commander of the Armoured Corps. Tal was not a man to consider the tank's failings an insoluble problem; on the contrary, his technical experience made him realise that he could vindicate the Centurion once and for all. He first assembled all tank officers above the rank of captain and lectured them on their own shortcomings, pointing out in great detail the deficiencies in gunnery maintenance and command procedures which he had observed in recent actions. Special maintenance crews were appointed to zero the tank guns, and gunnery courses for regular and reserve crews were set up. Maintenance procedures were worked out and enforced by strict discipline. Long-range tank gunnery areas were built and firing competitions between crews instituted. Promotions became geared to efficiency tests. As the results improved, morale rose.

Although General Tal achieved much by energy and efficiency, the Centurion still needed major modifications to turn it into a modern fighting machine capable of out-fighting newer Soviet-built tanks, and so a special team of experts was commissioned to build a modified Centurion prototype. First priority was given to replacing the obsolete and underpowered Meteor engine, whose short life often made it necessary to change engines in the field. This was an intricate and complicated technique, completely unsuited to field-maintenance conditions; it took five trained technicians, working with heavy ordnance equipment, 20 hours to complete the operation.

A suitable diesel replacement that would both improve performance and fit into the existing engine compartment was not easy to find. Finally, the American Continental AVDS-1790-2A 12-cylinder air-cooled engine (providing 750 horsepower at 2400rpm) was chosen. It also simplified logistics as this same engine was used in Israeli M48s and M60s, and the standardisation on diesel fuel eased the problems of the supply organisation. Fitting the new power pack into the engine compartment was an exacting task, however, necessitating over 300 modifications to the engine alone.

To improve performance further, the bulky Merritt-Brown gearbox, with five forward and two reverse gears, was replaced by a more up-to-date Allison automatic transmission with only two forward gears and one reverse. This made driving easier by eliminating constant gear shifting, which could hamper a crew's performance during long engagements. The clutch mechanism was entirely eliminated.

Improving the cooling system was the next challenge. A modern, easy-to-maintain air-cooling system was installed in place of the existing unreliable water-cooled type. Care was taken to produce a hermetically sealed system; special air filters were installed, suited to withstand the heavy desert dust of the Middle East.

An advanced steering mechanism, with a single handle, which improved both steering and turning, was introduced in place of the old two-lever driving

Below: Upgunned with a British 105mm L7 main armament an IDF Centurion climbs the Golan Heights. Most Centurions fighting on this front had their bazooka side-plates removed to prevent clogging by mud.

system. This facilitated manoeuvring and cut down the danger of the tank slipping out of control when changing direction at high speed. Driving downhill had always been a problem, as the dry-type brake drums tended to overheat and become unserviceable very quickly, resulting in the tank running out of control – a frightening experience if it happened on rocky and undulating ground. A new friction-disc, oil-cooled braking system was adopted to eliminate the problem.

The introduction of the British 105mm L7 main armament brought about a number of modifications to the fighting compartment that facilitated faster and more accurate fire. To improve the tank's range, a greater amount of fuel had to be stowed in the hull. However, the larger dimensions of the new engine and the added airflow channels made this an acute problem. To overcome it the team devised specially-shaped moulded fuel tanks which fitted snugly into every available corner of the engine compartment. The upgraded Centurion – as it was now called – had double the operational range of the Mark 5 on which it was based, as well as a superior maximum road speed of 43km/h (27mph).

In all, the development programme took 40,000 working hours spread over some three years, so that the new Centurion resembled the former models in little but shape. It was to become a highly effective combat system, the backbone of the Israel Armoured Corps – and it was soon to prove itself in battle.

Upgraded Centurions took part in a small but sharp action against a Jordanian stronghold in the Hebron hills shortly before the Six-Day War. Firing concrete-busting HESH (high explosive squash head) ammunition, they destroyed a Jordanian fortified police post within minutes. But this encounter was only the prelude to the main action: the first shots of the Six-Day War were fired on 5 June 1967 and Centurions were soon in the thick of combat.

In the battle for the Sinai peninsula a battalion of Centurions particularly distinguished itself during the engagement at Rafa. Knocking out several Egyptian

T34s dug in at the Rafa crossroads, Centurions smashed through the drawn-out Egyptian 7th Division defences and gained El-Arish, some 65km (40 miles) west of the ceasefire line within a few hours – a tremendous feat. Two reserve Centurion brigades of another division meanwhile made their way along an uncharted desert track, their new diesel engines achieving an unprecedented standard of performance in extreme desert conditions.

On the morning of the second day, the first Centurions were astride the main Sinai axis in time to ambush the advancing 4th Egyptian Armoured Division with its Soviet T55s. The Centurions caused devastation by firing APDS (armour piercing discarding sabot) ammunition at extreme ranges, before the T55s were able to get within range. By now the race to the Suez Canal was on. The Centurions won, reaching

Top: Carrying crew baggage, an upgraded Centurion – complete with Xenon infra-red searchlight – prepares for campaign service. Above: Tank crews of the 7th Armoured Brigade make a dawn inspection. Top right: A .5in Browning machine gun is mounted up-front on this Centurion in the Golan Heights. Right: A troop of Centurions pause on the Jordanian West Bank during the Six-Day War.

the Mitla Pass in time to close it before the retreating Egyptian armies. In the ensuing battle, they fired continuously, creating unprecedented havoc and destruction.

After the Six-Day War Israel purchased further Centurions from various sources, many of them Mark 5s. All were modified to IDF standards by the Ordnance Corps, which ran a regular production line.

During the so-called War of Attrition between 1969 and 1970, Centurions went into action both on the banks of the Suez Canal and on the Golan Heights. In a sharp clash with the Syrians in 1970, IDF Centurions knocked out several Syrian T54s. This encounter represented the first Syrian use of Snapper anti-tank missiles, but they had a negligible effect on the well-armoured Centurions.

About noon on 6 October 1973 – Yom Kippur – the Arab onslaught fell on IDF positions on the Golan Heights, and the Bar Lev line in the Sinai. At the time Centurions held the Golan sector, the Sinai being defended mainly by US-built M48 and M60 tanks. The M48s and M60s rushed forward to relieve the stricken Bar Lev outposts, only to be decimated by Egyptian infantry anti-tank teams. The Centurions on the Golan, however, stood their ground, although outnumbered by as many as 15 to 1. Their deadly 105mm L7 guns proved more than a match for the Soviet 115mm smooth bore T62 guns; firing APFSDS (armour piercing fin stabilised discarding sabot) ammunition the efficient gunnery of the

highly-trained Centurion crews knocked out hundreds of the Syrians' T55s and their latest T62s.

The Israeli reserves, mostly manning Centurions, finally broke the Syrian offensive and followed with a lethal counterattack. After a sharp encounter with Iraqi reinforcements and the destruction of the crack Jordanian 40th Armoured Brigade – also equipped with Centurions – the fighting in the Golan was over. The IDF Armoured Corps had gained a tremendous victory against great odds.

Meanwhile Centurions had also joined battle in Sinai, taking a leading part in the great tank battle of 14 October, when over 2000 tanks from both sides were locked in mortal combat. Firing from well-prepared positions, the Israeli Pattons and Centurions – all mounting lethal 105mm guns – knocked out more than 300 Egyptian tanks in a matter of hours. Shortly afterwards, a brigade of Centurions completely destroyed the Egyptian 25th Armoured Brigade on the banks of Bitter Lake, destroying over 100

T62s with no loss to themselves. Centurion tanks were also among the first to cross the Suez Canal at Deversoir on 16 October, roaming the Egyptian rear to the gates of Suez, where the last battles of the war were fought against the encircled Egyptian Third Army.

Although Israeli tank losses were heavy, many of the disabled Centurions were repaired under combat conditions and returned to battle. This – in addition to its combat performance – proved beyond doubt that the Centurion was a rugged fighting machine, able to withstand battle conditions as severe as any previously encountered in modern warfare.

The lessons learned with Centurions during the arduous battles in the Sinai and the Golan helped bring about the development of the Israeli-built Merkava tank. Despite the introduction of the Merkava, the Centurion remains a major combat weapon in the Middle East and is likely to remain so for many years to come.

Top: Israeli Centurions race across the desert sands of the Sinai Peninsula as part of a training exercise to keep the Armoured Corps of the IDF at peak readiness. Above: A Centurion pounds away at enemy positions as part of an Israeli defensive line between Yehudia and Hushnia on the southern sector of the Golan Heights. Well armed with the L7 series gun, the Centurions of the IDF have been able to inflict a series of bloody defeats on the numerically-superior Arab armies.

Battle for the north

How Chiang Kai-shek was outmanoeuvred in Manchuria

For about a year after the Japanese surrender in August 1945 an uneasy truce reigned between the communists and the Nationalists in China. Although talks were held they were doomed to failure, given the utterly contradictory aims of the two sides. At the same time the communists used the truce to consolidate their positions. They controlled most of Manchuria and northeast China while the Nationalists held the south and also the capital, Peking (now known as Beijing).

In 1947 the Chinese Nationalists mounted a series of fierce attacks against their communist enemies which initially suggested that they might be well on their way to winning the civil war. Communist forces were driven back in Manchuria; much of Shantung (Shandong) province was reconquered; and Yenan (Yanan), the headquarters of Mao's most famous base area, was occupied. Chiang Kai-shek boasted of his absolute superiority in terms of manpower, equipment, food, fodder and ammunition. The communists, he said, would be destroyed within six months.

Yet shortly after, one analyst highlighted a number of fundamental weaknesses which were to contribute to the Nationalists' ultimate defeat. He described the Nationalist (Kuomintang) Party as 'decrepit and degenerate' and as 'lacking standards of right and wrong'. He castigated officers for their lack of professional skill and spoke of their 'miniscule abilities'. They were specifically criticised for their ill-treatment of the men under their command, their lack of concern for soldiers' well-being, and their corruption. Senior commanders were accused of failing to cooperate and of acting like warlords. The communists, by contrast, were praised for their attention to the welfare of their soldiers, the willingness of officers to live as their men did, and their insistence on meticulous political and military education.

Over 30 years later few would disagree with these assessments. What is surprising, however, is the identity of the man who made them. It was Chiang Kai-shek himself. Chiang was fully aware of the deficiencies of his own supporters, which strengthens the case for describing him as 'the man who lost China'. The faults he described had long been present, yet he had recognised them only belatedly and, even when he had done so, he failed to act to rectify them. And it was in Manchuria that the chickens began to come home to roost.

Chiang himself was largely responsible for the decision to re-occupy Manchuria after World War II, despite advice from both Americans and Chinese that he should first establish complete control over China south of the Great Wall. Chiang did so because of an obsession with the prestige of his regime, which he tended to measure in terms of the numbers of cities it controlled. A more able leader might have learned from the fate of the Japanese invaders that even the

129

best-disciplined and best-equipped troops could face insurmountable difficulties by over-extending themselves in a vast agrarian country where over 80 per cent of the population lived in villages. Chiang failed to do so.

Instead, he deployed his troops in cities, often separated from each other by hundreds of miles and served by a poorly developed communications system which was hard to defend and maintain. Chiang's concept of strategy and tactics was essentially static and inflexible and bore little relation to military necessities. Prolonged garrison duty made his troops lazy and lax. A 'defensive mentality' pervaded Nationalist ranks and commanders came to regard it as a victory merely to beat off an enemy attack. As both political influence in Nationalist affairs and opportunities for profitable corruption were closely linked to the size of one's forces, senior officers were often content to leave the communists a route for escape rather than risk heavy losses by hot pursuit.

Mao, however, emphasised a war of movement and flexibility. He attached little value to holding territory for its own sake, even when it was of the symbolic importance of Yenan. China was large and there was always somewhere for his troops to move to if necessary. For him war was a question of annihilating the enemy by emphasising mobility in order to concentrate overwhelmingly superior forces against units which were weak. Whereas Chiang's forces were perpetually faced with immense logistical prob-

lems, the communists could speedily fade away into the countryside from where they had come. Mao's military genius lay in stressing the importance of linking the military struggle with political, economic and social movements. Long before 'winning the hearts and minds' became a cant phrase, Mao had preached the need for a 'people's war'.

In essence this was simplicity itself. Lacking the material resources of their enemies, the communists could only survive and flourish by being mobile. This in turn depended on relying on local sources for intelligence and supply. Mao's troops had to be what he called the 'fish' sustained by the 'sea' of the masses, and that meant acquiring popular support. From 1926 onwards Mao taught that the peasants were the source of real power, without whom no revolution could ultimately succeed. By trial and error, and a measure of luck, the communists evolved a code of 'good behaviour', as it were, which they applied in the areas where they operated. They permitted non-communists a reasonable degree of participation in local affairs, made their armed forces responsible for their own maintenance and introduced progressive reforms. Above all they focused on education, both in the narrow sense of establishing a sophisticated system of political commissions and instruction within the armed forces, and in the wider sense of disseminating propaganda among the rural population. In return the villagers supplied them with information, food and equipment, and a steady

Previous page: A Nationalist soldier stands guard at an outpost near Shanghai prior to the communist assault on 5 July 1949. He is equipped with a US Thompson submachine gun.

Below: Communist troops, some armed with Russian light machine-guns, storm a walled city near Mukden during the Manchurian campaign.

stream of strong peasant boys for their regular forces, guerrilla units and local militias.

Mao also used such tactics on the enemy. Captured Nationalists were well treated, subjected to propaganda and 'turned rural'. Sometimes they would be released in order to carry the message of the communists' humane behaviour back to their comrades. It was deliberate policy to encourage enemy soldiers to desert, and those who did so were rewarded and integrated into communist forces. In every respect Mao's all-encompassing vision and subtlety proved superior to Chiang's rigid and limited approach.

Thus, although Mao's forces suffered heavy casualties in 1947, they were able to extend their operations in many parts of north, central and east China and, moreover, began to show an increased willingness to attack Nationalist strongholds. And it was in Manchuria that General Lin Piao started to attack, isolate and ultimately destroy heavy concentrations of Nationalist troops.

At the beginning of 1947 Lin's assaults were successfully repulsed by one of Chiang's more able commanders, General Sun Li-jen. But as the year progressed Chiang engaged in a series of re-shuffles of the Manchurian command structure which served to confirm his unerring ability to remove generals of proven competence and replace them with mediocrities, partly on the grounds of personal loyalty to himself. Lin Piao again took the offensive in May and succeeded in surrounding Nationalist garrisons in the cities of Kirin (Jilin), Changchun and Szepingkai (Siping). The communists followed their usual tactic of cutting lines of communication and Chiang found himself faced with the problem of attempting to supply about 700,000 government personnel, of whom only about a third were effective combat troops. In the autumn of 1947 all the railway connections into the city of Mukden (Shenyang) were cut, and in the bitterly cold winter the communists captured a number of Nationalist strongholds. At the beginning of 1948 Chiang tried to improve the situation in another re-shuffle which made General Wei

Lin Piao, victor in Manchuria

Born into a peasant family in Hopeh province in 1907, Lin Piao was to become one of the most celebrated commanders of the Red Army and, at the height of his career, second only to Mao Tse-tung himself in the leadership of the Chinese Communist Party. He graduated from the Whampoa Military Academy in 1926 and joined the Communist Party the following year. By 1932 he was commander of the 1st Army Corps, which he led on the Long March (1934-35).

In the late 1930s he spent several years recovering from serious wounds in a Soviet hospital, but on the resumption of the civil war in China he played a crucial role and commanded the forces that routed the Nationalists in Manchuria and in the Peking-Tientsin campaign.

Following the communist triumph Lin rapidly acquired political power, becoming vice-premier in 1954, a member of the politburo a year later

and defence minister in 1959. During the Cultural Revolution, which began in 1966, he gave Mao the enthusiastic support of the armed forces. Soon afterwards, however, his career went into decline and he was ultimately disgraced. Lin is thought to have planned a military coup against Mao in 1971. When the plot was exposed he tried to flee to Russia by air but was killed when the aircraft crashed in Mongolia.

Li-huang commander in Manchuria in place of the more able Ch'en Ch'eng.

By this time, however, the problem was largely logistical. In the Mudken sector some 150,000 to 200,000 Nationalist troops had to be supplied by air because of communist success at cutting the railways. But air transport could cope with only a third of the tonnage required and the operation was unbelievably costly. In a secret report the minister of war revealed in September 1948 that the whole of the military budget for the second half of the year had been spent in air-lifting supplies into the single city of Changchun for a period of just over two months.

Matters were made worse by Chiang's personal interference. He held regular briefings to which only some of the key figures in the military command were invited and regularly issued orders without either consulting or informing those who should have been put in the picture. Ignorant of the generalissimo's wishes, other members of the high command issued their own orders, creating total confusion for the generals who were actually required to carry them out. In October 1948 Chiang went to Peking to be closer at hand to the area of operations. The quality of his orders improved, but by this time the situation was so muddled that they were not always obeyed. In any event, Lin Piao's final offensive was already underway.

By September, Lin had mustered a force of 600,000 men in Manchuria. A total of 65,000 surrounded Changchun, 183,000 were placed around Mukden, 179,000 between Mukden and Chinchow (Jinzhou), and 180,000 were held in reserve. Against them the Nationalists could deploy only 300,000 as a field army.

Lin first moved on Chinchow. Nationalist troops brought in from Formosa (Taiwan) through the port of Hulutao were successfully halted, as was a relief force sent from Mukden. On 17 October the Chinchow garrison of 100,000 men surrendered. Changchun, the capital of Manchuria and far to the north of Mukden, fell three days later. Its loss was a particularly bitter blow in that it was partly due to a revolt, in which one of its garrison units had opened fire on another. Five Nationalist divisions fell into communist hands.

Meanwhile Chiang had ordered a substantial part of the Mukden garrison to recapture Chinchow, in conjunction with the forces earlier landed at Hulutao. The actual commander of the Mukden troops was General Tu Yu-ming, a man whose position derived from personal friendship with Chiang rather than any demonstrable military skill. Tu preferred to remain in Mukden so the recapture of Chinchow was entrusted to Liao Yao-hsiang, a general who had fought with real distinction against the Japanese in Burma.

Lin Piao, however, moved briskly. With 200,000 men he fell upon Liao's advancing forces from the flank and rear. In three days of fierce fighting, Lin's troops attacked in human waves, supported by a murderous artillery barrage. Liao was killed early in the battle, and his entire force was routed by 30 October. Mukden, with its depleted garrisons, was now defenceless. Its commander defected to the communists and the troops surrendered. Communist forces were now supreme in Manchuria.

Altogether the Nationalists lost some 300,000 of their best troops together with all their weapons. The communists also acquired a number of arsenals,

The battle for Manchuria

March 1947

MONGOLIA
Sungari River (Songhua Jiang)
Harbin
Changchun • Kirin (Jilin)
Szeping (Siping)
Vladivostok
Chengte (Chengde)
Mukden (Shenyang)
Chinchow (Jinzhou)
Peking (Beijing)
Antung (Dandong)
Tientsin (Tianjin)
Paoting (Baoding)
Port Arthur (Lüshun)
Tsinan (Jinan)
YELLOW SEA   KOREA
□ communist held areas
■ Nationalist held areas

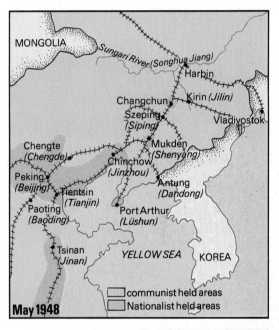

May 1948

MONGOLIA
Sungari River (Songhua Jiang)
Harbin
Changchun • Kirin (Jilin)
Szeping (Siping)
Vladivostok
Chengte (Chengde)
Mukden (Shenyang)
Chinchow (Jinzhou)
Peking (Beijing)
Antung (Dandong)
Tientsin (Tianjin)
Paoting (Baoding)
Port Arthur (Lüshun)
Tsinan (Jinan)
YELLOW SEA   KOREA
□ communist held areas
■ Nationalist held areas

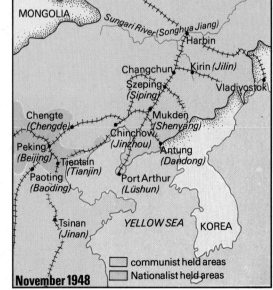

November 1948

MONGOLIA
Sungari River (Songhua Jiang)
Harbin
Changchun • Kirin (Jilin)
Szeping (Siping)
Vladivostok
Chengte (Chengde)
Mukden (Shenyang)
Chinchow (Jinzhou)
Peking (Beijing)
Antung (Dandong)
Tientsin (Tianjin)
Paoting (Baoding)
Port Arthur (Lüshun)
Tsinan (Jinan)
YELLOW SEA   KOREA
□ communist held areas
■ Nationalist held areas

'The condition of the conscripts and troops in Shensi and Kansu was very poor – so poor at times as to almost beggar description. This miserable condition of the conscripts, especially, is so general in the northwest that it is a universal subject of comment by both foreigners and Chinese. Almost everyone has several "horror" stories to tell.... When I have watched them eat they have had nothing but rice. It is usually a question of the strongest and fittest getting the most. The weak and sick get little. In Kwangyuan I saw a group of conscripts attack a crippled candy peddler. He was pushed over and all of his wares plundered in a matter of seconds. The guards paid no attention until after it was over. They then kicked several in the stomach and hit others with the butts of their rifles. The men seemed obviously starved.'

John S. Service, a US intelligence officer, reporting on Nationalist troops.

Above: Control of the great rivers of China was of paramount importance to the communist military leaders as these inland waterways provided important lines of communication and supply to front line troops. Here communist troops advance through a town on the Yangtse River.

Left: Communist troops advance across a river in Hopeh province. The manoeuvrability of the communist infantry and their seemingly unending forward momentum were in stark contrast to the rigid defensive tactics of the Nationalists.

including the one at Mukden, which was particularly well-equipped. Furthermore, victory in Manchuria enabled the communists to divert 400,000 of Lin Piao's troops south of the Great Wall, and these flooded into north China with a speed that astonished Nationalist generals there.

The outcome of the struggle for Manchuria showed that the nature of the civil war had changed decisively. The communists had proved conclusively that they were more than a guerrilla army capable of controlling large tracts of countryside but ill-equipped to conquer the urban bastions of the Nationalists. By the autumn of 1948 they had moved their style of warfare to a new and higher plane – that of conquering and holding great cities. They still retained the classic advantages of a guerrilla army – mobility and flexibility – but their iron discipline meant that they could make the transition to more conventional warfare with quite remarkable ease and outfight armies that had, ostensibly, great advantages over them.

The Nationalists, by contrast, had confirmed their ineptitude. Even in narrowly military terms they had failed to exploit their advantages. Their air superiority and their control of coastal ports proved unable to counter the communists' ability to dominate land communications. The loss of Manchuria, then, was the beginning of the end for Chiang Kai-shek. But defeats of even greater magnitude were to await him in the flat plains of central China between Hsuchow and the Huai River.   **John Gardner**

Mukden's final hours

Shortly before Mukden fell to the communists in November 1948 an American reporter, Roy Rowan, flew into the beleagured city. 'Mukden,' he wrote, 'is a ghost city. No preparation had been made for a last-stand defence. Most of the government troops were encamped near rail sidings awaiting evacuation. In the city itself, freezing blasts of wind whistled down the broad, empty thoroughfares.... [Mukden] looked as cold and desolate as the ragged, half-frozen refugees on every street. Only the railway station and the airports were active. Streets by the depot were jammed with refugees peddling old bits of belongings to buy food. Every few hours trains overflowing with yellow-clad troops left Mukden station and rattled south toward the evacuation port of Yingkow. At Pai Ling field, the last military airstrip, planes flew out whole companies and battalions of troops. Civilians also were flown out. And for them a little slip of white paper – a plane ticket to Tsingtao or Tientsin – was suddenly the most precious possession in the world.'

Above: The Nationalist commander of Mukden, General Wei Li-huang (centre), outlines his plans for evacuation of the city. Below: A Nationalist gun section prepare a water-cooled heavy machine gun for firing near Kalgan.

Final triumph

Hsuchow and the Nationalist collapse

The catastrophic loss of Manchuria was rationalised by Chiang Kai-shek when he publicly proclaimed it would permit his forces to concentrate more effectively on the defence of China proper. This statement gave little comfort to those who had advised him years earlier to avoid Manchurian entanglements in order to consolidate his hold on China south of the Great Wall. Their morale slumped further when they learned that Chiang proposed to make his next stand around the city of Hsuchow (now called Xuzhou) in the province of Anhwei (Anhui).

A number of his best strategists argued in favour of defending the Huai River, which runs approximately 160km (100 miles) north of the Yangtse and which was traditionally regarded as the natural line of defence for that populous and prosperous region. Yet again, however, Chiang ignored wise counsel and decreed that the major effort would be concentrated on Hsuchow, 160km (100 miles) north of the Huai. The city stood at the junction of the important Lunghai and Tsin-pu railways and constituted a gateway between north and south China.

It was a poor venue, nonetheless. Situated at the southern end of the north China plain, Hsuchow was the centre of a region which offered superb opportunities for the kind of war of manoeuvre at which the communists excelled. Chiang's obsession with maintaining large urban garrisons and the concomitant need to guard the extensive sections of railway line which connected them, made his forces an easy target

for the tactics of rapid thrusts, annihilating attacks on isolated units and encirclement – tactics at which Mao's generals had already proven themselves so adept.

The ensuing Huai-hai campaign, which derived its name from the territory between the Lunghai railway and the Huai River, was waged on an enormous scale. Even before it began, however, Hsuchow was in difficulties. Ch'en Yi, who commanded communist forces in east China, had already conquered most of the province of Shantung (Shandong) and threatened the city from the north. To the west of it, the communist forces of Liu Po-ch'eng dominated central China north of the Yangtse. Liu's men had already seized two important points on the Lunghai railway and were well placed to cut Hsuchow's communications with the south. Ch'en Yi, who had field command, was able to deploy 500,000 troops in the Huai-hai area.

Superficially, the Nationalists were equally strong in the sense that they possessed a similar number of regular troops. The Nationalist Second Army Group of 12 divisions was already stationed to the west of the city under the command of Ch'iu Ch'ing-ch'uan. To the east, Huang Po-t'ao's Seventh Army Group of 10 divisions stretched along the Lunghai railway as far as the coast. In and around Hsuchow were the Armoured Corps and the garrison forces of the Hsuchow Bandit Suppression Headquarters. The Eighth Army Group lay to the west of the city and the Sixth to the south. Chiang also ordered the Thirteenth and Sixteenth

Two Nationalist soldiers rest for a few moments during action in 1949. Although relatively well equipped, the Nationalists were unable to match the commitment and will to win of Mao's forces.

Nationalist troops in trenches near Hsuchow await an imminent communist attack.

Army Groups to march to join the forces already in position and, at a later stage, ordered Huang Wei's Twelfth Army Group to march north to join the battle. All in all, some 51 Nationalist divisions were committed, including some which were American-equipped and trained. The Nationalists also enjoyed total air supremacy.

Nationalist equality, however, was more theoretical than real. Even in terms of numbers, the communists had a real superiority because of their unique 'people's war' which assigned military roles to a host of individuals who were not, strictly speaking, first line troops. If one includes logistical and guerrilla support units, total communist strength in the Huaihai campaign may have given them a ratio as high as six to one over the Nationalists. Moreover, half-starved and subject to brutal discipline, Nationalist troops lacked the motivation to fight and were often willing to defect to the enemy at the first opportunity. The contrast with the highly indoctrinated, well-disciplined soldiers in the communist ranks was marked.

At the highest echelons, too, differences were apparent. The communist side enjoyed a remarkable degree of unity. Ch'en Yi was nominally in control and his East China Field Army was roughly twice the strength of Liu Po-ch'eng's Central Plains Field Army. Yet Ch'en was reportedly willing to defer to Liu, the 'one-eyed dragon', on strategy decisions. Together they formed the 'hammer and the brains' of the communist forces, and their staffs and commanders worked in harmony.

The Nationalist command, however, was riven by deep-seated factionalism; at least four rival cliques constantly squabbled among themselves and took a peculiar delight in sabotaging each other's operations in the interests of short-term personal advantage. The confusion which resulted was further exacerbated by Chiang Kai-shek's insistence on master-minding the campaign from Nanking (Nanjing). He kept interfering, issuing orders which were out-of-date by the time they arrived, and bypassing established chains of command in favour of direct communication with his personal favourites.

The campaign began in earnest on 6 November

1948 when communist forces seized a county town near Hsuchow. The next day they destroyed the 181st Division, and the Eighth Army Group to which it belonged promptly opted for a speedy retreat south to the Huai River. The Nationalist forces' poor morale was amply demonstrated on 8 November when four divisions to the north of Hsuchow defected to the communists. A couple of days later the communists drove a wedge between Huang Po-ta'ao's Seventh Army Group and the city. On 11 November it was reported that one million troops were locked in combat along a 320km (200 mile) front.

Cut off from Hsuchow, Huang Po-t'ao desperately sought to safeguard his position by pulling back those of his units at the coastal end of the Lunghai railway, but this only served to complete his isolation for communist forces immediately moved into the evacuated area, encircling Huang's army and denying it access to the sea. What then followed was a classic example of the factionalism that existed among the Nationalists. On becoming aware of Huang's predicament, Chiang Kai-shek ordered Ch'iu Ch'ing-ch'uan to lead the Second and Thirteenth Army Groups to his assistance. But Ch'iu's dislike of Huang was such that he chose to leave his 'brother officer' to stew in his own juice. Ten days after embarking on the 'relief operation', Ch'iu's powerful force of 15 divisions had covered only 13km (8 miles) and was still 20km (12 miles) from Huang's western-most position.

While this was happening, Liu Po-ch'eng mounted an attack on Suhsien (Su Xian), a town on the Tsin-pu railway to the south of Hsuchow. The Sixth Army Group lost two divisions to the troops of the 'one-eyed dragon' and immediately followed the example of the Eighth Army by retreating to the Huai River. The Sixteenth Army Group withdrew to Hsuchow, having lost one division. Suhsien fell on 15 November and with it Hsuchow's rail communications to the south were severed. The Second, Seventh, Thirteenth and Sixteenth Army Groups were now isolated in the Hsuchow sector.

The communists next attacked both the Second and Seventh Army Groups in an attempt to prevent them from linking up. The Seventh tried to break out of its

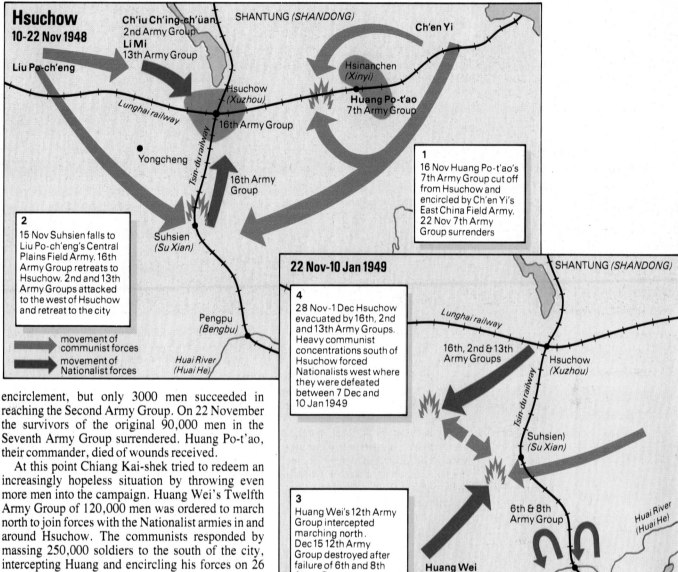

Hsuchow
10-22 Nov 1948

SHANTUNG (SHANDONG)

Ch'iu Ch'ing-ch'üan
2nd Army Group
Li Mi
13th Army Group

Ch'en Yi

Liu Po-ch'eng

Hsinanchen
(Xinyi)

Hsuchow
(Xuzhou)

Huang Po-t'ao
7th Army Group

Lunghai railway

16th Army Group

1
16 Nov Huang Po-t'ao's
7th Army Group cut off
from Hsuchow and
encircled by Ch'en Yi's
East China Field Army.
22 Nov 7th Army
Group surrenders

Yongcheng

16th Army
Group

Tsin-du railway

Suhsien
(Su Xian)

2
15 Nov Suhsien falls to
Liu Po-ch'eng's Central
Plains Field Army. 16th
Army Group retreats to
Hsuchow. 2nd and 13th
Army Groups attacked
to the west of Hsuchow
and retreat to the city

22 Nov-10 Jan 1949

SHANTUNG (SHANDONG)

4
28 Nov-1 Dec Hsuchow
evacuated by 16th, 2nd
and 13th Army Groups.
Heavy communist
concentrations south of
Hsuchow forced
Nationalists west where
they were defeated
between 7 Dec and
10 Jan 1949

Lunghai railway

16th, 2nd &13th
Army Groups

Hsuchow
(Xuzhou)

Pengpu
(Bengbu)

Tsin-du railway

Suhsien)
(Su Xian)

Huai River
(Huai He)

→ movement of
communist forces

→ movement of
Nationalist forces

3
Huang Wei's 12th Army
Group intercepted
marching north.
Dec 15 12th Army
Group destroyed after
failure of 6th and 8th
Army Groups to
reinforce

Huang Wei
12th Army Group

6th & 8th
Army Group

Huai River
(Huai He)

Pengpu
(Bengbu)

encirclement, but only 3000 men succeeded in
reaching the Second Army Group. On 22 November
the survivors of the original 90,000 men in the
Seventh Army Group surrendered. Huang Po-t'ao,
their commander, died of wounds received.

At this point Chiang Kai-shek tried to redeem an
increasingly hopeless situation by throwing even
more men into the campaign. Huang Wei's Twelfth
Army Group of 120,000 men was ordered to march
north to join forces with the Nationalist armies in and
around Hsuchow. The communists responded by
massing 250,000 soldiers to the south of the city,
intercepting Huang and encircling his forces on 26
November.

Chiang then ordered his forces in Hsuchow, which
still numbered some 250,000 men, to break out and
link up with Huang Wei's Twelfth Army Group. Liu
Chih, commander-in-chief in Hsuchow, prudently
chose to fly to safety in Pengpu (Bengbu) on the Huai
River, as did the commander of the Thirteenth Army
Group and Colonel Chiang Wei-kuo, commander of
the still-unused Armoured Corps and son of the
generalissimo himself.

Other Nationalist generals, however, attempted to
follow Chiang's orders. The commander of the Sixteenth Army Group left Hsuchow with his three
remaining divisions and struck south towards
Suhsien. Ch'iu Ch'ing-ch'uan then led a force composed of the Second and Thirteenth Army Groups and
the Armoured Corps out of Hsuchow on 28 to 30
November. On 1 December Tu Yu-ming led the
rearguard from the city.

Hopes that it would be possible to link up with the
Twelfth Army Group were quickly dashed by the
massive communist concentrations to the south of the
city, and the Hsuchow forces veered west after sustaining heavy losses. Hampered by heavy equipment,
personal possessions, families and camp followers,
the Nationalists moved very slowly. About 32km (20
miles) from Hsuchow their progress was halted by
communist troops who had dug three lines of deep

trenches. The Sixteenth Army Group was annihilated
when it tried to break through on 7 December. Thus
Tu Yu-ming's and Huang Wei's forces remained
isolated from each other to the northwest and southwest respectively of Suhsien. The Sixth and Eighth
Army Groups, already noted for their willingness to
run away, were ordered north from the Huai but
showed a marked reluctance to seek out the communists and, indeed, cleverly avoided those areas where
the enemy was to be found in strength. Subjected to
relentless artillery bombardment, Huang Wei's
Twelfth Army capitulated on 15 December.

The communists then concentrated their efforts on
the hapless forces of Tu Yu-ming and by late December had moved 300,000 men into position around
them. On 6 January 1949 they launched a general
attack, supported by heavy artillery. At this stage any
remaining willingness among the Nationalist forces
to continue to resist was destroyed by news reaching
them of a proposal which was unbelievably callous
and inept, even by the standards of Chiang Kai-shek.
Faced with the prospect of the imminent loss of much
valuable equipment, it was suggested in Nanking that

The first soldiers of the communist People's Liberation Army enter Nanking, the Nationalist capital. There was no looting and pillaging from this victorious force; their policy towards the civilian population was expressed in their 'three commandments': 'Do not take even a needle and thread; consider the people your family; all that you borrowed, you must return.'

this should be destroyed by air bombardment regardless of the effects on Nationalist troops! Tu Yu-ming's forces surrendered without delay. General Ch'iu Ch'ing-ch'uan was killed in the final stages of battle, and Tu Yu-ming was captured trying to escape disguised as an ordinary soldier.

On 10 January the Huai-hai campaign was over. In 65 days the Nationalists had lost about 550,000 men, some 327,000 of whom the communists claimed to have taken prisoner. The impact on the course of the civil war was dramatic. Between September 1948 and the end of January 1949 Nationalist forces had been reduced to about 1,500,000 men of whom approximately only 500,000 were service troops. In the space of four and a half months the Nationalists had lost 45 per cent of their total troop strength. Communist strength, by contrast, had mounted to over 1,600,000, virtually all of whom were combat effectives.

Red China's fighting men

Soon after the communist triumph in 1949 Lieutenant-Colonel Robert B. Rigg of the US Army reported that 'the soldiers of present-day Red China as a group can probably outmarch those of any other nation, including the majority of our own. Like the Japanese, they can get along on less food than can US soldiers. Their attitude toward death is not necessarily one of indifference, but they obey orders that other troops would challenge. PLA men are products of a stiffer and more brutal system of discipline than are our own. Their health is below the standards we apply to our military service. Their training is below American standards of completion, but this is compensated for by the fact that the greater part of these Chinese soldiers have been in actual combat for years. Their stealth is superior.'

The communists were now unstoppable, and the Nationalists' belated attempts at negotiation were contemptuously rejected. In north China Fu Tso-yi entered secret negotiations with the communists who, as a result, were able to occupy the key cities of Tientsin (Tianjin) on 15 January and Peking (Beijing) eight days later. Attention could then be devoted to the Nationalist bastions of the Yangtse (Chang Jiang). The Nationalist capital of Nanking fell to Ch'en Yi on 23 April and on 25 May Shanghai was occupied.

Thereafter the Nationalists continued to offer resistance, and to engage in final attempts to raise new levies from a dispirited and resentful population. It was not until 27 December 1949 that Chengtu (Chengdu), the capital of Szechwan (Sichuan) province fell to communist forces. Guerrilla forces remained in some of the more remote provinces, but what was left of Chiang's regular armies had by that time retreated to the island province of Formosa (Taiwan). With the confidence that their victory was absolute the communists proclaimed the establishment of the People's Republic on 1 October 1949, and made Peking their capital.

Thus a civil war, which had been fought intermittently since 1927, was brought to a close. The Nationalists lost China because of military incompetence. But their defeat also demonstrated their weakness in other spheres. Chiang's regime was despotic and corrupt and succeeded, over time, in alienating the vast majority of the Chinese population.

The communists were victorious, not only because of their superiority in strategy and tactics, but primarily because they offered the Chinese people a better deal. In the areas they controlled the communists provided reasonably honest administration and a host of valuable political, social and economic reforms which were of particular benefit to the peasantry but which also appealed to other groups. Based in the great cities, the Nationalists cared little for the peasant majority. In essence they lost China because, as one writer has put it, 'the soldier of Chiang Kai-shek knew not why he fought'. **John Gardner**

The will to win

Is morale the single most important factor in war?

Most rational people fear death and are apprehensive about the nature of its coming. They will go to great lengths to avoid situations in which death is a possibility and will strive to achieve the basic requirements of long life – health, an adequate diet and personal security. But in war this changes. Ordinary human beings, possessing no gift of immortality, are expected consciously to face the probability of death, mutilation and pain, while trying hard to inflict the same punishment upon the enemy. It is an unnatural and frightening experience, often played out in an alien environment under conditions far removed from normal life. The natural, instinctive reaction is to escape by whatever means are available – flight, surrender or mental collapse.

Unfortunately such reactions do not win battles, so the primary task of all military leaders, at whatever level of command, is to prevent them occurring. Men must be made to forget their natural instincts, sublimating the desire to escape beneath a veneer of courage, cohesiveness and corporate strength, for if this can be achieved the chances of victory increase. As early as the 4th century BC the Greek writer Xenophon recognised the potential: 'You know, I am sure, that not numbers or strength bring victory in war; but whichever army goes into battle stronger in soul, their enemies cannot withstand them.'

In more modern times such 'strength of soul' has been defined as 'morale', but its intangible nature remains. It is not something which can be imposed; it is a feeling which must come from the soldiers themselves, manifested in a desire to win and a will to withstand the pressures of war. 'High morale,' as

Field Marshal Viscount Slim of Burma has said, 'means that every individual in a group will work – or fight – and, if needed, will give his last ounce of effort in its service.'

But the creation and maintenance of morale is by no means easy. Commanders in the past often ignored its desirability entirely, preferring to substitute iron discipline for individual willpower. At the battle of Waterloo in 1815, for example, British soldiers were expected to withstand the terrifying ordeal of French artillery and cavalry attacks not through their personal resolve but under the threat that, if they did not, flogging or execution would result. Nor is this process completely ignored in the more modern age: the ritualistic 'oathing' ceremonies of the Mau Mau in Kenya in the 1950s promised instant death or tribal disgrace to disloyal recruits in the campaign against the British.

Yet it is widely accepted that threats cannot succeed on their own. All armies need a certain amount of imposed discipline, of course, if only to ensure a coherent command structure, but as fighting units have become smaller and more isolated on the modern battlefield, soldiers no longer come under close supervision and have to fall back on their own resources. A foot-patrol on the streets of Belfast, a guerrilla group in the mountains of Afghanistan or the crew of a tank or aircraft have to be capable of producing their own discipline and sustaining their own morale. As Lord Moran wrote in *The Anatomy of Courage*, 'a man with high morale does things because in his own mind he has decided to do them.'

A key factor in this decision is undoubtedly lead-

The ability to keep going under fire is one of the keys to success. The Israeli forces that poured into the Lebanon in 1982 (above) were secure in the knowledge of their superiority, and their morale was correspondingly high.

ership, for any soldier will feel more secure and better able to cope with the pressures of battle if he has confidence in his officers. A good leader, at any level of command, should care for the men under him, understand what they are capable of achieving and be prepared to set an example of courage, resolution and common sense. In Lord Moran's words again, he should be able to 'frame plans which will succeed and . . . persuade others to carry them out in the face of death'. If this is achieved, regardless of the type of military formation involved, morale will begin to emerge out of cohesiveness and loyalty. The peasants who followed Mao Tse-tung on the Long March in 1934-35 were reacting to the leadership of political officers of the Chinese Communist Party, just as the soldiers of the 1st Battalion of the Gloucestershire Regiment, surrounded at Choksong on the Imjin River in Korea in April 1951, looked for inspiration to their officers and continued to resist, literally until overrun by communist forces. Obviously if the leaders fail to act as good examples to their men, morale will suffer – the Egyptians left leaderless in the Sinai desert in June 1967 showed this by following their natural instincts to flee or surrender to the advancing Israelis – but the emphasis placed upon effective leadership in all armies implies that this is a lesson already well learnt.

One way of producing the necessary leaders is through careful training, and this applies equally to the ordinary soldiers in the sense that the natural fears of war can be lessened through preparation. Intensive training, designed to provide a series of rehearsed responses to the stimuli of battle, is the favoured method in most armies, guerrilla as well as regular, for if a soldier has something definite to do when faced with enemy action, he is less likely to pause and allow his fears to materialise. As J. T. MacCurdy in *The Structure of Morale* points out, 'there is nothing so conducive to fear as not knowing what to do', so time spent on the seemingly mundane and repetitious tasks

of weapons drill, advance-to-contact, digging-in or defending unit locations is rarely wasted. If, in addition, the soldiers are educated in the tactics and weapons capabilities of the enemy, they will be less vulnerable to surprise and better able to face the traumatic experience of battle.

But care needs to be taken, for if the soldiers are geared to specific enemy actions which do not then eventuate – if, for example, the enemy uses new tactics or unexpected weapons – they may become confused and open to panic. A case in point is the impact of German blitzkrieg tactics, with their novel use of dive-bombers and fast-moving armour, upon Allied troops in France in 1940, although the process of demoralisation need not always be that dramatic. If soldiers are told in training that the enemy has certain material deficiences which weaken his capabilities and then they suddenly find out that this is not so, the effects can undermine rather than quickly destroy morale. American troops discovered this in Vietnam in early 1968.

During the night of 6/7 February 1968 an American Special Forces camp at Lang Vei, southwest of Khe Sanh in South Vietnam, was overrun by North Vietnamese regular troops. In itself this was not particularly remarkable – the camp was isolated and its

The regimental tradition of the British Army has usually been seen as a considerable aid in maintaining the morale and resolve of its soldiers. Seemingly irrelevant ceremonials, such as trooping the colour (below), may well add to the fighting efficiency of the Brigade of Guards. Bottom: Guardsmen prepare to move forward in the Falklands in 1982.

defences were weak – but the effects were far-reaching. For the first time in this war the North Vietnamese used tanks (11 Soviet-built PT76s) in their assault and this sent a shock-wave which spread rapidly through the American forces elsewhere in Vietnam. Michael Herr, in his memorable book *Dispatches,* describes a typical reaction: 'Jesus, they had tanks. Tanks! . . . After Lang Vei, how could you look out of your perimeter at night without hearing the treads coming?' American soldiers, already unsure about the war and the reasons for their own involvement, were suddenly presented with evidence which ran counter to their belief that the enemy was unsophisticated and poorly equipped. Their morale suffered accordingly.

So training alone cannot guarantee high morale; it can only act as a reinforcement to something far deeper in the soldier's psyche which strengthens his will to resist. In most organisations, civilian as well as military, this may be created through group loyalty, for if someone values the well-being of his friends he will be more likely to work hard in the interests of the group rather than for purely personal gain. In a military context this is extremely useful, overlaying a soldier's natural fears with something which is of more importance to him and which he will be prepared to protect even to the extent of endangering his life.

In the British Army this has been largely achieved through the 'regimental system', a unique organisational framework which thrives on group loyalty. When a soldier enlists he does not join 'the army' as such, but a small part of it – his regiment. In most cases he is trained for that unit and may be expected to spend his entire service life within it. He comes to regard it as his 'family', with all the emotional ties of loyalty which that entails. Lieutenant-Colonel John Baynes, in his book *Morale,* made a detailed study of one such unit – the 2nd Battalion of The Cameronians (Scottish Rifles) – under the pressures of war in 1915 and he places regimental loyalty at the top of his list of

requirements for high morale. When it is added that the system also produces a strong feeling of tradition, which the individual soldier is loath to break by bringing disgrace upon his regiment in battle, it may be appreciated that it is a worthwhile organisational exercise. Indeed, many American commanders are convinced that their system of producing soldiers for the army as a whole, with no regimental continuity or tradition, contributed to the decline in morale in Vietnam. They are in favour of an extension of the British pattern to the United States.

At the present time, however, the British system is the exception rather than the rule, so we must look elsewhere for a universally applicable answer to the question of loyalty. There are many possibilities. If, for example, the soldier is dedicated to a cause then he is more likely to be prepared to make personal sacrifices and stand firm in battle. One of the most obvious such causes is patriotism, enhanced dramatically if the country itself is directly threatened, and in this the Israeli defence forces provide the best modern example.

In October 1973 they were surprised by a coordinated Egyptian and Syrian assault which threatened the existence of the Jewish state. Furthermore, as Israeli reserves were mobilised and rushed to the Sinai and Golan fronts, they encountered weapons which undermined the very basics of their tactical doctrine – precision-guided anti-tank and anti-aircraft missiles capable of destroying the traditional tools of Israeli victory. In such circumstances morale should have been weakened, especially as Syrian tanks approached the Jordan River. But the Israelis stood firm, even finding time to perfect successful counters to the missiles in the midst of battle before going over to the offensive. It was a remarkable achievement, given the problems. Many agree that this was only possible because of the deeply-held conviction that the Israeli forces were all that stood against the complete destruction of the state. If the state was to survive, sacrifices had to be made, far outweighing the personal fears of individual soldiers.

Patriotism may be only a part of the soldier's loyalty. In many guerrilla armies, particularly those which follow the teachings of Mao Tse-tung, the difficult problem of motivation may be eased by providing a political aim which transcends the logic of instinct. A poor peasant, landless, starving and repressed, may be mobilised to military action by promises of a better life, even to the extent of accepting that his own death may be required to guarantee improvements for future generations. Such an appeal may be further reinforced by a desire for political independence, especially from colonial rule. The hordes of

Keeping soldiers clean and fed is important if they are to fight at their best. Above: An Israeli field shower in the Sinai in 1967. Left: South Vietnamese troops snatch a meal in a mountain strongpoint they are defending against communist forces.

Above: Religious rather than professional or nationalist motivation assumed a new importance to the Iranian Army after the downfall of the Shah and the establishment of a fundamentalist Islamic regime. Below: For many soldiers the sight of death on the battlefield can be overwhelming – as this US Marine found on Hill 881 in Vietnam in May 1967.

people were openly critical of their political leaders, many soldiers soon came to regard Vietnam as a place for which it was not worth making sacrifices. Similar problems affected the French Army in Indochina (1945-54) and Algeria (1954-62) and the Portuguese forces in Africa (1961-74). In all cases the results were civil-military alienation and political disaffection among demoralised armed forces.

Good morale must therefore have its roots in self-discipline, leadership, training, loyalty and belief, but there is one other factor worth considering. A soldier's resolve may be dramatically weakened if he is not cared for in the physical sense. Battle is traumatic enough without having to worry about such things as food, water, medical support or contact with home, so most armies – guerrilla as well as conventional – will devote considerable effort to this aspect. Mao Tse-tung's emphasis upon the creation of 'safe base areas', within which his revolutionary fighters could gain shelter, food and rest through a sympathetic population, is a pertinent example, equivalent to the enormous administrative 'tail' which now accompanies most conventional armies. Only if this 'back-up' works, will the soldier fight at his most efficient level.

This was a point well understood by Field Marshal Slim in Burma in 1942-43 when he devoted enormous resources to improving the health and welfare of the British Fourteenth Army, transforming it from a number of demoralised units into an effective fighting force. But if problems abound, morale will swiftly crack. The defeat of insurgents in both Malaya (1948-60) and Kenya (1952-60) was virtually guaranteed once the British forces had cut them off from their sources of food supply.

Most military commentators have agreed that morale is probably, in the words of Field Marshal Lord Montgomery of Alamein, 'the greatest single factor in war'. If it exists, soldiers of any type or background will face the pressures of battle; if it does not, chaos will ensue as the soldiers lose all evidence of military cohesiveness and rapidly regress to their original characters – ordinary human beings, frightened out of their wits by the trauma of war. In such circumstances, no amount of discipline or punishment will prevent defeat, but if the ingredients of morale are mixed in the right proportions, the chances of victory are enhanced. And once that happens, a self-supporting process may begin: as Montgomery observed, 'the best way to achieve a high morale in wartime is by success in battle.' **John Pimlott**

Viet Minh fighters who hurled themselves time after time against French defences on the Red (Hong) River in 1951 and at Dien Bien Phu three years later undoubtedly felt this way, achieving remarkable long-term results despite enormous casualties. Finally, religious belief may create the same effect. The unexpected resolve shown by the Iranian armed forces since the Iraqi attack of September 1980 owes much to their belief in the Islamic revolution preached by the Ayatollah Khomeini.

Obviously if such beliefs are ever undermined then morale will begin to crack. The lack of domestic support for the war in Vietnam, manifested by the peace movement of the late 1960s, contributed to the decline in American service morale, principally by casting doubts in many soldiers' minds about the moral justification for the conflict. As the United States was clearly not directly threatened and its

Previous page: One of the Soviet Union's more effective surface-to-air missiles, the highly mobile SA-4. Above: The SA-1 was the first missile in the Soviet SAM series; although a technological breakthrough in the 1950s this SAM was soon superseded by smaller and more flexible types.

Soviet military thinking has always emphasised the role of anti-aircraft defence within its armed forces, and the Soviet Army is well protected by a dense AA (anti-aircraft) umbrella made up of both guns and missiles. To carry out its demanding requirements Soviet AA equipment has to be highly mobile and be capable of accompanying mechanised and armoured forces into the combat zone. In addition these forces must be able to withstand the inhibiting effects caused by nuclear, biological and chemical warfare, a commonplace factor in a full-scale superpower conflict.

The theory behind heavy battlefield anti-aircraft defence has largely been vindicated through the Vietnam and Yom Kippur Wars. In both these conflicts considerable numbers of American and Israeli combat aircraft were committed to air-defence suppression sorties; and over North Vietnam anything from 25 to 50 per cent of US aircraft were forced into this role, thus reducing substantially the number of aircraft available for bombing missions.

The Soviet Union fields an awesome array of anti-aircraft guns, but the most important elements within their AA armoury are the SAM (surface-to-air missile) systems. Designed to provide a full range of combat functions, Soviet SAMs range from hand-held infantry weapons to vast missiles capable of carrying out semi-strategic missions.

Estimated to have come into service as early as 1954, the SA-1 Guild represented a considerable breakthrough in Soviet missile technology; it was the first operational SAM in the world apart from the Swiss RSC series. Due to its considerable size and weight – 12m (39ft 5in) and 3200kg (7055lb) – the SA-1 has been considered as part of the Soviet Union's fixed strategic defences and since 1960 it has

steadily been replaced by more advanced models.

The SA-2 Guideline became operational in 1957 and since then has become the most combat-tested SAM to see operational service, having been used extensively in Vietnam and the Middle East. The SA-2 came to the attention of the West in 1960 when one shot down the American U-2 'spy' plane piloted by Francis Gary Powers over the Soviet Union. From then on even the highest-flying aircraft were vulnerable to surface-to-air missiles. Since the late 1950s a number of modifications have been incorporated into the SA-2 in the light of combat experience, but despite these improvements the SA-2 system has been characterised by its simplicity and robustness which has enabled it to be operated by technologically unsophisticated customers, most notably Egypt, Syria and North Vietnam. .

The simplicity of the SA-2's operation has, on the other hand, meant that it can be outwitted by well-trained air crews, either through ECM (electronic countermeasures) as employed by the Americans in Vietnam, or by relatively simple evasive manoeuvres of the type used by the Israelis in the Middle East. Once the SA-2 had been spotted, the pilot could swing his aircraft towards the missiles and then swiftly dive below it, a manoeuvre the ungainly SA-2 would be unable to follow.

As the SA-2 was designed for high-level aircraft interception it was supplemented in 1961 by the SA-3 Goa, produced to take on aircraft at medium and low altitudes. First used in combat in the Middle East in the late 1960s and in North Vietnam in 1972 it had some initial success, but like the SA-2 its ability to knock-out advanced combat aircraft has been rendered almost negligible. During the 1970s both mis-

siles were replaced in the Soviet Union by more advanced types though they are still used by the Warsaw Pact and in other countries which deploy Soviet weapons.

The SA-4 Ganef marked a considerable improvement on its predecessors, being capable of in-depth defence against aircraft flying at a variety of altitudes, while at the same time being carried by a highly-mobile launch vehicle. Consisting of two missiles mounted on a tracked launcher the SA-4 has the ability to advance with the swiftest mobile forces and yet provide effective air-defence protection to a range of 70km (43 miles). Introduced in 1964 the SA-4 has not been used in combat; although a number were stationed in Egypt during 1970-72 they were withdrawn prior to the Yom Kippur War in 1973. An updated version was brought into operation in 1974 with improved capabilities at low altitudes and it is thought that this missile may have its own terminal radar-homing system.

The SA-5 Gammon can hardly be considered a conventional SAM, for with a launch weight of 10,000kg (22,050lb) and a range of 250km (155 miles) it forms part of the Soviet static defence system.

When the SA-6 Gainful was first observed in a Red Square parade in 1967 few Western observers had any idea of the capabilities of this self-propelled, triple-launcher missile system. In 1973, Egyptian SA-6s destroyed a considerable number of Israeli aircraft during the first few hours of the Yom Kippur War and it rapidly gained a fearsome reputation. This was largely unjustified, however, for despite its manoeuvrability, sophisticated terminal radar guidance and low-level capability, by the end of the fighting Israeli

Above: A captured SA-2 of the Egyptian armed forces is inspected by curious Israeli troops following the campaign in the Sinai during the Six-Day War of 1967. Right: SA-2s have been distributed throughout the Warsaw Pact and here a detachment of Polish troops answers an alert during an exercise held in 1981.

pilots had come to terms with the SA-6, having mastered it through a combination of evasive action techniques and by the timely release of 'chaff' clouds which disturbed the missile's guidance system. The SA-6's weaknesses were revealed further during the Israeli invasion of the Lebanon in 1982 when Israeli defence suppression aircraft wiped-out the Syrian SA-6 air-defence system with contemptuous ease.

Although the SA-6 had proved a useful and mobile weapon the Soviet authorities saw its limitations and in 1974 brought out the SA-8 Gecko. Considerably more advanced than the SA-6, the SA-8 is considered to have the necessary acceleration to hit fast-moving aircraft at low altitudes. The launch vehicle allows four missiles to be carried, which can be fired in pairs at separate targets. The tracking radar is carried on the launch vehicle (especially designed for amphibious operations) and provides the SA-8 missile with a maximum range of up to 15km (9 miles). Not having been used in combat, little is known of its true capabilities, however, although its radar guidance system is thought to be supplemented by an infra-red terminal homing system.

Distinct from the radio-command guidance systems of most SAMs are the SA-7 Grail and SA-9 Gaskin missiles which use a very simple infra-red homing system designed to lock onto the exhausts of passing aircraft. The SA-7 can be carried by individual infantrymen and the latest models are capable of shooting down slow-moving aircraft at ranges of up to 5.6km (3.5 miles). More advanced, the SA-9 is quad-mounted on scout cars and is equipped with a larger warhead. The great advantage of these portable weapons is that they allow units as small as an infantry section to have their own SAM defence, and their cheapness and simplicity of operation make them available to insurgent groups the world over. But as with other simple weapon systems, the SA-7 and SA-9 are easily countered and few modern combat aircraft would experience real problems from such weapons, although helicopters and slow-moving counter-insurgency aircraft remain vulnerable.

The latest generation of Soviet SAMs are the

Below: East German SA-4s are prepared for action.
Opposite top: SA-4s carry out manoeuvres in Eastern Europe. In the advent of war with Nato the SA-4 would play an important role in attempting to fend off Western strike aircraft from disrupting the advance of the Soviet Army.
Opposite bottom: The portable and cheap SA-7 infra-red SAM is given a firing demonstration by a Soviet soldier.

SA-10 and SA-11 which have been designed to counter low-flying strike aircraft such as the US F-111 and the European Tornado as well as US cruise missiles. The SA-10 is a long-range weapon of high manoeuvrability combined with exceptional acceleration, and it is thought to pose a real threat to Nato strike forces. The SA-11 is a shorter range SAM and is fitted on triple or quadruple launchers. From 1978 it began to replace the ageing SA-6 batteries within the Soviet Union.

The strength of the Soviet SAM system lies not in any one particular missile – for any missile can be mastered over time – but in the fact that Soviet military planners see the whole SAM programme as a continually evolving one, each new development providing a springboard for further improvement. Because of this the Soviet Union has been able to develop missiles as advanced as the SA-10 and SA-11 that look set to provide Nato air forces with their greatest challenge yet.

Overleaf top: SA-8 launchers (left) stand side-by-side with truck-borne SA-2s. Soviet air defence theory emphasises integrating all aspects of the SAM system. Overleaf bottom: An SA-9 launcher is shown here with only its two outer missile boxes in position on the launcher rails.

THE KEY SOVIET SAMs

SA-2 Guideline
Length 10.6m (35ft)
Launch weight 2300kg (5065lb)
Guidance Radio command
Fuel 1st stage, solid; 2nd stage, liquid
Maximum speed Mach 3
Maximum range 35km (21.7 miles) – later models 50km (31 miles)
Warhead 130kg (287lb) high explosive

SA-3b Goa
Length 6.1m (20 ft)
Launch weight 950kg (2094lb)
Guidance Radio command
Terminal homing Semi-active radar
Fuel Two-stage solid fuel
Maximum speed Mach 3.5
Maximum range 18.3km (11.4 miles)
Warhead 60kg (132lb) high explosive

SA-4 Ganef
Length 8.8m (28ft 10in)
Launch weight 2500kg (5512lb)
Guidance Radio command
Terminal homing Semi-active radar
Fuel Four solid-boost motors, plus ramjet sustainer
Maximum speed Mach 2.5
Maximum range 70km (43.5 miles)
Warhead High explosive; weight unknown

SA-6 Gainful
Length 6.2m (20ft 4in)
Launch weight 550kg (1213lb)
Guidance Radio command
Terminal homing Semi-active radar
Fuel Two-stage solid boost motor, plus ramjet
Maximum speed Mach 2.8
Maximum range 37km (23 miles)
Warhead 80kg (176lb); half of which is high explosive

SA-7 Grail
Length 1.3m (4ft 5in)
Launch weight 9.2kg (20.3lb)
Guidance Infra-red homing
Fuel Two-stage solid fuel
Maximum speed Mach 1.5
Maximum range 3.5km (2.2 miles) – later models 5.6km (3.5 miles)
Warhead 1.8kg (4lb)

SA-8 Gecko
Length 3.2m (10ft 6in)
Launch weight 200kg (441lb)
Guidance Radio command
Terminal homing Infra-red (or possibly semi-active radar)
Fuel Dual-thrust solid fuel
Maximum speed Mach 2
Maximum range 15km (9.3 miles)
Warhead 40kg (88lb) high explosive

SA-9 Gaskin
Length 1.37m (4ft 6in)
Launch weight 50kg (110lb)
Guidance Infra-red homing
Fuel Solid
Maximum speed Mach 2
Maximum range 7km (4.4 miles)
Warhead 5kg (11lb)

War on the Red River

French attempts to hold on to Indochina met with bitter resistance

There is a story that in September 1943, in remote Kwangsi province in south China, the military governor Chang Ta-k'uai released an exiled communist Vietnamese from the prison where he had been incarcerated for subversive activities. The communist leader claimed that he could pass on valuable information about the Japanese forces in Indochina from his guerrilla contacts there. Chang badly needed this intelligence, and so he agreed to support the communist guerrillas with arms and money. He suggested, however, that as the communist leader was a known agitator, he should change his name in case the central Chinese government refused to countenance the support he was to receive. And so Nguyen Ai Quoc assumed the name Ho Chi Minh ('He who enlightens') and his guerrillas received the help they needed to become the force that pursued one of the most bitter struggles in modern history.

The wars in the region that was once known as French Indochina, comprising the areas of present-day Vietnam, Laos and Kampuchea (Cambodia), have been among the largest of all the conflicts since 1945. What began as a communist-nationalist revolt against French rule in Indochina turned into a series of confrontations that have engaged the attention of the entire world.

The French had taken control of Indochina during the second half of the 19th century. The region was divided into five territories: Cochin-China, Annam and Tonkin (respectively, the south, centre and north of what is now Vietnam), Cambodia and Laos.

Previous page: In the fight for the delta regions, amphibious assault vehicles played a major role. Here French soldiers refuel their amphibious load-carrier. Right: Young members of the Cao Dai militia undergo weapons training.

During the 1920s and 1930s, nationalist movements had begun to grow up: the National Party of Vietnam (Viet Nam Quoc Dan Dang or VNQDD) was formed in 1927, and in 1929, Nguyen Ai Quoc formed the Indochinese Communist Party. Failed revolts in 1930 and 1940, however, seemed to demonstrate that the French were still firmly in control. But the French position itself was soon to be in peril. The collapse of the French armies in Europe in May and June of 1940, the subsequent armistice with Germany and the partition of the country had left the French administration in Indochina out on a limb, unable to count on any help from the Vichy government. One power that was swift to take advantage of this was Japan, which was engaged in a war of conquest in China and wanted to cut all supplies reaching the Chinese government from Indochina. The first Japanese ultimatum came in June 1940. Gradually Japanese control was extended, and they took over completely in March 1945 in a lightning coup that was resisted by the French and resulted in some French forces being massacred.

This new order in Indochina had profound long-term effects. The most important of these consequences was the revival of the fortunes of the Indochinese Communist Party. Many of the leaders of this party, including Nguyen Ai Quoc, had fled to Kwangsi province in China in 1939, and in May 1941, after a conference with leaders of other nationalist groups, had formed the League for the Independence of Vietnam (Viet Nam Doc Lap Dong Minh Hoi, soon shortened to Viet Minh), which put independence above the class struggle on its list of priorities. The first active move the new grouping took was to agree to the appointment of Vo Nguyen Giap to form guerrilla bands to operate in Cao Bang province in the north of Tonkin.

Using Chinese Nationalist money, obtained after Ho Chi Minh's accord with the Kwangsi governor, the Viet Minh extended its guerrilla network, although little actual fighting, either against French or Japanese, was undertaken. As Japanese defeat came nearer, Giap moved his guerrilla forces towards the Red (Hong) River Delta, and when the sudden Japanese surrender came in August 1945 his men were the only ones on the spot able to take advantage of the situation. The French troops had been disarmed by the Japanese since March; and so, on 17 August, there was little to stop Giap when his men raised the red flag with its inset yellow star all over Hanoi, and took over administrative authority on behalf of the Viet Minh.

In Cochin-China, the collapse of the Japanese saw a combination of many nationalist parties, the United National Front, agree to combine with the Viet Minh to set up a Provisional Executive Committee. Of the nine members of this committee, six were communist. In Annam (central Vietnam) the Emperor Bao Dai who had been nominal ruler under the French and then the Japanese, abdicated in favour of the Viet Minh; and so over all the area of Vietnam, the Viet Minh had asserted control. On 2 September 1945, Ho Chi Minh, from Hanoi, proclaimed the independence of Vietnam.

At the Potsdam conference in the summer of 1945, the great powers had agreed that Chinese Nationalist troops should arrange for the surrender and repatriation of Japanese troops north of the 16th parallel, and for British troops to organise this process in the south of the country. Major-General Douglas Gracey and his forces helped pave the way for the return of the French administration in the south, and by the beginning of 1946, French forces under General Philippe Leclerc were in control of Saigon and large areas of the surrounding countryside. The situation in Tonkin, however, was very different.

In Tonkin the arrival of the Chinese Nationalist forces in September 1945 may have reduced the authority of the Viet Minh, but it also prevented the immediate return of the French.

In fact, it was not until March 1946 that French forces landed at Haiphong and, in spite of an agreement on French re-occupation having been signed with the Chinese, some fighting took place. The Viet Minh leaders acceded to the French landing and a French military presence in return for limited recognition of their independent republic. By the end of June almost all Chinese troops had gone, and complex negotiations between the Viet Minh and the French were under way. What the French were offering was some degree of autonomy and inclusion within the French Union and a federation of Indochina; the preliminaries to such agreements were signed with Cambodia in January 1946 and with Laos in May 1947. But the Viet Minh wanted a united, independent Vietnam under their control, and this the French would not agree to.

During the summer of 1946, negotiations took place in France itself, at the close of which Ho Chi Minh signed an agreement which would have placed the Hanoi regime within the Indochinese federation. But no real agreement was possible between parties with such widely divergent aims, and fighting broke out in November when French forces attacked Viet Minh troops in Haiphong, even employing a naval bombardment of the town. In December, Viet Minh attacks on French garrisons in Tonkin saw the final breakdown of any possibility of compromise. The Viet Minh retreated to their base areas in the northern mountains, the Viet Bac, and the French set about restoring their authority in earnest.

The fighting over the next four years, until the Viet Minh successes on the Cao Bang ridge, had several unusual features that are essential to an understanding of what took place. The first of these lay in the unusual demography of Vietnam. The vast bulk of the popula-

Above and right: The problems of resupply and lack of barbed wire often meant that French bases were forced to employ the use of bamboo stockades. A line of tin cans along the inside warned of possible night attacks. Below: As the French, equipped with US arms, fight their way into Hanoi in 1946, these troops in their rooftop location cover the streets with a Browning machine gun.

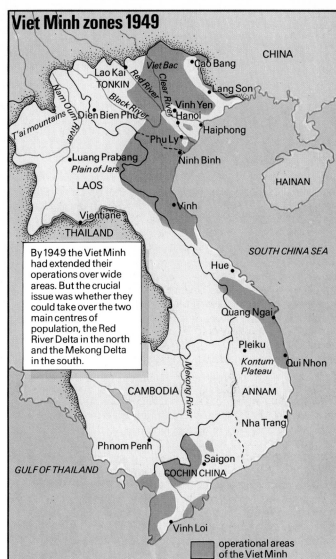

Viet Minh zones 1949

By 1949 the Viet Minh had extended their operations over wide areas. But the crucial issue was whether they could take over the two main centres of population, the Red River Delta in the north and the Mekong Delta in the south.

operational areas of the Viet Minh

tion was concentrated in two deltas – that of the Red River in the north and of the Mekong in the south. There was a thin band of fairly dense population along the eastern coast, but the great mass of the central highlands was very sparsely peopled, and that mainly by hill tribes traditionally hostile to the Vietnamese. So the struggle for control of the Vietnamese people was concentrated in two areas that were very far apart.

A second aspect of the war that assumed great importance was the situation of the French. They were (ostensibly at any rate) not fighting to retain colonial control, but to establish autonomous states within the French Union. Their constant objective was to find an indigenous Vietnamese grouping that they could rely on to resist the Viet Minh and yet consent to remain within the French Union. The former Emperor of Annam, Bao Dai, was involved in negotiations in 1947, and at various times the French seemed to be succeeding in their policy. There were, indeed, many nationalists, such as the survivors of the VNQDD, who had little cause to love the Viet Minh, and many of these were prepared to negotiate with the French.

The existence of many anti-Viet Minh groupings made the situation far more complex than a straight conflict between the French and the communists. These groupings were various. There was, for example, a very important Catholic element in Vietnam –

Eye for an eye

A peasant victim of a French reprisal raid.

During the early stages of the war in Indochina, terrorism and atrocities between the two sides were a regular occurrence. In one incident in Dalat in May 1951, a French police officer, outraged at the cold-blooded murder of his superior by guerrillas, decided upon immediate reprisal.

Twenty hostages were taken from a group of prisoners who were being held on suspicion of activities against the Bao Dai regime. The hostages, 16 men and 4 women, were led into the street and shot. They were left dying in the road.

In another incident a month or so later, General Chanson, the French Commissioner and commander of the French Union forces, was brutally murdered. The general, while on tour of the Sadec district, entered a town square where he was to be greeted by officials of the local administration. As he entered the square a Vietnamese 'volunteer of death' pushed his way through the police cordon and ran towards the general. On reaching him the guerrilla ignited two grenades which he had in his trouser pockets. The general, mortally wounded, died in hospital without regaining consciousness.

Above: An armoured patrol moves into a village which has just been attacked by a Viet Minh unit, hoping to both surprise and engage the guerrillas. Right: A French amphibious unit crosses the Mekong delta on the way to a forward battle area.

about 1,700,000 people in all. The leaders of the Catholics tried to demonstrate that they were not necessarily pro-French; and the two vicariates of Phat Diem and Bui Chu, on the coast in south Tonkin, maintained their independence with the aid of their own militia.

Nor was Catholicism the only minority religion. In Cochin-China two sects, the Cao Dai and the Hoa Hoa, had grown up as syncretic religions before World War II and had many supporters. In January 1947 the Cao Dai signed an agreement with the French and the Hoa Hoa followed suit in May, the latter after one of their leaders had been murdered and his body sawn in half by the Viet Minh.

Add to this mix of varied nationalists and religious groupings the hill tribes (Montagnards) and various bands of river pirates (Binh Xuyen) who flourished on the Mekong, and the situation in Vietnam during the late 1940s can be seen to be complex; and these complexities did not help the French formulate a coherent policy. Nor was the French cause helped by the political situation at home. The Fourth Republic was notoriously unstable. Some governments only lasted a matter of days, and the presence of a strong communist minority in the legislature contributed to ambivalent feelings about the future of Indochina. The French forces in Indochina were kept at levels well below those which would have been necessary to allow a sustained offensive against the Viet Minh; and no conscripts were permitted to be employed there – only regulars. Just before the main Viet Minh attacks in 1950, the French government even proposed to reduce its commitment by 9000 men.

This combination of weakness at home and the complexity of the situation on the ground, meant that when the French should have been taking the initiative against the militarily much weaker Viet Minh and promoting effective local nationalists to destroy the Viet Minh's base of popular support, they were unable to do so. Ho Chi Minh and Giap, secure in the mountains of the Viet Bac in north Tonkin, did not risk any of their main units during 1947 and 1948, but they continued to extend their guerrilla networks wherever they could.

This was a nasty little war, in which torture and atrocity were commonplace. The Viet Minh steadily put pressure on the rural population and encouraged the French to retaliate wildly; the French, for their part, displayed no mercy in their attitude to the Viet Minh but felt bitter that they were not receiving the support they needed from France itself. There was resentment in the French forces, too, at the residual corruption in the cities of Vietnam, where a black market in the piastre (the currency intended for the Indochinese Federation) was flourishing, and at the arguments between nationalist politicians. This squalid world hardly seemed worth fighting to preserve.

French strategy was essentially defensive; the characteristic sight of the war was a line of wooden watchtowers protecting railways and roads. As soon as troops were concentrated in one area the Viet Minh seeped into others that had been denuded. It was not that the Viet Minh were overwhelmingly popular in the countryside. They certainly enjoyed great support amongst a certain percentage of the population, but the widespread popularity they had enjoyed in August 1945 as the major nationalist group had tended to evaporate during the months of famine in late 1945 and early 1946. Where there was a rival popular force – as in the areas the Cao Dai controlled in Cochin-China or in the Catholic parts of Tonkin – then the Viet Minh made little headway. But over most of the country there was no such rival, only the French presence. And the French were feared and resented; the atrocities committed by legionaries or Senegalese troops did not endear them to the local population.

The Viet Minh, too, committed atrocities; but theirs were more selective, and always to an end – not vicious responses to unseen assailants. To many Vietnamese it seemed obvious that the only alternative to French rule was the Viet Minh, however unpleasant that might be. And this feeling was reinforced in 1949, when the communist Chinese won their civil war against Chiang Kai-shek.

The communist victory in China altered everyone's perspectives on the war in Vietnam. In spite of a tradition of Vietnamese hostility to the Chinese stretching back over 1000 years, the Viet Minh could now see a new source of weapons, and totally safe

training areas. The French high command also realised this, and whereas previously they had been able to feel content at having confined the insurgents to a remote area where they could do little damage, they could now see them inexorably building up their strength. Communist Chinese victory did hold the promise of some advantage to the French: American aid was now likely to be forthcoming to stop the red tide sweeping south. On 8 May 1950, Dean Acheson, American Secretary of State, announced that he considered the situation to be such as to warrant the provision of economic and military aid.

It was, however, to be the communists that reaped immediate benefits from Mao Tse-tung's success to the north. In the summer of 1949 the French Army's chief of staff, General Revers, had recommended that French troops withdraw almost completely from the mountains of north Tonkin and concentrate on keeping control of the Red River Delta. If the Viet Minh could be kept out of this populous area and denied any food supplies from it, then their safe base areas in the Viet Bac would be largely valueless. Some parts of the Revers Plan were carried out in 1949, but the garrisons on the remote Cao Bang-Lang Son ridge were still kept in place – perhaps in order to inhibit Chinese supplies to the Viet Minh.

In February 1950, Giap announced that the guerrilla war was ending and the war of movement beginning. With better artillery support than they had ever enjoyed before, the Viet Minh attacked the post of Dong Khe on the Cao Bang ridge in May 1950; and although the French forces recaptured the fort, the writing was on the wall. They had failed to take the initiative when they had the chance in 1947 and 1948; France was soon to pay dearly for this failure.

Ashley Brown

Soldiers and civilians

How modern warfare
involves the whole population

the enemy's strength to be maintained in the battle area, in the 20th century it became possible to use the long reach of air power to destroy the *sources* of such supplies – the enemy's factories, resource areas and working population. The bombing of cities such as Coventry, London, Hamburg, Berlin and Tokyo during World War II represented attempts to achieve this new strategic aim, and civilians inevitably suffered. Of the estimated 50 million people killed between 1939 and 1945, the vast majority were what would be traditionally termed non-combatants.

The atomic attacks upon Hiroshima and Nagasaki in August 1945 were the ultimate expressions of this policy, but the advent of weapons of such instantaneous devastation has led to a change of emphasis. As the prospect of nuclear holocaust emerged, destruction was replaced by deterrence, and although civilians continued to have a part to play – this time as hostages rather than victims of war – the avoidance of 'total' conflict seemed to offer them a certain immunity. Indeed, with the evolution of strategies of 'limited war', designed specifically to avoid an escalation to levels which would produce civilian 'mega-death', it might be presumed that civilian involvement in warfighting has declined in the period since 1945.

But this would be a false picture. The apparent immunity arising from deterrence affects civilians living in the nuclear-capable states only, leaving vast numbers of people in the world still vulnerable to the full rigours of war. In early 1982, for example, it was estimated that wars or military campaigns were actually being conducted in areas which contained more than 700 million civilians, producing a catalogue of death, injury, disease and deprivation which makes the Thirty Years War and probably even World War II pale into insignificance.

This state of affairs has been made much worse by the fact that in few of the affected areas are the civilians merely innocent bystanders caught up in military action, for since 1945 there has been a significant shift in the types of war being fought. It is still possible to find examples of campaigns in which rival armies are expected to decide issues between states – the Falklands conflict is a case in point – but it has become usual to see military techniques being used to open the way to a usurpation of political power within a state.

The rash of independence struggles which has accompanied the often-reluctant withdrawal of Western powers from their imperial possessions, coupled to the spread of communist revolutionary ideology, has produced an emphasis on guerrilla rather than conventional campaigns. As guerrilla forces emerge from and are dependent upon the continued support of the ordinary people, civilian involvement in the struggle is both essential and unavoidable.

The first person to recognise this was undoubtedly Mao Tse-tung as he searched for a method whereby the existing government of China could be overthrown and a communist regime put in its place. He found a ready source of support among the oppressed peoples of rural China, but the establishment of alternative, communist societies – of states within the state – could hardly be expected to go unnoticed by the ruling authorities. Mao had to protect his bases and, lacking a regular army, he had to turn to the people both to provide and to sustain guerrilla fighters. The guerrillas were the cutting-edge of revolution, capable of gradually wearing down the strength and

The recent wars of the Middle East have seen a blurring of the line between civilian and soldier. Left: For these Lebanese Christian phalangists civilian involvement in war became part of their daily lives, while for the Afghan tribesmen (top) there has never really been a distinction between civilian or soldier. Above: A civilian Arab becomes an unwitting victim of hostilities between Arab terrorists and British soldiers in Aden. Two soldiers administer first aid.

It would be naive to pretend that there has ever been a time when civilians were not involved in war. Even when the ideal was for bodies of professional soldiers to meet in the clinical isolation of battle to decide an issue by pure force of arms, non-combatants were unavoidably drawn in, if only because the fighting took place over ground which they occupied. During the Thirty Years War of the 17th century, for example, it has been calculated that the civilian population of Germany fell by a third as a direct result of military activity or its associated deprivations. Attempts may have been made to impose 'rules' of war, stressing the need to minimise civilian casualties, but in the end it has always been the ordinary people who have suffered.

Armed forces depend upon continuous supplies of equipment, weapons and ammunition to be effective. Rather than allow such supplies to be delivered and

morale of the government forces preparatory to open battle on more equal terms and, eventually, a takeover of political power. But without the people, they were nothing: 'the people are water, [the guerrillas] are fish; without water the fish will die.'

Mao's main task was therefore to ensure popular support, and this could only be achieved if relations between civilians and guerrilla soldiers were good. For this reason, Mao compiled a simple list of 'rules of behaviour' which his soldiers were expected to obey throughout their dealings with the civilian population. The troops were instructed to 'Replace all doors [used as beds or stretchers] when you leave the house; return and roll up the straw matting on which you sleep; be courteous and polite to the people and help them when you can; return all borrowed articles; replace all damaged articles; be honest in all transactions with the peasants; pay for all articles purchased; be sanitary, and especially establish latrines at a safe distance from people's houses'.

To a peasant class whose only previous experience of soldiers had been the ill-disciplined, rapacious and oppressive members of warlord or government forces, the respect inherent within these rules must have been a pleasant surprise and one which could be exploited by the communist political teachers. If the people could be persuaded that the new ideology and its practitioners did not pose a threat, they were more likely to lend their support, even if that meant suffering the inevitable consequences of guerrilla or open war.

This apparently straightforward process of logic has been copied successfully outside China by other revolutionary or nationalist guerrilla leaders. Ho Chi Minh and General Vo Nguyen Giap used similar methods to create popular opposition to continued French rule in Indochina in the 1940s and early 1950s; Colonel George Grivas and his EOKA guerrillas in Cyprus in the mid-1950s enjoyed strong support from the Greek-Cypriot population in their desire for union with Greece and an end to British rule; Fidel Castro gained widespread popular backing in Cuba in the late 1950s for his fight against the repressive regime of President Fulgencio Batista.

But problems may be experienced. Elements of the civilian population may not agree with the guerrillas' ideology, regardless of its promised advantages, because they already believe in something far stronger, as Viet Minh and, later, Viet Cong activists discovered to their cost among the Catholic sects of southern Indochina throughout their long revolution. Similarly, some of the guerrillas may not obey the 'rules', acting towards the peasants in a high-handed or oppressive manner which merely alienates and offends; widespread Kikuyu opposition to the Mau Mau in Kenya after the Lari massacre of 20 March 1953 illustrates the point.

In such circumstances, with popular support declining, the guerrillas may turn in desperation to intimidation rather than respectful persuasion, instilling fear into the hearts of the people to force them to support the aims of the insurgency. This was certainly the case in South Vietnam where, between 1957 and 1972, an estimated 37,000 people, chiefly from those areas where Catholicism was strong, were murdered by Viet Cong guerrillas.

But no insurgency is ever one-sided, for while the guerrillas try by whatever means available to gain popular support, the armed forces of the existing government are also doing all they can to maintain civilian loyalty. They can do this in a variety of ways. The most effective, at least in the long term, is to mirror the ideas of Mao by persuading the people that government policies and actions merit continued support. This may be done by a simple process of reform to rectify social problems which could be exploited by the insurgents, a policy successfully carried out by President Magsaysay in the Philippines in the early 1950s, or by giving to the people through the existing machinery of government the very things which the guerrillas are striving for illegally, something which the British did in 1952 by promising independence to Malaya despite communist activity. An equally simple process of propaganda, stressing the advantages of settled government and the need for loyalty, may also achieve results.

Such counter-insurgency policies usually go under the title 'hearts and minds', but they rarely work on their own, affecting, at best, those civilians only who were already wavering or uncommitted to the guerrilla cause. This may make the aims of the insurgents more difficult to achieve, but will do little to destroy the hard core of the revolution, which may remain as a basis for future expansion long after government forces have celebrated their counter-insurgency 'victory'. So long as hard-core civilian support persists, the guerrillas can survive; if the insurgency is to be destroyed completely, the link between the two must be cut and the guerrillas isolated, preparatory to their military defeat.

This was certainly the approach adopted by the British in both Malaya (1948-60) and Kenya (1952-60), with impressive results. In Malaya whole villages, situated close to known guerrilla areas, were moved to new locations and the inhabitants protected from fresh communist infiltration; the supply of food to villagers was closely monitored to prevent its delivery to guerrillas; and aggressive military action was initiated deep into the jungle environment of the enemy. Similar tactics were used in Kenya, with the added refinement of concerted action against the Mau

During periods of civil strife, the soldier often becomes the butt for the anger of the civilian population, as in Northern Ireland (above). But the 'invisibility' of the enemy means that whole sectors of the population must be screened. Huge sweep and search operations often lead to violence, as in Aden during the troubles of 1967 (below). Above right: US forces in Vietnam attempted to restrict the activities of the Viet Cong by interrogating large numbers of villagers. Right: A US soldier shares K-rations with an old Japanese woman after the occupation of Okinawa.

Mau 'passive wing' in Nairobi, where in Operation Anvil (24 April 1954) security forces swept through the city detaining all suspect members of the Kikuyu people. In both emergencies, success may be gauged by the fact that guerrilla gangs were forced deeper and deeper into hostile terrain, cut off from their civilian sources of food, recruits and intelligence and, eventually, left to choose between starvation or surrender.

Such policies have to be very carefully controlled, containing as they do all the ingredients for civilian alienation. It would be disastrous, for example, to have one part of the security forces pursuing hearts and minds or resettlement while another was intent upon the destruction of suspect civilian areas. Yet this problem was created by both the French in Algeria (1954-62) and the Americans in Vietnam (1965-73), where it was not unknown for a 'new' or 'pacified' village, carefully nurtured to ensure support for the government, to be bombed or attacked at the first sign of guerrilla activity in the area.

Faced with such a failure of their counter-insurgency methods, security forces may resort to other techniques which continue the process of civilian alienation. Most regular armies dislike having to fight guerrillas, preferring open battle in which superiority of firepower, technology and numbers can be brought to bear; when confronted by the problems of unconventional war, they may over-react. American servicemen in Vietnam, for example, found it exceptionally frustrating to march for days over difficult terrain without making contact with enemy forces, particularly if during that time they were subjected to the classic guerrilla tactics of ambush, sniping, mines and booby-traps. A Marine lieutenant summed it up: 'You walk through the bush for three days and nights without sleep. Watch your men, your buddies, your goddam kids get booby-trapped. Blown apart. Get thrown six feet in the air by a trap laid by an old lady and come down with no legs.' The experience was often traumatic and, as guerrillas could not be distinguished from ordinary civilians, the temptation to 'kill them all' was strong. After the death of a close friend, one American soldier felt that he 'couldn't look at [the Vietnamese] anymore without thinking "gook, dink", anything to show how much I hated them'. It was a combination of anger, frustration and latent racism which often condemned the hapless civilian to yet more suffering.

In most cases these feelings would be manifested in low-level personal abuse and indifference, negating all hopes of a successful hearts and minds campaign, but occasionally the anger would boil over into the worst type of atrocity against the civilian population. On 16 March 1968, for example, American soldiers of the Americal Division, after days of ambush and booby-traps, reacted by destroying the hamlet of My Lai in Quang Ngai province, burning the houses and killing an estimated 175 to 200 South Vietnamese civilians, many of them women and children. This was not an isolated incident nor a reaction confined just to American troops in Vietnam – on 12 December 1948, for example, British soldiers killed 24 civilians at Batang Kali in Malaya – but the fact that soldiers of any nation may carry out such acts emphasises the vulnerability and involvement of civilians in modern war. As hostages, contributors or victims, ordinary people can no longer remain isolated from hostilities and relations between them and the fighting soldiers may often hold the key to victory. **John Pimlott**

Disaster at Cao Bang

When France's crack troops were annihilated in the jungle

When the Viet Minh had withdrawn their main forces into the mountains of the Viet Bac in 1947, the French Army had not been slow to follow. French troops were moved into the old colonial forts in the mountains of north Tonkin. Bringing the Viet Minh to battle proved almost impossible, however, and even with the help of certain of the hill tribes, the French garrisons were able to do little more than maintain a defensive presence.

There was little large-scale fighting, but the isolated garrisons proved a steady drain on supplies without putting any pressure on the Viet Minh. Thus, in 1949, the scheme put forward by General Revers for a withdrawal from all areas north of the Red River Delta seemed to make good sense. French troops would be concentrated in the populous areas most under threat, and if the Viet Minh's supplies of rice from the delta could be cut, then no amount of activity in the hill country could help them.

The essentially defensive nature of Revers' plan did not please some senior members of the French high command, however. General Alessandri had devised a scheme for taking the offensive in the Viet Bac using small, lightly armed units able to survive without an extensive logistics network, but attached to a central base; and this also seemed an attractive option. The success of Mao's communist forces in China in 1949 confused French thinking still further, in that garrisons near the Chinese border might interrupt possible Viet Minh supply routes.

The French resolution of these contradictory suggestions was to evacuate most of the forts in north Tonkin, but to leave strong garrisons, 'hedgehogs' as they were called, on the Cao Bang-Lang Son ridge, along Route Coloniale 4 (RC4). The two main fortresses were Cao Bang and Dong Khe, with a smaller garrison at That Khe. The fortresses were considered too strong to be taken by the Viet Minh and suitable for use as bases for offensive activity if the necessity for such action arose.

Unfortunately for the French, Giap's Viet Minh were now about to take the offensive, and they began by making RC4 almost impassable for traffic. Re-supply became an enormous problem as convoys had to fight their way along the road; and they needed such large escorts that they could barely feed themselves, never mind carry enough to re-stock the beleagured fortresses.

The thinking of the French high command in establishing the 'hedgehogs' was that although the Viet Minh were extremely proficient in the jungle they were, after all, only a guerrilla army with no real chance of attacking and taking fortified positions. But the French grossly underestimated their opponents, for in 1949 and 1950 the nature of Giap's army was undergoing a profound change. All along the Chinese frontier a huge workforce of some 100,000 coolies was building military supply routes through the

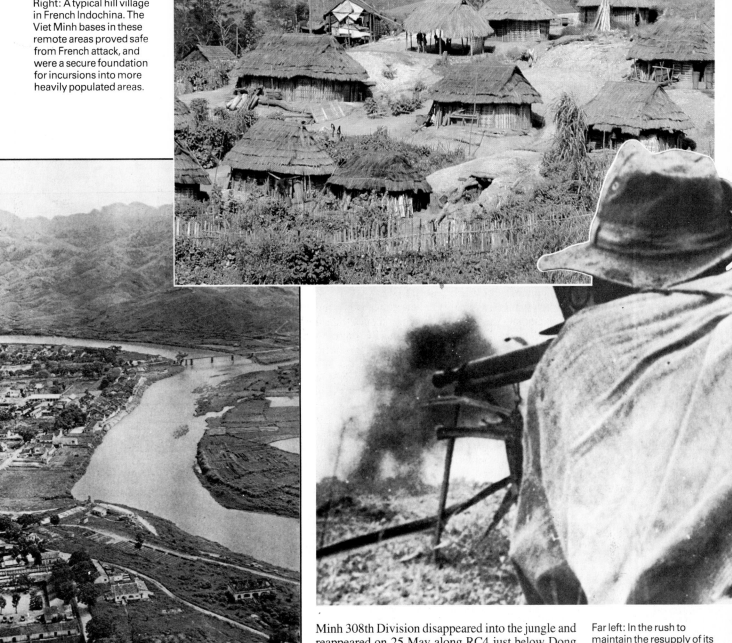

Right: A typical hill village in French Indochina. The Viet Minh bases in these remote areas proved safe from French attack, and were a secure foundation for incursions into more heavily populated areas.

jungle towards objectives along RC4. Large supply dumps were established at the end of these roads and as Chinese-trained units of Viet Minh recrossed the border into Indochina they would stop at these dumps to be issued with smallarms and artillery. By early 1950 Giap's armies had acquired a firepower that would shock the French.

The French high command remained oblivious to these changes despite Giap's declared intention of February 1950 to change from guerrilla war to open offensives. They believed that the Viet Minh would continue to refuse open battle. But the nature of the war began to change in the spring of 1950.

After a minor action in the area of Lao Kay, the Viet

Minh 308th Division disappeared into the jungle and reappeared on 25 May along RC4 just below Dong Khe. Four battalions of Viet Minh, supported by a concentrated barrage from mortars and artillery, advanced rapidly against the fortress after a 'softening up' barrage of 48 hours. The attack was completely successful and by 27 May the French garrison was forced to withdraw. The attack had coincided with a period of bad weather which had prevented the French from flying in reinforcements from Hanoi or Lang Son. A break in the weather shortly afterwards, however, allowed a complete parachute battalion to be dropped into the area from a flight of some 30 Junkers aircraft. Within a few hours the French had retaken Dong Khe and the relief column, which had set out from That Khe, arrived to find the paras sitting at their ease among the ruins of the fortress.

At this point it would have been easy for the French to effect the evacuation of Cao Bang and withdraw their forces to the south, but no such decision was taken. The ease of the recapture and the continuing dispute in the high command over the possibility of using the 'hedgehogs' as bases for offensives in the mountains persuaded the French to refortify the Dong

Far left: In the rush to maintain the resupply of its northern garrisons, the French Army was forced to use jungle routes for its convoys. These isolated routes were extremely vulnerable to attack from Viet Minh units. Here one such column has been virtually wiped out. Left: The 'hedgehog' fortress of Cao Bang. Although the fort was heavily protected, the surrounding hill country gave perfect cover for Viet Minh artillery units allowing them to continually harass the French garrisons without incurring casualties. Above: During mopping-up operations, a French machine-gunner gives covering fire to advancing units of the French Expeditionary Force.

Khe position and increase the strength of the garrison.

At Cao Bang the garrison, mainly legionaries, was well aware of the presence of large numbers of Viet Minh in the surrounding jungle. Only occasionally supplied by parachute, the men divided their time between guard duty and erecting defences. All legionaries who were not on guard were building with home-made concrete, stones and any other material that would withstand an artillery bombardment. An experienced commander, Colonel Charton, was flown in, and the men waited for the enemy attack.

During the summer monsoon, the Viet Minh continued their massive military build-up and then, on 18 September, just as the rainy season was drawing to a close, they began their offensive against Dong Khe. During the first day artillery fire that was far heavier than the French had ever expected rained down on the defences. By the second day over half the defending legionaries had been killed or wounded. By the third day the much-vaunted 'hedgehog' had fallen. There was no French counter-attack, for the French were completely stunned by this overwhelming victory and were finally convinced that to pour more troops into the area would result in even greater losses. The great symbol of French strength in Indochina had finally fallen, and with it the 'hedgehog' system was discredited.

To the French high command, Giap's intentions were plain. After the fall of Dong Khe it was inevitable that the Cao Bang garrison would be the next target, and so the evacuation of the garrison was ordered.

Under the codename Operation Thérèse, the French chose a withdrawal along RC4 as opposed to an airlift or a retreat southwestwards down RC3, but this plan had been conceived when the Viet Minh were still weak and when Dong Khe was still held by the French. The plan was that a relief column from Lang Son under Colonel Lepage would advance to

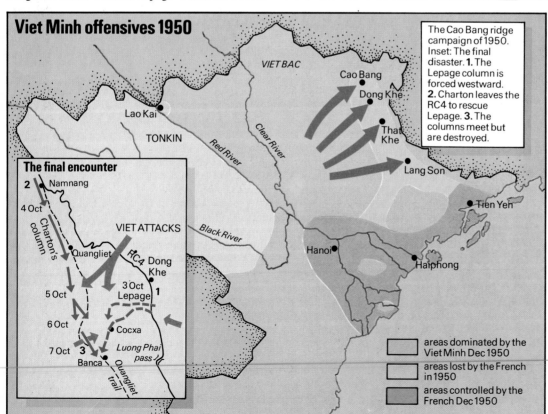

Above: One of the great strengths of the Viet Minh guerrilla was his ability to survive in difficult conditions with few supplies. The emphasis was firmly on manoeuvrability. Here a unit of Viet Minh march out of dense jungle into a clearing, carrying very little in the way of bulky equipment. Right: A mortar section of the French Foreign Legion, occupying a base to the east of Cao Bang, is about to fire a 120mm HE shell at a Viet Minh hillside emplacement.

Viet Minh offensives 1950

VIET BAC

Cao Bang
Dong Khe
That Khe
Lang Son

Lao Kai

TONKIN

Red River

Clear River

Black River

Tien Yen

Hanoi

Haiphong

The Cao Bang ridge campaign of 1950. Inset: The final disaster. 1. The Lepage column is forced westward. 2. Charton leaves the RC4 to rescue Lepage. 3. The columns meet but are destroyed.

The final encounter

2 Namnang

4 Oct

Charton's column

Quangliet

VIET ATTACKS

RC4 Dong Khe

5 Oct

3 Oct Lepage

1

6 Oct

Cocxa

7 Oct 3

Banca

Luong Phai pass

Quangliet trail

☐ areas dominated by the Viet Minh Dec 1950

☐ areas lost by the French in 1950

▨ areas controlled by the French Dec 1950

Change of tactics

Lieutenant Planey, the commander of a French para unit sent to relieve the strongpoint of Pho Lu, was one of the first French officers to witness the new Viet Minh tactics in the spring of 1950.

'We had not been dropped on the post itself, but in the jungle on the other side of the Red River nearly 20 miles [32km] away. There were 115 of us altogether. We marched along the track for hours until we reached the river bank over against Pho Lu, which was still holding out – but we stumbled right into the middle of the Viet concentration .... Fifteen battalions were attacking Pho Lu, but two had been left on our side of the river. They closed in on us at once .... We could not resist and we had to get out by the only gap that might still be open. We destroyed our equipment and our loads and practically all the radios so as to move faster .... We could see thousands of Viets swarming across the river to join in the kill. They were crossing at a ford, up to their necks in water, holding their rifles above their heads. It was then that I made the appalling decision to abandon our dead.'

When he returned to base nobody believed the lieutenant's story; but soon all French officers on the Cao Bang ridge had experience of facing these massed suicidal attacks.

within 30km (20 miles) of Cao Bang where it would link up with the evacuating garrison. The two columns would then force their way south to That Khe. On 15 September Lepage set out from Lang Son with a hurriedly-put-together force consisting almost entirely of North Africans. He was unaware of what his precise mission was; all he had been told was that he was to advance towards That Khe along RC4.

Mine craters, landslides and blown bridges along RC4 soon forced Lepage's column to abandon all their artillery, trucks and heavy equipment and to continue on foot. By 19 September the column had reached the lip of the That Khe depression where they then linked up with the garrison of Foreign Legion parachute troops. Lepage had received no orders for a further advance; and so his men installed themselves alongside the legionaries at That Khe. But over the next few days it became patently clear that there was a good deal of mistrust between the Legion and Lepage's Moroccans, and in order to minimise friction the Moroccans were sent on minor operations around That Khe. Morale was not, therefore, very high when, on 30 September, a coded signal was received ordering all troops at That Khe to advance on Dong Khe and take it by 2 October. In the eyes of Lepage this was an order tantamount to suicide, for he had only 2000 men and very little intelligence about the enemy. All he knew was that in the general area of Dong Khe were tens of thousands of Viet Minh. The French, who had been forced to abandon their heavy equipment, could only rely on such armament as they could carry; the Viet Minh were known to have artillery support. In desperation Lepage radioed Lang Son, hoping to persuade the high command of the futility of any such action. But the reply categorically ordered him to set out for Dong Khe at once.

On the evening of 30 September, after a meeting between Lepage and the commanders of the individual units, the four battalions began the advance towards their objective. Most of the time the convoy travelled along RC4 with the legionaries on the road and the Moroccans scouting to the front and flanks. They encountered no Viet Minh resistance, but just beyond the Luong Phai Pass some legionaries encountered a Viet Minh patrol. They killed three of them, but two escaped. For fear of losing the element of surprise, Lepage then ordered the column to advance at full speed. A forward section managed to advance to within 750m (800 yards) of Dong Khe before they were forced to withdraw under sustained and accurate enemy fire.

The next morning Lepage ordered his force to move into the jungle, hoping to advance upon Dong Khe in a pincer movement, but his men stumbled upon the main concentrations of Viet Minh. Enmeshed in the dense foliage of the jungle, both sections of the French force floundered under constant attack. Withdrawal from the area was essential to the survival of the force and Lepage radioed for such permission. The answer was emphatic: the Cao Bang garrison could only evacuate along RC4 and if Lepage could not take Dong Khe he was to strike out for Namnang through the jungle and rendezvous with the garrison there. At last Lepage knew what his mission was – after two weeks of enforced ignorance. He regrouped his men and began to make for the proposed rendezvous but almost immediately came under such fierce attack that his men were pinned down.

On 3 October, Charton set out from Cao Bang with a force some 2600 strong (including 1000 hill tribesmen). He had ordered the complete destruction of any materiel that might be of use to the Viet Minh, so that upon their departure the fortress of Cao Bang was a ruin. Charton's column made good time and, although observed by the communists, was at no point attacked. But when the column reached the proposed rendezvous, Charton rightly feared the worst, for Lepage was nowhere to be seen. Shortly after reaching his objective, Charton received a radio message that explained clearly the plight of Lepage's force. Charton was ordered to move off RC4 into the jungle, take the old Quangliet track and rescue the trapped relief column.

The move was to be completed within 24 hours. All heavy equipment was jettisoned and the column plunged into the jungle in search of the trail; although they found it fairly quickly, it had become so over-

Below: Keeping a sharp lookout for French air movements, a well-camouflaged unit of Viet Minh anti-aircraft gunners train a captured French 8mm Model 1914 Hotchkiss machine gun skywards. Although the Hotchkiss had been the principal machine gun of the French Army during World War I, its reliability was such that it was still being used some 40 years later.

grown that the column's advance was considerably slowed and at some points they were forced to advance in single file. In fact it took Charton's column almost three days to reach the area in which Lepage's column was besieged. But by 6 October Charton had established a base along a ridge overlooking the Cocxa Valley where the Lepage force were. In the late afternoon Charton managed to make radio contact with Lepage, and requested that he be allowed to continue to That Khe whereupon he would muster all available reinforcements and return to rescue Lepage. Lepage, in reply, insisted that Charton remain.

As night fell Charton organised his defences, with the hill tribesmen holding the peaks along the edge of the ridge. Two companies were sent forward to the Quichan peaks near the Cocxa gorges where it was hoped that Lepage's column would make contact. As darkness descended, however, the Viet Minh launched an attack. The offensive lasted most of the night, and although the legionaries managed to repulse the Viet Minh, it was clear to Charton that the attack had been a mere preliminary to the main onslaught.

At 0600 hours on 7 October the communists launched a full-scale attack against Charton's positions. The situation seemed hopeless, yet the column managed to hold some of its ground. By the time the first survivors of Lepage's column walked out of the jungle, just before dawn, Charton's men held only a small saddle some 900m (1000 yards) long. In a desperate attempt to break away from the ridge Charton ordered a battalion of the Legion to counterattack, but the casualties were enormous and the battalion was virtually wiped out. Finally he decided that the only hope was to reach the jungle and strike out for That Khe, and so he led the survivors into the jungle. The French had hardly advanced 1km when they came under artillery and mortar fire. As the barrage ceased Viet Minh units made mass attacks. Although Charton's men managed to resist the first assaults, the Viet Minh soon overwhelmed them through sheer force of numbers and the result was a massacre. Only 23 survivors reached That Khe.

The loss of the Cao Bang ridge was a severe blow to French prestige, and gave a corresponding boost to communist morale, while Giap's forces now controlled almost all the hill country in northern Tonkin. But the war was far from over, for the next struggle would be for the Red River Delta itself, where French advantages in artillery and air power would still apply. **Alexander McNair-Wilson**

Key Weapons

The F-4 PHANTOM II
part 1

Development of the F-4

Top, left and right:
Phantom development –
the 1954 single-seat mock-
up designed for the US
Navy (left) and the 1956
mock-up with two-seat
cockpit and Sparrow air-to-
air missiles. An early F-4A
undergoes carrier trials on
USS *Independence* (above
right) while an F-4B on USS
Enterprise is brought up to
the flight deck (above
centre). Above: The
thousandth Phantom takes-
off, an F-4B for the US
Navy.

The McDonnell Douglas F-4 Phantom II is considered by many aviation experts to be the finest combat
aircraft built since World War II. A remarkable
aircraft by any standard, it was a record breaker even
before its introduction into service at the end of 1960
and its production run continued on into the 1970s,
exceeding 5000 models – a considerable manufactur-
ing feat for a military aircraft outside full-scale war
production.

Ironically, the story of the Phantom II started with a
failure when, in 1953, McDonnell lost a naval design
competition for a supersonic carrier fighter to its
competitor the Vought F8U Crusader. Undeterred,
McDonnell went to great lengths to investigate future
US Navy requirements, and as early as mid-1953 the
company began design on a new carrier-borne aircraft. The new project was designated F3H-G/H and a
full-size mock-up, completed in August 1954, revealed a single-seat fighter with two Wright J65
reheat engines – intended to provide a maximum
speed of Mach 1.5 – and four internally-mounted
20mm cannon.

Although the aeronautics bureau of the US Navy
approved the basic design in October 1954, only six
months later the specification was virtually rewritten
and called for a two-seat, long-range, high-altitude
interceptor equipped with an APQ-72 radar and
armed only with missiles. This major redesign was
completed in only two weeks; in July 1955 the
designation became F4H-1 and the name Phantom II
was adopted (the title Phantom I had been assigned to
McDonnell's first jet aircraft).

Production began in August 1956 and incorporated
two basic modifications: the tailplane was given a
considerable anhedral angle of 23 degrees (that is,
pointed downwards) and the outer wing panels were
provided with 12 degrees of dihedral (pointed upwards). With these features now integral with the
main design, a prototype model was given its maiden
flight at Lambert Field, St Louis, on 27 May 1958.
Able to operate over a combat radius of at least 460km
(285 miles) and able to loiter for up to two hours, the
Phantom was equipped with advanced avionics that
allowed it to detect and destroy enemy aircraft within

its radar range – in contrast to other aircraft of the time that still needed separate ground-based radar assistance. By the end of 1958 the Phantom had convincingly beaten Vought's XF8U-3 Crusader III in a fly-off evaluation trial, and in the following years it went on to break many speed and flight records including absolute height (30,040m; 98,556ft) on 6 December 1959, speed at low altitude (1452km/h; 902mph) on 28 August 1961 and absolute speed (2585km/h; 1606mph) on 22 November 1961. Carrier suitability trials had begun in February 1960 and first deliveries to the Navy were made that December.

Following the acceptance of the Phantom, McDonnell regained its position as a leading supplier of jet fighters to the US Navy. The first major production version, the F-4B, had an APQ-72 radar and an ACF infra-red detector under the nose. Among a series of improvements the cockpit was raised – the new canopy being higher than the top line of the fuselage to improve view on carrier approach. From the outset, the primary air-to-air weapons of the Phantom were the Sparrow and Sidewinder air-to-air missiles, both well tested and designed for long and short-range attacks respectively.

During the 1960s two separate events had a great influence upon the Phantom's future development

and career. The first of these occurred in 1961, when the US Air Force staged Project Highspeed, in which it evaluated the Phantom closely against the best Air Force air-defence interceptor, the Convair F-106 Delta Dart. When McDonnell's fighter outstripped the F-106 in speed, ceiling, climb, weapon load and accuracy of delivery, only one decision was possible and in March 1962, with an order for 280 aircraft, the Phantom became the first-ever US Navy fighter to be adopted in quantity by the Air Force. Known initially as the F-110A, the Air Force F-4C version eventually equipped no fewer than 16 of the 23 wings in the USAF's Tactical Air Command.

The USAF introduced its own modifications to the Phantom. The refuelling probe was replaced by a boom receptacle, the Navy tyres were replaced by tougher models better suited to airstrips, braking was improved, the General Electric engines were fitted with a cartridge/pneumatic starter, and more comprehensive dual controls were fitted for the crew, which at first comprised two pilots. There followed the redesigned RF-4C tactical reconnaissance Phantom, without armament but equipped with an extremely sophisticated camera, forward and sideways-looking radar and high frequency communications systems. The F-4D was produced from scratch as an Air Force

Top: The XF4H-1 prototype which out-flew the competition during the US Navy flight-evaluation trials in 1958. Above: The seventh production model of the F-4A, seen here with a raised cockpit canopy.

Above: Two F-4J Phantoms of the US Navy. Left: A Westinghouse APQ-120 radar installed in an Israeli Phantom is revealed for inspection as is the 20mm Vulcan cannon below it.

USAF McDonnell F-4E Phantom II
336th Tactical Fighter Squadron,
4th Tactical Fighter Wing

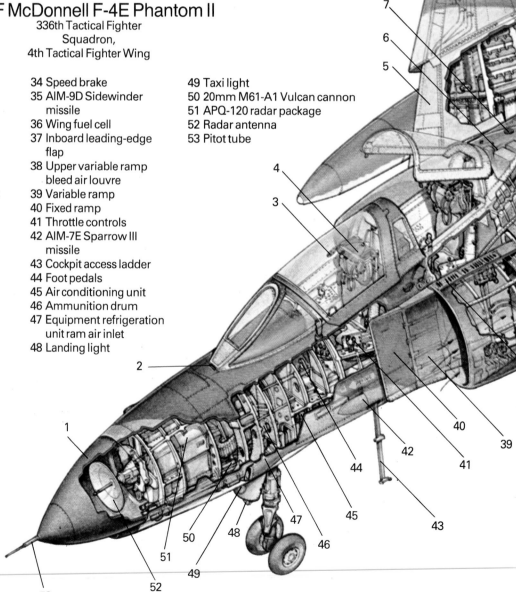

1 Radome hinged door
2 Rain removal air nozzle
3 Face-curtain ejector handle
4 Mk 7 ejection seat
5 Centre leading edge flap
6 IFF antenna
7 Fuselage light
8 Outboard leading edge flap
9 Starboard wing-tip position light
10 Starboard join-up light
11 Fuel vent and dump mast
12 Airflow spoiler
13 General Electric J79-GE-17 engines (two)
14 Fuselage fuel cells (seven in all)
15 Cooling air duct
16 Anti-collision light
17 Pressure probe
18 Tail light
19 Rudder
20 Fuel vent mast
21 Drogue chute compartment
22 Slotted stabilator
23 Stabilator actuator
24 Fuel tank cooling air exit
25 Arrester hook
26 Variable area exhaust nozzle
27 Afterburner
28 Trailing-edge flap
29 Port aileron
30 Wing fold actuator
31 Air duct
32 Main landing-gear jack pad access door
33 External wing tank (370 US gallons)

34 Speed brake
35 AIM-9D Sidewinder missile
36 Wing fuel cell
37 Inboard leading-edge flap
38 Upper variable ramp bleed air louvre
39 Variable ramp
40 Fixed ramp
41 Throttle controls
42 AIM-7E Sparrow III missile
43 Cockpit access ladder
44 Foot pedals
45 Air conditioning unit
46 Ammunition drum
47 Equipment refrigeration unit ram air inlet
48 Landing light

49 Taxi light
50 20mm M61-A1 Vulcan cannon
51 APQ-120 radar package
52 Radar antenna
53 Pitot tube

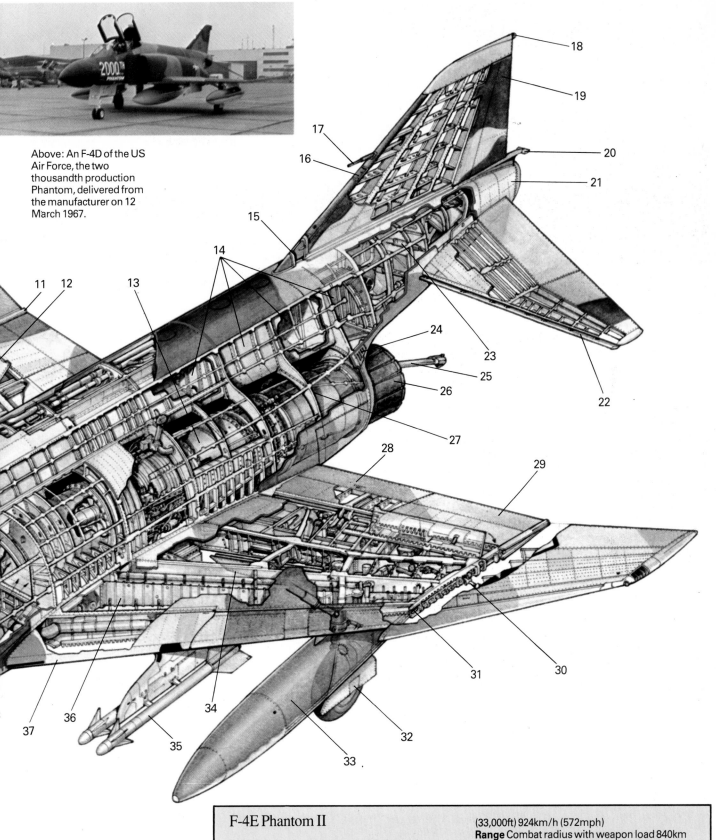

Above: An F-4D of the US
Air Force, the two
thousandth production
Phantom, delivered from
the manufacturer on 12
March 1967.

F-4E Phantom II

Type Twin-seat multi-role fighter/strike aircraft
Dimensions Span 11.68m (38ft 4in); length 19.20m
(63ft); height 5m (16ft 5in)
Weight Empty 14,461kg (31,853lb); maximum
take-off 28,055kg (61,795lb)
Powerplant Two 8127kg (17,900lb) General Electric
J79-GE17 afterburning turbojets
Performance Maximum speed Mach 2.17 or 2304
km/h (1430mph); cruising speed at 10,050m

(33,000ft) 924km/h (572mph)
Range Combat radius with weapon load 840km
(520 miles); maximum ferry range 2593km (1610
miles)
Ceiling 17,907m (58,750ft)
Armament One 20mm L61A-1 Vulcan multi-barrel
cannon, four AIM-7E Sparrow missiles
semi-recessed under fuselage, and various
combinations of missiles and stores up to a total
weight of 7258kg (16,000lb) carried on a centreline
pylon and four wing pylons

Above: A flight of F-4E Phantoms on display in Hawaii as part of the US Air Force's 'Thunderbirds' display team. Right: Basic Phantom armament as carried by an RAF FGR Mk 2 – four Sparrow air-to-air missiles and two Sidewinders carried under each wing, plus a 20mm SUU-23/A cannon pod.

attack aircraft with totally new avionic and weapon-delivery systems, while in August 1965 the F-4E made its first flight.

A multi-role USAF fighter (air superiority/close support/interdiction), the F-4E became the most numerous of the many Phantom versions, a total of 1517 aircraft being built. Armed with a 20mm Vulcan M61A-1 multi-barrelled cannon fitted under the forward fuselage, the F-4E proved popular with air crews who preferred to have the addition of a properly-mounted gun to their otherwise all-missile armoury. Retrospectively fitted with later improvements the F-4E was also subsequently equipped to deliver the laser-guided 'smart' bombs that proved so effective in Vietnam.

In 1965 the interceptor/ground attack F-4J was introduced to both the US Navy and the Marine Corps. Some 522 models were built and as an upgraded F-4B it was provided with more powerful engines as well as having an improved ground-attack capability.

The second major influence on the Phantom's career came about through America's involvement in the war in Vietnam, where the F-4C was first deployed in June 1965. In fact, the SOR (specific operational requirement) for the F-4C, issued in August 1962, had been preceded five months earlier by that for the RF-4C tactical-reconnaissance version whose part in early operations in Vietnam was equally valuable though less well known.

Besides stimulating demand for this aircraft, Vietnam taught the US services two important lessons concerning the Phantom. First, the lack of a built-in gun was a distinct disadvantage. The external pod-mounted Vulcan cannon, while both formidable and reliable, suffered from pylon distortion which affected its accuracy; moreover, its parasitic drag degraded the fighter's performance. This problem was largely solved by the introduction of the Vulcan cannon fitted under the fuselage. Second, although the Phantom's general manoeuvrability was excellent, violent twists and turns at high operating weights caused the onset of serious stall and spin problems. After more than 100 aircraft had been lost, the decision was taken to fit a powerful slatted leading edge, this being introduced on the F-4E line in June 1972. So great was the improvement that the Navy im-

mediately adopted the slatted wing, and several other features of the USAF Phantoms, for its later models.

Improvements to the basic aircraft continued and new variants were developed to meet specific tactical requirements; they included the QF-4B drone, the F-4N, a remanufactured B-model with extended fatigue life and completely new avionics, and the F-4G Wild Weasel electronic warfare platform. The Wild Weasel Phantoms first flew in 1975 and were fitted with ECM (electronic countermeasure) equipment to locate and disrupt enemy electronic installations.

Only since the introduction of new types of advanced aircraft like the F-14, F-15 and F-16 has the position of the Phantom come under real challenge. Employing the most advanced avionic equipment, coupled with exceptional combat manoeuvrability this new generation of US aircraft has now pushed beyond the high standards set by the Phantom. Despite these new developments, however, the Phantom will continue to see service for a number of years yet, and in the hands of highly skilled pilots will remain an aircraft to be reckoned with.

Berlin under siege

Blockade, airlift and the start of the Cold War

The Grand Alliance of the Western powers and Soviet Russia which had led to victory over Hitler's Germany in World War II did not long survive that victory. Strains in the alliance were apparent even before the war ended, when it became clear that Stalin had no intention of abandoning Russia's revolutionary role in world affairs and would continue to regard the capitalist West as fundamentally hostile to Soviet aims.

The Russians were constantly at odds with the Western governments over the future of Germany. In the countries of eastern Europe, despite promises to promote democratic freedoms, the Soviet government pressed ahead with the imposition of regimes dominated by communists who were mostly imported from Russia, where they had spent the war years. Watching this process, Winston Churchill was led to remark in March 1946 that an 'iron curtain' had descended on Europe, dividing East from West.

It was not until 1947 that the Western governments reacted decisively to Soviet aggressiveness. The first clear move was made by President Harry Truman who, in March 1947, announced that America was ready to provide substantial military and economic aid to any country trying to resist the inroads of communism. This became known as the Truman Doctrine. It was followed in June by an offer from Secretary of State George Marshall of large-scale economic aid to the countries of western Europe – the Marshall Plan. If the Americans could not force the Russians out of eastern Europe or persuade them to tolerate a measure of democratic freedom there, they could at least put the vast productive capacity of American industry to the task of restoring prosperity in western Europe and so resisting the spread of communism.

The Russians responded by political measures. In September 1947 they founded the Communist Information Bureau (known as Cominform), linking the communist parties of eastern Europe with those of France and Italy. It amounted to a clear threat to the stability of western Europe. In February 1948 the communists in Czechoslovakia, under pressure from Moscow, carried out a successful coup and thus completed the 'communisation' of eastern Europe. East and West were now sharply divided. The Grand Alliance was dead; the United States and the Soviet Union were now engaged in vituperative confrontation.

By 1948 this so-called Cold War was in full swing. But neither side had yet tested just how far the other was prepared to go. That crucial test came with the breakdown of the four-power administration of Berlin and the Russians' imposition of a blockade on all surface communications with the city from the West.

At the Potsdam conference in July 1945 Truman, Stalin and Churchill (later replaced by Clement Attlee) reached agreement on the administration of Germany. It was to be divided into four zones – Soviet, American, British and French – with a joint Control Commission established in Berlin, the former capital. Berlin itself was to be similarly divided into four sectors and placed under four-power control. The underlying purpose of this arrangement was to prevent the recrudescence of a strong and united Germany with an effective central government. Its main weakness was that it left the city of Berlin landlocked inside the Soviet zone of occupation, 160 km (100 miles) from the nearest point in the American zone. All road and rail communications between the Western zones of Germany and the Western sectors of Berlin had to pass through the Soviet zone, and air

As Western powers made efforts to strengthen their hold on West Berlin during the late 1940s, the communists responded with a blockade. During a period of 10 months in 1948-49 a massive airlift supplied West Berlin's beleaguered citizens. Here a Douglas C-54 is loaded with supplies for air-corridor flight to Berlin.

Prague '48

14 September 1948: the funeral of Dr Beneš.

In 1947 there was one important anomaly in the otherwise straight-forward division of Europe between East and West: Czechoslovakia remained a democratic, multi-party state which had a relatively advanced and largely undamaged industry, was not occupied by the Red Army, and was led by a much-respected statesman, Eduard Beneš, who had spent the war years, not in Moscow but in London. True, the Prime Minister, Klement Gottwald, was a communist and the Communist Party had obtained 46 per cent of the vote in the first postwar election. But the government was a coalition which included non-communist parties; Czechoslovakia was still far from being a communist-ruled 'people's democracy'. Stalin, however, made it quite clear to the Czechoslovak communists that he expected them to bring the country quickly into line with Russia's other 'satellites'.

The communist bid for power began on 20 February 1948. In protest at the high-handed behaviour of the communist minister of the interior, 12 non-communist ministers tendered their resignation to President Beneš in the hope that he would support them and bring the communists to order. The communists then accused the other parties of planning to overthrow the government.

Gottwald urged the president to accept the resignation of the 12 ministers. But Beneš stood firm, so Gottwald decided to bring the whole apparatus of the Communist Party into action – the police, the mob, the Action Committees and the Workers' Militia. The communist-controlled police occupied the radio station and other important public buildings. The mob arrived in trucks from throughout Bohemia to take part in meetings over the next few days. Action Committees were ordered to be formed in villages, towns, factories and offices. The Workers' Militia armed themselves, ready to intervene if necessary. The Action Committees then proceeded to take control of every organisation in which they had been formed. They made changes in personnel and policy as they pleased. Without referring to the existing institutions they changed the whole machinery of government. It was a bloodless revolution, but a very thorough one.

The non-communist parties had no way of replying to the communist assault. They were prevented from speaking over the radio and their newspapers were sabotaged by communist cells. They were divided in their views and had no contingency plans. So everything depended in the end on the president and on who could bring to bear the greatest pressure on him.

The next day, a Sunday, there were more mass meetings. The word went around that Valerian Zorin, formerly Soviet ambassador in Prague and now deputy foreign minister in Moscow, was in town and playing a part in events. President Beneš regarded his arrival in Prague as a clear sign that Stalin was determined to back Gottwald to the hilt. At the same time there were rumours, impossible to confirm, that Russian troops were massing on the frontier and had even entered the eastern part of the country. All this tended to raise tension and to intimidate the population. Throughout the country anti-communists were being arrested or dismissed from their jobs. On the 23rd four non-communist ministers were prevented from entering their offices and the secretary of the National Socialist Party was arrested. At the same time the communists kept up an almost continuous demonstration in the centre of Prague.

On the 25th the exchanges between Gottwald and Beneš continued; Beneš insisting on a parliamentary and democratic solution. Gottwald proposed that he should form a new government with representatives of non-communist parties of his own choosing. In the afternoon Gottwald met Beneš again and proceeded to harangue the ailing, exhausted president. After listening to what the communist leader had to say Beneš gave in, accepted Gottwald's proposal and approved the new government.

The most significant casualty of the crisis was President Beneš himself. After swearing in the new government on 27 February he announced that he was leaving his official residence of Hradčany Castle for his private home in the country. He returned to Prague only once – to attend the funeral of his friend and supporter Jan Masaryk, the foreign minister, who was found dead on the cobblestones beneath the window of his flat on 10 March. In a final, and futile, act of protest Beneš resigned the presidency on 7 June. He died on 3 September 1948.

David Floyd

communications had to fly along agreed air corridors. This meant that the Russians were able, whenever they wished, to cut West Berlin off from the sources of supply in the West upon which 6500 British, American and French troops and the 2.5 million West Berliners depended for their existence. The Russians held a potential stranglehold on Berlin.

The four-power administration worked reasonably smoothly throughout 1946 and 1947; but as the Russian grip on eastern Europe tightened and East-West relations deteriorated, Berlin also came under threat. By the beginning of 1948 all the countries of eastern Europe had been brought under Soviet political control and communist-dominated governments installed in power. At the same time the Russians had gone a long way towards making their zone of Germany into an exclusively Soviet dependency.

In 1948 a six-power conference took place in London at which the participants – the United States, Britain, France, Belgium, the Netherlands and Luxembourg – agreed on a programme for the future of the three western zones, providing for their amalgamation and the creation of a federal German government. The three zones became a single economic unit and in June 1948 the Western powers announced a currency reform and the introduction of the Deutschmark in their zone.

Early in 1948 it became clear that the Russians were no longer interested in making the four-power administration of Berlin work, though they hoped to be able to place the blame for its breakdown on the shoulders of the Western governments. On 20 March Marshal Vasili Sokolovsky, the Soviet representative on the Allied Control Commission, broke up a meeting of the Commission with an angry attack on the British, American and French representatives. Their behaviour, he claimed, proved that 'they no longer consider the Control Commission to be the four-power authority in Germany'. The Western representatives, surprised at the strength of the attack, replied in kind. After heated exchanges the Russian gathered up his papers and walked out of the meeting.

Soviet pressure on the West continued to increase. On 1 April 1948 the express train from Frankfurt-on-Main to Berlin, carrying 300 US officers and men as well as civilian passengers, was stopped at the frontier crossing by Russian officers who demanded to examine all the Americans' documents. The Americans refused to comply, on the grounds that they were not subject to Soviet control. But, faced with a choice between authorising the Americans to use their weapons to fight their way through to Berlin and ordering them to back down, the US military governor and commander of the US forces in Germany, General Lucius Clay, chose the latter course.

At that point Clay really had no choice. He could not take action likely to lead to open conflict without the backing of his government, and Washington was firmly against doing anything provocative. General Omar Bradley, the US Army Chief of Staff, said the Pentagon doubted 'whether our people are prepared to start a war to maintain our position in Berlin'. But Clay took a different view. 'If we retreat from Berlin, then after Berlin will come Western Germany,' he said. 'If we mean . . to hold Europe against communism, we must not budge.'

Through May and June the Russians kept up their harassment of Western communications with Berlin. On 20 June the currency reform came into effect in the

Above: The Potsdam conference of July-August 1945 saw Attlee, Truman and Stalin (seated, left to right) discussing the future of the world in ostensible accord. But amicable discussion did not last long. By 1947 when the Marshall Plan began to help western Europe along the road to economic recovery, the countries behind the Iron Curtain were effectively cut off from the West.

Above: A German poster extolling the virtues of the Marshall Plan.

Western sectors, which prompted Sokolovsky to claim that the city had already been 'integrated economically into the Soviet zone'. General Clay in turn replied: 'I reject *in toto* the Soviet claims to the city of Berlin.' It was clear that the Russians planned to starve Berlin and the Berliners into submission, and just before midnight on 23 June the Soviet-controlled news agency ADN put out a brief, ominous statement: 'The Transport Division of the Soviet Military Administration is forced to halt all passenger and freight traffic to and from Berlin as from 0600 hours tomorrow because of technical problems.' Next day the Russians proceeded to cut all road and rail communications with West Berlin and stopped the supply of coal and electric power from the Soviet zone.

General Clay's immediate reaction was to threaten to fight it out. He told newsmen at Tempelhof air base that evening: 'The Russians are trying to put on the final pressure. But they can't drive us out of Berlin by anything short of war.'

His first plan for beating the blockade was to drive a passage through the Russian barriers by sheer force. He made preparations for sending an armed convoy of 200 lorries along the Helmstedt-Berlin autobahn with a powerful military escort and all the engineering equipment necessary for carrying out repairs to roads and bridges along the way. He intended to call the

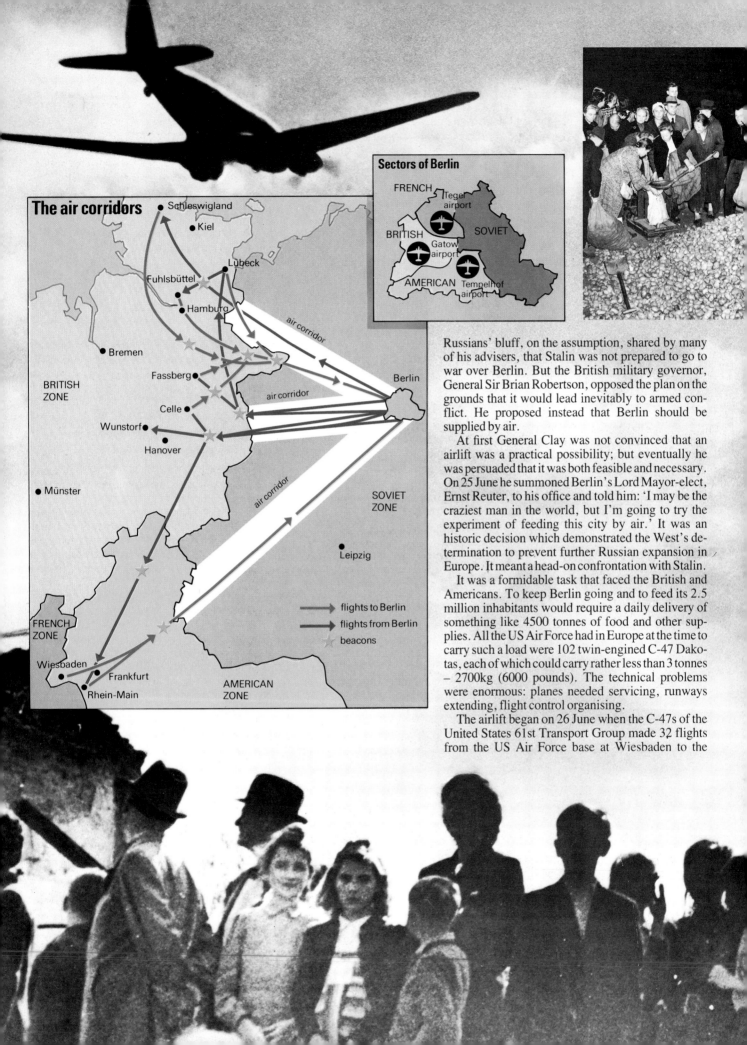

The air corridors

Schleswigland
Kiel
Lübeck
Fuhlsbüttel
Hamburg
Bremen
Fassberg
BRITISH ZONE
Celle
Wunstorf
Hanover
Münster

FRENCH ZONE
Wiesbaden
Frankfurt
Rhein-Main
AMERICAN ZONE

air corridor
air corridor
air corridor

Berlin

SOVIET ZONE

Leipzig

→ flights to Berlin
→ flights from Berlin
★ beacons

Sectors of Berlin

FRENCH
Tegel airport
BRITISH
Gatow airport
AMERICAN
Tempelhof airport
SOVIET

Russians' bluff, on the assumption, shared by many of his advisers, that Stalin was not prepared to go to war over Berlin. But the British military governor, General Sir Brian Robertson, opposed the plan on the grounds that it would lead inevitably to armed conflict. He proposed instead that Berlin should be supplied by air.

At first General Clay was not convinced that an airlift was a practical possibility; but eventually he was persuaded that it was both feasible and necessary. On 25 June he summoned Berlin's Lord Mayor-elect, Ernst Reuter, to his office and told him: 'I may be the craziest man in the world, but I'm going to try the experiment of feeding this city by air.' It was an historic decision which demonstrated the West's determination to prevent further Russian expansion in Europe. It meant a head-on confrontation with Stalin.

It was a formidable task that faced the British and Americans. To keep Berlin going and to feed its 2.5 million inhabitants would require a daily delivery of something like 4500 tonnes of food and other supplies. All the US Air Force had in Europe at the time to carry such a load were 102 twin-engined C-47 Dakotas, each of which could carry rather less than 3 tonnes – 2700kg (6000 pounds). The technical problems were enormous: planes needed servicing, runways extending, flight control organising.

The airlift began on 26 June when the C-47s of the United States 61st Transport Group made 32 flights from the US Air Force base at Wiesbaden to the

Tempelhof base in the American sector of Berlin. They transported altogether 80 tonnes of milk, flour and medicines. It was a good but small start.

On the morning of the 30th some C-54 transports arrived in Wiesbaden from Alaska, Hawaii and the Caribbean and made their first trip to Berlin the same day. At the beginning of July the Royal Air Force brought in two squadrons of Sunderland flying boats, which operated from Finkenwerder, near Hamburg. By mid-July work had started on building a new runway at Tempelhof, while the British had completed an 1800m (2000 yard) runway at Gatow, in their sector. The Americans now had 54 C-54s and 105 C-47s, while the British had 40 Yorks and 50 C-47s. By the end of the month the aircraft were delivering more than 2000 tonnes a day to Berlin. The British were using three converted Lancasters for the transport of liquid fuel.

The tonnage carried increased day by day. In mid-August the British and Americans together delivered 4742 tonnes, the first time they had exceeded the 4500 tonnes that the Berliners were reckoned to need for survival. By the end of August the total tonnage delivered was over the 100,000 mark. Meanwhile, work was started on the construction of new runways at Tegel, in the French sector of Berlin, and at Celle in the British zone.

As winter approached the Americans installed CPS-5 radar equipment to make ground control approach landings in bad weather possible. By the end of November 1316 such landings had been made at Gatow alone. By the end of the year the airlift had transported more than 700,000 tonnes of supplies to Berlin in just over 100,000 flights. The quantities continued to rise in the early months of 1949, so that by 18 February the millionth tonne had been delivered, and on 26 February a new record was set for one day's work: 8025 tonnes in 902 flights.

All kinds of records in the handling of aircraft were being broken. The US Air Force 61st Maintenance Squadron at Rhein-Main claimed a new record for rebuilding engines – 154 in the month of March. On 7 April the flight controllers at Tempelhof handled a plane every four minutes for 6½ hours non-stop. A C-54 from Fassberg completed the round trip to Berlin and back in just 1 hour 57 minutes. By 22 April the airlift deliveries over a five-day period equalled what the Berliners had normally been receiving by rail before the blockade started. In the same month a record total of 232,263 tonnes was transported, an average of 7845 tonnes a day for the month.

It had been clear since the end of January that the Russians were beginning to recognise that they were beaten and that they would not succeed in starving Berlin into submission. Although they indulged in a good deal of harassment of the British and American pilots as they performed their difficult task, they did not go so far as to shoot a plane down. There were many cases of close flying, radio interference, 'buzzing', and actual firing by the Russians; but none of the relatively few crashes that took place during the airlift were attributed directly to Russian interference. They were not really looking for a straight fight with their wartime allies.

On 21 March the Soviet delegate at the United Nations hinted that the blockade could be lifted in the near future. On 4 May the four powers reached agreement. Eight days later, on 12 May, the railways and roads to Berlin were reopened, and the first train from the West arrived in Berlin at 5.32 am that day. The airlift continued, however, until 30 September so as to build up ample stocks in the city.

The airlift involved about 700 planes altogether. The Americans contributed 441 (309 C-54s; 105 C-47s; 21 R5Ds; 5 C-82s; 1 C-97.) The Royal Air Force brought in 147, of which about a third were Dakotas, plus 35 Yorks and 26 Hastings. In addition about 104 British civil aircraft were used. A total of 277,804 sorties were flown, the Americans completing 189,963, the Royal Air Force 65,857 and the British civil planes 21,984. The total tonnage flown in was finally estimated at about 2,325,000. Less than a third of this consisted of food; three out of every five tonnes were coal.

The airlift was undoubtedly a major defeat for the Russians. Stalin had been advised that, if sufficient pressure were put on them, the British and Americans would not make any serious effort to stay in Berlin. It apparently did not occur to the Russians that the Western powers would choose to defeat the blockade in the air, where they had overwhelming superiority. Moreover, the Americans had ample supplies of all the necessities of life that the Berliners needed. Ever a realist, Stalin recognised that he was involved in a confrontation which he could not win and he was not prepared to order the Soviet Army to attack the Berlin air-bridge and provoke an armed conflict with Britain and America. So he backed down. But he had to have scapegoats for his defeat: shortly before the blockade was lifted both Marshal Sokolovsky and his political adviser were summarily withdrawn from Berlin.

David Floyd

Top: As the Russian blockade began to bite, food was distributed in the street as quickly as it was flown in by US C-47s and C-54s, like those being unloaded above. Below: A group of children watch as supply planes begin their descent into Berlin.

Shielding the West

How Nato was born

On 4 April 1949, in the presence of President Harry S. Truman in Washington, the North Atlantic Treaty was signed. Signatories to the document were the foreign ministers of 12 Western states – Belgium, Canada, Denmark, France, Iceland, Italy, Luxembourg, the Netherlands, Norway, Portugal, the United Kingdom and the United States. The treaty had its origins in the development of the Cold War, for it was the perception of a Soviet threat in the years following World War II that prompted western European governments to take collective defence measures and to seek American involvement in their efforts.

The process began with the signature of the 50-year Treaty of Alliance and Mutual Assistance – The Dunkirk Treaty – between Britain and France on 4 March 1947. At this stage, despite suspicions in western Europe about their future relationship with the Soviet Union, the Dunkirk Treaty was actually aimed at preventing renewed German aggression. But when President Truman went before Congress on 12 March 1947 he committed the United States to support Greece and Turkey and by implication western Europe against Soviet encroachment. This policy became known as the Truman Doctrine and was followed by the Marshall Plan for economic help announced on 5 June. Despite these initiatives, however, the Americans remained cautious about

becoming directly involved in any permanent European defence agreement. The Europeans therefore moved the process further along with the Brussels Treaty, a 50-year pact of economic, social and cultural collaboration and collective self-defence that was signed by the foreign ministers of Belgium, France, Luxembourg, the Netherlands and the United Kingdom on 17 March 1948. Still, as with the Treaty of Dunkirk, the objective was to contain Germany, while at the same time trying to build an understanding between Germany and her western neighbours as a defence against the Soviet Union. It was around the Brussels Treaty that the Nato alliance would be built.

As a result of events in eastern Europe, and especially the communist coup in Czechoslovakia in February 1948, British Foreign Secretary Ernest Bevin approached the United States Secretary of State, George Marshall, with the idea of concluding an Atlantic pact. Secret negotiations began in Washington on 22 March but there seemed to be no satisfactory way by which the United States could be linked to the Brussels Treaty.

The objective was assisted by the adoption of the so-called Vandenberg Resolution in the US Senate on 11 June 1948. Senator Arthur Vandenberg of Michigan was the influential Republican Chairman of the Senate Foreign Relations Committee, and his resolution called for the United States to associate itself with

Guaranteeing the future of the West against the threat of Soviet expansion, Harry S. Truman signs the North Atlantic Treaty, thus officially creating Nato.

VIGILANCE the price of LIBERTY

Above: A pamphlet cover depicting Nato as a shield for the West against the communist threat. Above right: The opposite viewpoint in a Russian cartoon accusing Nato members of having fought the fascists only to take over from them.

regional arrangements for individual and collective self-defence. The US administration was thus given the support of Congress to negotiate an alliance with Europe which would deter aggression. The onset of the Berlin Blockade on 24 June provided further impetus, and on 6 July talks began between the Brussels Treaty powers, the United States and Canada.

The talks continued into the winter of 1948. The seven negotiating governments invited Denmark, Iceland, Italy, Norway and Portugal to join what would be known as the North Atlantic Treaty. They accepted, and together the 12 formed the new Atlantic Alliance.

The treaty, which consists of 14 Articles and came into force on 24 August 1949, is dedicated to the defence of the territories of the member states. The aim of the alliance is set out in the preamble to the treaty: 'to safeguard the freedom, common heritage and civilization of their peoples, founded on the principles of democracy, individual liberty and the rule of law', and 'to promote stability and well-being in the North Atlantic area'. The commitment is for member states to consult when any one of them is threatened, and to regard an armed attack against one or more member states as an attack against them all.

The alliance is an international military agreement for collective defence as defined in Article 51 of the United Nations Charter, and collective defence was to be pursued through a combination of deterrence and defence. In peacetime the alliance was to have a substantial organisation and structure – hence the title North Atlantic Treaty Organisation (Nato). The civilians, in the form of the politicians, were to have overall control in a suitable administrative structure. The military also created an administrative system, to strengthen forces, plan strategy, organise a command structure, integrate national forces and procure and exercise personnel and equipment.

The Korean War, which began in June 1950, had the effect of speeding up the detailed creation of Nato's integrated military structure. There was the appointment of a Supreme Allied Commander, Europe (SACEUR) and his Headquarters (SHAPE) at Rocquencourt near Paris. In October 1950 both Turkey and Greece became associated to Nato in preparation for their eventual entry into the alliance on 18 February 1952. It was also in late 1950 that the Nato Defence Committee opened discussions with the Federal Republic of Germany about a West German contribution to Nato. This was to lead towards the full entry of West Germany into Nato on 5 May 1955.

At the Nato meeting in Lisbon in February 1952, the now-famous Lisbon Goals were announced. The goals referred to an agreement to adopt a military target of 50 divisions and 4000 aircraft by the end of 1952 – an objective that was not achieved then nor has been since. On 14 May 1955, the Soviet Union, partly in retaliation for the West's inclusion of West Germany in Nato, concluded the Warsaw Pact, the eastern bloc equivalent to Nato. Ever since then the two alliances have faced each other in ideological adversity, political and economic competition, and military confrontation which has led the world, on occasion, to hold it's breath – but which has also managed to preserve peace between East and West.

David Johnson

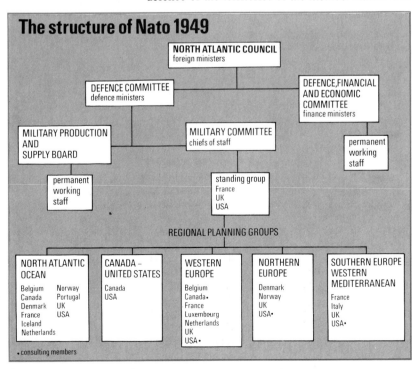

The structure of Nato 1949

| | | NORTH ATLANTIC COUNCIL
foreign ministers | | |

DEFENCE COMMITTEE
defence ministers

DEFENCE, FINANCIAL AND ECONOMIC COMMITTEE
finance ministers

MILITARY PRODUCTION AND SUPPLY BOARD

MILITARY COMMITTEE
chiefs of staff

permanent working staff

permanent working staff

standing group
France
UK
USA

REGIONAL PLANNING GROUPS

NORTH ATLANTIC OCEAN	CANADA – UNITED STATES	WESTERN EUROPE	NORTHERN EUROPE	SOUTHERN EUROPE WESTERN MEDITERRANEAN
Belgium Norway Canada Portugal Denmark UK France USA Iceland Netherlands	Canada USA	Belgium Canada• France Luxembourg Netherlands UK USA•	Denmark Norway UK USA•	France Italy UK USA•

• consulting members

Undercover war
The world of intelligence and spying

When the Russians test-fire a new ballistic missile at one of their proving grounds, orbiting satellites, previously launched from an American site thousands of kilometres away, monitor the whole operation. Not only do they take photographs; they eavesdrop on the missile's performance by picking up the signals which the missile transmits back to the Soviet scientists from equipment installed in it for that purpose. In turn the Russians do all they can to spoof the satellites in the hope that they will record false information.

One vital piece of equipment in the missile that is monitored in this way is called an accelerometer, and in fairly recent tests the Russians went out of their way to give the impression that they were having trouble with it. They installed three accelerometers in each test missile so that the Americans would believe that the instruments were so poor that they were having to average the results of three readings instead of being able to rely on one. At the same time the Russians sent spies to the United States to go through the motions of trying to find out the secrets of the American accelerometers and followed this up with agents who tried to buy one. These moves were designed to strengthen the American belief that the Russians were behind in an important aspect of the ballistic missile arms race. Had the Americans been fooled they could have been lulled into a false sense of security by wrongly believing themselves to be ahead of the Russians in the accelerometer field.

Such operations, which are extremely costly, are a modern expression of the ancient art of gathering information about a potential adversary and of countering such efforts. This information is called intelligence and all governments whether they be monarchies, dictatorships or republican democracies have regarded it for centuries as an essential compo-

nent of power. Up-to-date intelligence is more necessary than ever in the nuclear missile age when devastating attacks or threats of attack can be mounted at short notice, when subversion and sabotage are part of the policy of many governments, and when terrorism is a declared tool of governments as well as minorities.

The major effort of intelligence-gathering is concerned with defence. Governments need to know the strength of foreign forces, their locations and movements. They need to know about their armaments, the performance of individual weapons and their potential for improvement. The most important intelligence of all, however, is concerned with the intentions of foreign governments – what they intend to do with their military hardware. The recent conflict in the Falklands illustrates the difference. Britain had excellent information concerning the movements of the Argentinian fleet and the nature of the materials and men. But British planners did not know the intentions of the Argentinian rulers when the fleet put to sea on what appeared to be another maritime exercise.

There are two main ways of securing intelligence. The first (and easier) is from open sources – information published in newspapers, technical magazines and sessions of Parliaments or gleaned from events like military displays and diplomatic conversations. The second is information from clandestine sources, obtained against the wishes of the target country.

In the past, clandestine information was obtained almost exclusively by spies operating on the ground. The best known of these were the wartime and postwar Russian agents like Klaus Fuchs, who secured the innermost secrets of American and British atomic bombs. Today much of this effort has been

A photograph of New York taken by a spy-in-the-sky satellite. Such advanced surveillance technology allows pictures to be returned to earth which can show troop movements, defence installations and other subjects of intelligence interest. Previously film was returned to earth via an aircraft collection procedure but today's technology allows 'real-time' satellites to return immediate pictures direct to base.

superseded by spy-in-the-sky satellites and by the interception and decoding of secret messages sent by radio between the agencies of foreign governments and their various out-stations. The sophistication of these operations is staggering. Orbiting satellites are capable of returning to earth photographs showing fine detail of troop movements, defence installations and other objects of intelligence interest. The film was, until recently, returned in packages which were caught by waiting aircraft fitted with catching nets; but now there are 'real-time' satellites transmitting immediate high-definition pictures direct to base.

The latest techniques for intercepting conversations are equally extraordinary. One type of American eavesdropping satellite is able to record radio-telephone conversations between the cars of officials travelling about Moscow. When the Post Office Tower was built in London to transmit telephone messages by microwaves, it was believed that there were far too many channels for Russians in the London embassy to tap specific messages out of it. The Russians solved this, however, by importing a computer-analyser which recorded only those picked-up messages emanating from certain telephone numbers in which Soviet intelligence was specially interested. This has been so successful that really secret messages now have to be sent by undersea cable, while computers are now used for the decoding of secret messages to such a degree that no code or cypher is totally reliable unless changed very frequently.

Warships and ships disguised as trawlers and merchant vessels are specially equipped for gathering radio-intelligence at sea and while docked in foreign ports. There is, for instance, a Soviet ship always on station near the mouth of the Clyde, off Scotland, to monitor the movements of British and American nuclear submarines based there.

To carry out all these intelligence functions requires elaborate organisations. In Britain the two most important are the Secret Intelligence Service (SIS, often called MI6) and Government Communications Headquarters (GCHQ) which is a euphemism for the interception agency. Britain has no independent capacity for launching and operating surveillance satellites but under an agreement with the USA the results of American satellite surveillance are supplied to GCHQ and to the Ministry of Defence.

The Secret Intelligence Service is responsible for espionage in foreign countries and for countering the activities in foreign countries of agents whose task is to prevent British espionage. The corresponding agency in the US is the Central Intelligence Agency (CIA) and in the Soviet Union the Komitet Gosudarstvennoi Bezopasnosti (KGB). The headquarters of the SIS is at Century House in London and the staff there, headed by a Director General called 'C', consists of career officers and a supporting staff which is mainly administrative with technical and scientific backing.

In any agency it is important to distinguish between Secret Service *officers* who plan and control espionage operations and the *agents* who carry them out. Though officers are often recruited because of linguistic ability it is difficult for them to carry out active spying in foreign countries. They therefore employ nationals of that country who can more easily insinuate themselves into various sensitive positions or are already in them. For example, when the Russians

The first defector

In 1945 the illusion of future East-West co-operation was delivered a severe blow by an event which, if it did not change the course of history, did much to reveal the true nature of Soviet intentions towards the West. This was the defection from the Soviet embassy in Ottawa of Igor Gouzenko, a cypher clerk. On the evening of 5 September 1945 he walked out of the embassy determined never to return. He took with him a collection of secret documents, all concerned with Soviet spying.

Gouzenko was not himself a spy and was not a very important person in the Soviet embassy. But in the course of encyphering and decyphering messages passing between Moscow and the principal intelligence officer in the embassy, Colonel Zabotin, he learnt about many things of which he disapproved, and in particular that the Soviet government was operating a vast spy network in Canada and the United States and trying to penetrate the most secret institutions of a country which was supposed to be a friend and ally. In the course of two years' service Gouzenko had come to like Canada and its democratic ways and he had decided to stay there and bring his family up away from the restraints and shortages of a communist state. When he defected he was already under threat of being recalled to Moscow.

It took Gouzenko the whole of the next day and the best part of the following night before he could persuade the Canadian authorities that

Gouzenko, hooded, gives a television interview after his defection.

he had something of great importance to tell them and that they should take him under their wing. Throughout the day of 6 September Gouzenko was being sought by secret police from the embassy, who did not stop at breaking down the door of his flat in their efforts to get their hands on him. He was saved by another man, equally obscure, a sergeant in the Canadian Air Force who lived next to the Gouzenko's and who came to his aid.

The documents Gouzenko had taken with him contained incontrovertible proof that the Russians were operating a large and successful spy network in Canada, the United States and Britain. With the assistance of the Canadian Communist Party the Russians had recruited more than a score of high-ranking government officials, scientists and researchers. Through them they had obtained a vast amount of detailed information on research taking place on explosives, radar, aerial photography and other areas of secret military endeavour.

But the greatest success of the Canadian network was to obtain for Moscow an up-to-the-minute account of progress on the development of the atomic bomb, a description of how the bomb was manufactured, and samples of the uranium used. This information was provided by a British physicist, Dr Alan Nunn May, who was arrested in 1946, tried and sentenced to 10 years in prison.

David Floyd

wanted access to top secret naval information they blackmailed a British clerk in the Admiralty, John Vassall, to spy for them, while in order to secure Soviet rocket secrets the British employed the Russian colonel, Oleg Penkovsky, who worked in Moscow.

For any kind of espionage operation in a foreign country it is essential to have cover – some apparent position that will not arouse the suspicions of the target country's counter-spy agencies. For officers this is usually provided by the embassies abroad. SIS officers are posted in the guise of diplomats, being listed as second secretaries, counsellors and so on. Such cover carries the advantage that if a spy is detected he is automatically protected by diplomatic immunity and cannot be prosecuted. Instead he is deported and, since his cover will have been broken, he will then be required to resign from the service or will be given some desk appointment in Britain. Trade delegations are also used for cover, especially by the KGB, as are the United Nations organisations in New York, Geneva and elsewhere. In 1971 Britain formally expelled 105 Soviet intelligence agents who had been sheltering in the embassy, trade delegations and organisations such as Aeroflot, Tass and other ostensibly commercial agencies. The figure indicates not only the size of the KGB effort against Britain but the fact that the spy on the ground is still very important.

Large areas of major embassies like the Soviet embassy in London and the British and American embassies in Moscow have to be allotted for the technological war which is now waged between intelligence services. Tunnels are driven under opposing embassies so that listening devices can be inserted not only to eavesdrop on conversations but to record the chatter of cipher machines in the hope that it can be decoded. Laser beams are played on windows because vibrations on the glass caused by human speech can thereby be picked up and deciphered. Embassies are bombarded with microwaves for similar purposes to such an extent that there have been fears of injuries to staff. Rooms have to be 'swept' at regular intervals by sweepers using electronic devices to detect hidden microphones and other instruments surreptitiously introduced by adversaries. Perhaps the deepest insult to ambassadorial dignity has been the necessary construction in the basements of modern embassies of a room, cantilevered out from the walls, and surrounded by protective wire-netting and other physical precautions to prevent eavesdropping. There the ambassador has to sit, virtually in a cage, with distinguished visitors (such as his prime minister) so that really secret matters can be discussed in private.

The KGB attaches such importance to preventing adversaries from securing intelligence that on at least one occasion its agents have invaded the British embassy and destroyed eavesdropping equipment. This was achieved by the simple expedient of starting a fire and then sending in 'firemen' with hatchets.

Those intelligence officers posing as diplomats and trade officials are known as 'legals', while spies insinuated into a country in various guises and operating on their own, usually communicating with their headquarters by clandestine radio, are called 'illegals'. If illegals are caught they have no immunity and can be prosecuted and jailed as was Gordon Lonsdale, the KGB spy who ran the so-called Navy Secrets

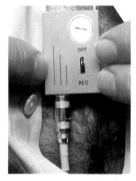

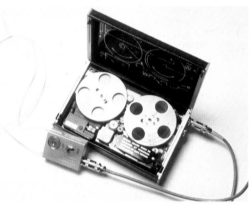

Right top and bottom: Two centres of the intelligence war. The Lubyanka in Moscow (top) home of the KGB, and the headquarters of the CIA in Langley, Virginia (bottom).

spy-ring in Britain. Illegals must have cover, and small businesses like bookshops and photographic studios are commonly used. So is the profession of journalism, which offers an excuse for general nosiness and requests for access to organisations and officials. Among spies who have used journalism for cover, the best-known are Richard Sorge, who spied with great success for Russia in China and Japan between 1933 and 1941; Philby, who is thought to have operated in Spain before joining the Secret Service, and possibly Sir Roger Hollis, a Director General of MI5 who worked as a freelance journalist in China as well as for a tobacco company.

One of the most substantial sources of information available to intelligence-gathering units is the defector, an employee of one government who wishes to transfer information of value to another. To reduce the damage inflicted by defectors Russia has developed techniques for casting doubt on the information they bring with them. One way of doing this is to send over fake defectors with false information – what has become known as 'disinformation'. Some of these have been remarkably successful, the best-known recent example being a Russian employed in a technical capacity in the United Nations headquarters in New York.

This man offered his services to the American Federal Bureau of Investigation, the counter-spy agency, in 1962 claiming that his Soviet masters had swindled him out of part of his pay. He then began to feed information about the KGB and other Russian secrets over a period of 10 years and this was believed to be so genuine that some of it was passed on directly

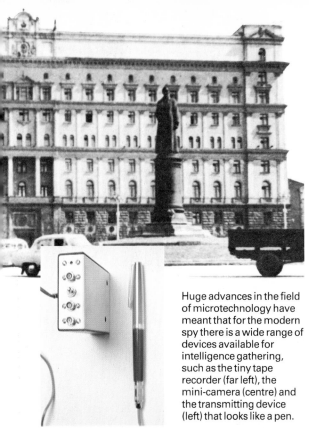

Huge advances in the field of microtechnology have meant that for the modern spy there is a wide range of devices available for intelligence gathering, such as the tiny tape recorder (far left), the mini-camera (centre) and the transmitting device (left) that looks like a pen.

to the American President. It has since been admitted by the FBI that this 'spy', who had been code-named Fedora, was really a KGB disinformation agent. He is now safely back in Russia and the FBI is still trying to sort out how much of his information was nonsense and how much was genuine material provided by the KGB to establish Fedora as a reliable spy.

When spies on the ground can still be so important it is obviously necessary to do everything feasible to counter their activities. All major countries have counter-espionage organisations, Britain's being known as the Security Service or, more popularly, as MI5. Its functions have been described by a former Director General as 'the defence of the realm as a whole from external and internal dangers arising from attempts at espionage and sabotage, or from actions of persons and organisations, whether directed from within or without the country, which may be judged to be subversive to the security of the State'.

The heart of any counter-spy organisation is the registry containing the dossiers on suspects and potential suspects from which leads can be developed. Those of MI5, said to number about 2 million, are now computerised, which has led to fears that computer technicians suborned by an enemy power could easily tap them. Adversaries do all they can to penetrate their opponents' counter-spy agencies, and even when the windows of MI5 headquarters in Curzon Street, London, are cleaned, every document has to be cleared off the desks in case they are photographed. The most effective way of penetrating such an agency is to introduce a spy onto the staff. The Russians have been extremely successful at this, both in MI5 and in MI6.

The major leads to spies operating in Britain, and probably also in the United States and the Soviet Union, now mostly come from radio-intercepts of secret messages and from defectors. The Foreign Office spy Donald Maclean was identified from an intercept while George Blake (the MI5 spy), Vassall of the Admiralty and the Navy Secrets spy-ring were given away by defectors.

The mass of intelligence and counter-intelligence material flowing in day and night requires a large staff of analysts to deal with it. The 'raw' intelligence is collated with previously held material and summarised, giving an up-to-date picture of the various situations of immediate interest. In Britain these summaries are passed to the Joint Intelligence Committee which has a sizeable staff for reducing the summaries still further so that brief accounts can be written for those politicians and officials who need to see them. Inevitably the raw intelligence is sometimes misread in this process, as certainly seems to have happened in the days preceding the Argentinian invasion of the Falkland Islands in 1982.

Although spying has always been regarded in a somewhat romantic light, there is indeed nothing romantic about a business which propagates the liquidation of individuals, blackmail, corruption and manipulation – often with the aquiescence of the parent state. In the foreseeable future, however, with no likely diminuation of the distrust between East and West and with intelligence techniques becoming ever more sophisticated, there can be little doubt that information about adversaries and their intentions will be regarded as increasingly crucial to the preservation of peace and to the strengthening of defences against possible conflict. **Chapman Pincher**

Gordon Lonsdale (top) was brought to trial in 1961 with four others, accused of running a communications centre and bank for a Soviet spy-ring from a bungalow in Ruislip. George Blake (above) succeeded in a dramatic escape from Wormwood Scrubs in 1966. Blake had received a British-record sentence of 42 years for selling secrets to the Russians and betraying other British agents.

Traitors or idealists?

The spies who gave the Soviets the secrets of the atom

Flanked by agents of the FBI, Julius Rosenberg is escorted into the Federal Building in Manhattan, New York. He was later charged with leaking atom bomb secrets to the Russians, found guilty, and in 1953, after numerous appeals had failed, he was executed.

The Russians were probably as shocked as the rest of the world when the Americans dropped an atomic bomb on Hiroshima in August 1945. But their surprise was due to the realisation that President Harry Truman was ready to *use* the new weapon, and not to the fact that such a terrifying means of destruction existed. For one thing, Josef Stalin had already been told by Truman at Potsdam in July that America possessed such a bomb. But, far more important, the Russians had been kept well informed, at least until the end of 1945, about the progress of atomic research in the West by the 'atom spies' Alan Nunn May, Klaus Fuchs, Donald Maclean, and Julius and Ethel Rosenberg. Thanks to their traitorous efforts there can have been very little that the Russians did not know about the development of the atomic bomb, and by 1945 Russia's own nuclear physicists were already on the way to building their own atomic reactors and weapons.

Klaus Fuchs, who admitted passing secret information to the Russians from 1941 to 1945, was probably the most valuable of the spies, because he let them into the secret of how the bomb was manufactured. He had worked on nuclear research in the United States, Canada and Britain, and there was little he did not know about the subject. 'I suppose it could be said that I *am* Harwell,' he once boasted, referring to the principal British atomic research centre. In his confession he wrote: 'I concentrated mainly on the product of my own work, but in particular at Los Alamos I did what I consider to be the worst I have done, namely to give information about the principle of the design of the plutonium bomb.'

Alan Nunn May provided Soviet agents with samples of uranium (U-233 and U-235) and wrote them reports on the progress of atomic research. Julius Rosenberg passed on sketches of the bomb's design. Donald Maclean, though not a scientist, worked in the British embassy in Washington, had access to the United States Atomic Energy Centre and was able to extract material from its archives.

But how much real damage did the atom spies do? To what extent did their activities benefit the Russians? The answer seems to be that, in the long run at any rate, they had very little effect on the nuclear arms race that was to dominate the postwar years.

Soviet scientists had been engaged in nuclear research ever since the 1920s and were very well informed about work in the West on splitting the atom. One of Russia's leading physicists, Peter Kapitsa, worked under Ernest Rutherford at the Cavendish Laboratory in Cambridge until he was recalled by Stalin in 1935. Another of Russia's outstanding scholars, Vladimir Vernadsky, spent years at the Curie Radium Institute in Paris and was one of the few people to forecast the part atomic energy would eventually play in the modern world. Nuclear research was being carried out in Leningrad, Moscow and Kharkov in the 1930s and by 1937 the Radium Institute in Leningrad had a cyclotron, the first in Europe. In 1940 a committee was set up to study the question of uranium supplies. The following year Kapitsa went so far as to warn of the frightening power of an atomic bomb.

The German invasion of Russia in 1941 brought all such scientific research to an end. Until the tide of war turned in 1943 the Soviet government had neither the time nor the means to mount an operation comparable with the Manhattan Project in the United States.

Alan Nunn May

A brilliant physicist who distinguished himself at Cambridge University, Alan Nunn May was invited to work on atomic research at the Cavendish Laboratory in 1942 and a year later was sent to Canada to work on the joint Anglo-Canadian atomic project. Although not directly involved in the development of the atomic bomb he had access to much information about it. His great service to the Russians was to provide them with samples of the uranium being used in the bomb.

May, born in 1912, came from a comfortable, middle-class background. Like many other young people in the 1930s he was affected by the economic crisis in the West and the growth of fascism in Europe, and he made no secret of his Marxist views. But he did not become involved in politics. The only clear sign of the way his mind was working was a visit he made to Russia in 1936. Soon after his return he joined the editorial board of the official journal of the Association of Scientific Workers, which was under strong communist influence at that time. It was through information provided by Soviet defector Igor Gouzenko that May's treachery came to light.

After his arrest in 1946 May made a full confession of his spying on behalf of the Russians. He said he had done it to make sure that 'the development of atomic energy was not confined to the USA' and that he felt he was contributing to 'the safety of mankind'. May was sentenced to 10 years in prison. He was released in 1952 and later became professor of physics at the University of Ghana.

Klaus Fuchs

By far the most important of the 'atom spies', Klaus Fuchs had access to practically all the atomic research being carried out in Britain and America as well as to the work being done on the manufacture of an atomic bomb. His ability as a nuclear physicist gained him a position on the Manhattan Project in the United States and later as head of the department of theoretical physics at Britain's atomic research centre at Harwell. Up to the moment of his arrest in 1950 there was very little that Fuchs did not know about the development of the atomic bomb in Britain and America, and he kept the Russians fully informed.

He was born in 1911 in Rüsselsheim in what is now West Germany, the son of a Lutheran pastor who later joined the Quakers and became a socialist. But Fuchs soon abandoned Christianity and socialism to become an active member of the Communist Party. When Hitler came to power in 1933 he was forced to escape, first to France and then to England. He settled in Bristol and went to university there, but kept his political views to himself and had no contact with the British Communist Party, although in 1934 the German consul in Bristol informed the police that Fuchs was a communist.

After the outbreak of World War II Fuchs became more deeply involved in atomic research and was subjected to security 'vetting' on two occasions. Each time the German consul's report was dismissed as coming from a tainted source. On the second occasion, in 1942, Fuchs was cleared and granted British citizenship. By then he had established contact with the Soviet spy network in Britain. He continued to live a double life until his arrest. Sentenced to 14 years in prison, he was released in 1959 and went to East Germany where he took a senior job at the Nuclear Research Institute.

Above: An extract from the *Daily Express* in 1951. Maclean's escape to the Soviet Union with Guy Burgess was a clear indication that British intelligence had been thoroughly penetrated by the Russians.

Donald Maclean

One of the two 'missing diplomats' (the other was Guy Burgess) who fled to Russia in 1951, Donald Maclean acted as a spy for the Russians for probably 15 years before he faced exposure. At the time of his disappearance he was head of the American department in the British Foreign Office.

Maclean was born in 1913 the son of Sir Donald Maclean, Cabinet minister and a leader of the Liberal party, a Scot of strongly Christian views. Maclean attended a good public school,

went up to Cambridge in 1931, took a first-class degree and did well in the examination for entrance into the Foreign Office. He had become a communist while at Cambridge and appears to have been recruited by the Soviet intelligence service, but he did not go out of his way to advertise his political views. He performed his diplomatic duties in exemplary fashion, though his personal behaviour and his drinking bouts revealed the strain to which his double life was subjecting him.

Unlike 'Kim' Philby, who also served the Russians from inside the British Foreign Office, and who wrote about his experiences and boasted of his prowess as a spy, Maclean avoided publicity and did not attempt to defend his actions publicly. On his defection he was provided with a flat and a pension by the Soviet government and led a low-key life in Moscow where he is believed to have acted as an advisor to the Soviet government on policy towards the West, and is said to have published political articles under an assumed name. He died in March 1983.

which had been set up in 1942 with the objective of building an atomic bomb.

Soviet scientists resumed their researches in 1944, and by 1947 their first nuclear reactor, a copy of the American Hanford 305, was in operation. In August 1949 they exploded their first atomic device. That was remarkable enough, but the main Soviet achievement was to move from this primitive atomic device to the development of a usable thermonuclear bomb in a very short time. Just four years later, in 1953, they detonated a nuclear bomb small enough to be delivered by plane or missile. The Americans, by contrast, did not test their first usable nuclear bomb until 1954.

The information which the atom spies provided was almost certainly of great value to the Russians in the initial stages of their work on the bomb, if only because it told them that there *was* a way of making such a bomb and indicated the way to go about it. Their access to Western secrets at that time probably advanced the detonation of their first atomic device by a year or so. But the speed with which they then advanced further to possess the nuclear bomb was probably due primarily to the enormous resources which the Soviet government was prepared to invest in nuclear research and weapons development. In peacetime the advantage in this respect was on the Soviet side. While governments in the West were under strong pressure to reduce expenditure on armaments and to concentrate on economic reconstruction, the Soviet system enabled its leaders to ignore popular pressure and to concentrate on acquiring the new weapon. But equally important was the outstanding ability of the Russian scientists engaged in nuclear research. Men like Igor Kurchatov, Lev Davydovich Landau and Andrei Sakharov were the equals of their counterparts in the Western world. There can be little doubt that, with their ability and the unqualified support of the Soviet government behind them, the Russian scientists and engineers would have caught up with the West in any case.

The main consequences of the exposure of the atom spies appear now to have been political and moral. It served to jolt the governments of the West out of the illusion that Stalin and the Soviet government were going to collaborate with the 'capitalist' world in peacetime. It also served as a warning to the West that there were traitors in their midst, some of them in very sensitive and important places. The lesson was not well learned, however, and there were many more unpleasant surprises ahead.

David Floyd

Key Weapons
The F-4 PHANTOM II
part 2

The Phantom in Vietnam

During the war in Vietnam, US armed forces had almost complete air superiority and so US aviation carried out its major task of direct support for the forces on the ground. Nonetheless the tasks carried out by the US Air Force, Army, Navy and Marine Corps were many and diverse and called for a correspondingly wide range of aircraft, anything from helicopter gunships to giant B-52 strategic bombers. However, the plane that established itself as *the* aircraft of the conflict was the versatile and redoubtable F-4 Phantom II. This American aircraft proved to be highly successful at carrying out many tasks: battlefield ground-support, long-range interdiction, air superiority, defence suppression and reconnaissance.

As the American involvement in Vietnam deepened during the 1960s so too did that of the Phantoms. By the time of the Gulf of Tonkin Incident on 2 August 1964 (when US ships were attacked by North Vietnamese surface craft) the Phantom was fully operational with both the Navy and the Air Force.

Initially the Phantom was intended to carry out its role as a weapons delivery system and its substantial weapons load of over 7000kg (15,000lb) made it an ideal aircraft for tactical assaults on ground targets. But it was not long before US aircraft came under attack from North Vietnamese MiGs and the Phantom found itself involved in dog fights to protect other less effective US aircraft. Although the Phantom became

Previous page: A US Navy Phantom over South Vietnam. Above: A Phantom from USS *Enterprise* fires its rockets in support of ground-forces. Below: An F-4E loaded with bombs and a 600-gallon drop-tank. Opposite page: An F-4B fires a Sparrow III AAM (top); Randy Cunningham and his radar intercept officer Willie Driscoll pose jubilantly on their Phantom (centre); an F-4J completes its landing run (bottom).

known as the 'MiG killer', the smaller, less sophisticated North Vietnamese fighters could hold their own
given the right conditions.

Both the MiG-17 and MiG-19 caused US pilots a
number of problems though they were solved in the
end, as Vietnam's first 'ace' Lieutenant-Colonel
Randall H. Cunningham explained. 'The MiG drivers were out-manoeuvring our missiles and our aeroplanes. A study of those early encounters revealed
that the F-4 was heavier and less manoeuvrable than
the MiG series. The Phantom wouldn't out-turn the
MiG series at speeds below 420 knots and its weapons
just wouldn't hack the turns and the g-loads that the
MiG could pull to defeat them. As a result of that
study, the Navy established its Fighter Weapons
School to train pilots in air-to-air-combat. There we

Top: A flight of F-4C Phantoms take in fuel from a KC-135 aerial tanker. Above right: The armed reconnaissance Phantom – the RF-4C – takes off on a dawn mission from the US air base at Da Nang. Above: Armament on an F-4D; the lower slung missile is a test round of the TV-guided Hughes Maverick ASM.

were taught how to fight and survive in the air, much of which was based on the "dicta" set down by Oswald Boelcke, the German ace of World War I.'

The F-4 Phantom II lost few dog-fights during almost eight years of aerial conflict over Vietnam. The first North Vietnamese aircraft fell victim to the Phantom on 17 June 1965 when two F-4Bs from USS *Midway* shot down two MiGs near Gen Phu in North Vietnam. In all some 146 MiGs were destroyed by Phantoms, 38 by the Navy and 108 by the Air Force.

The type of warfare that Phantom pilots had to contend with was illustrated by Lieutenant-Colonel Cunningham when on a mission to protect a US strike force from enemy attack over North Vietnam in January 1972. After drawing considerable automatic anti-aircraft and surface-to-air missile fire from the

Quang Lang area, Cunningham and his wingman Lieutenant Grant were ordered to fly a MiG/CAP (combat air patrol) in that region. 'Our job was to keep any MiGs off the strike force,' Cunningham recalled, 'but on our way into and over the airfield, 17 SAMs were fired at us – in pairs. You can't do much in the way of looking for MiGs when you're dodging all of those SAMs.

'I was just coming out of my third SAM break, going down almost purely vertical, trying to get energy, when I looked up and saw a couple of glints. I know there weren't supposed to be any aeroplanes up there, north of Quang Lang, because all of the strike force was behind me, I thought they might have been [Vought] A-7s, off target and going after some SAM sites. But I saw a glow at their tailpipes and A-7s don't have afterburners. You never think you're going to see a MiG because everyone has told you that you won't. So I put my nose toward the glint and pressed on until I got within visual range of the aircraft I had spotted. Coming down on them, I saw two of the prettiest silver delta-wing aircraft I had ever seen. One was 700 to 800 feet above the trees and his wingman was on his starboard side, slightly stepped up. I came down behind the one on the port side.'

The MiG-21 pilot must have seen the American

Above: The prototype of the F-4G/Wild Weasel defence-suppression aircraft. The role of the Wild Weasel in Vietnam was to locate, identify and suppress or destroy enemy electronic installations, most specifically North Vietnamese SAM sites.
Right: A combat-battered Phantom is overhauled by American ground crew.

Below: A heavily-laden F-4B lumbers onto the runway at Da Nang, bearing the markings of Marine Fighter Squadron 323 – known as the 'Death Rattlers'.

Phantom just as the Sidewinder missile was fired because he executed a very hard 'break' turn to the right. The missile was unable to sustain the turn and exploded beneath the MiG. As the MiG pilot continued his roll to the right, Cunningham started a lag pursuit roll to the left, half expecting the other MiG-21 to come after him, but at the first sign of trouble, the second MiG fled the scene. Cunningham then came out of the roll and was back behind the first delta-wing MiG. He fired a second Sidewinder which, Cunningham noted, 'just took off his whole tail. The aeroplane pitched, head over heels, and came down near a village.' On a mission later in the year Cunningham shot down three MiGs including that of Colonel Toon, North Vietnam's highest scoring ace.

By the early 1970s bombing technology had undergone a succession of far reaching improvements, and with the introduction of laser-guided bombs the Phantom acquired the role of a precision bomber able to hit difficult targets such as bridges and power stations with virtually 100 per cent accuracy. Operating in pairs Phantoms would approach the target, with one aircraft – acting as the 'illuminator' – sending out a laser beam to 'lock-on' to the target which would then send out a cone of reflected laser light that would be picked up by the second aircraft carrying the LGB (laser-guided bomb). Once released the bomb's computerised guidance system would seek out the cone of reflected laser light and by adjusting steering vanes in its tail it would ride down the cone onto the target.

One pilot, Lieutenant Colonel Ray Stratton, described how even tanks could be destroyed by laser-guided bombs. 'I found two tanks just north of the Marines' position on the My Chanh River. It was at twilight. There was a PT76 and a T54; the PT76 was trying to pull the T54 out of a dry stream bed. They were just about a mile to the east of Route 1 and about a

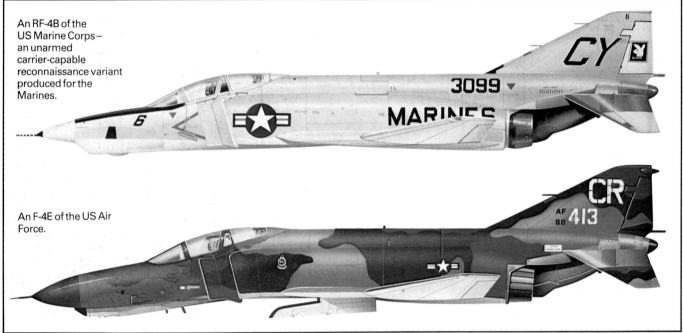

An RF-4B of the US Marine Corps – an unarmed carrier-capable reconnaissance variant produced for the Marines.

An F-4E of the US Air Force.

Top: An F-4E armed with fuse-extended Mk 82 bombs prepares to make a bombing run against targets in North Vietnam.

mile and a half north of the town of My Chanh. I called for ordnance and there was none available. I waited and finally ''Schlitz'' and ''Raccoon'', two Phantoms out of the Ubon, showed up. They were equipped with a laser-guided bomb system known as Paveway One. ''Racoon'' was the illuminator; he carried the laser gun used to direct the laser energy onto the target. ''Schlitz'' carried the laser-guided bombs.

'They checked in with two or three minutes of ''playtime'' left – that is, they were running short on fuel. I briefed them on the way to save time. I put the smoke down marking the target. By this time, the illuminator, ''Racoon'', was in orbit; he asked me which tank we wanted to hit first. I suggested the one that was not stuck. Within about 30 seconds he said ''I've started the music'', meaning the laser beam was on the target. ''Schlitz'' was already in position for the drop – the LGB hit right on that PT76, blew the turret off and flipped the tank over. The blast covered

the second tank with mud, so I put another smoke rocket down; ''Racoon'' ''started the music'' again. ''Schlitz'' meanwhile had pulled right back up on the porch for another run. The whole operation was over in three minutes. Two bombs – two tanks destroyed.'

When the US Army began to disengage from the Vietnamese conflict in the early 1970s the importance of the Air Force commitment grew correspondingly. During the Easter offensive of 1972, when North Vietnamese columns broke through the lines of the South Vietnamese Army, the role of the Phantom became critical. Able to halt the communist forces through pin-point bombing of key positions, they took the momentum out of the North Vietnamese assault and bought valuable time for the forces of the South. But after the 1973 ceasefire, US aerial support came to a close and the Phantoms were withdrawn. The South was now an easy target and could put up little resistance when the communists launched their final offensive in 1975.

Turmoil in Malaya

Communist insurrection and the British response

The communist-inspired outbreak of violence in Malaya in June 1948 was but one of a number of serious crises which confronted the Western world at that time. The Soviet Union was, or so it seemed, bent on forcing the Western Allies out of Berlin; political democracy had just been overturned by communists in Czechoslovakia; Ho Chi Minh and the communist-dominated Viet Minh were waging war against the French in Indochina and, most significant of all, Mao Tse-tung was on the brink of success in China. At the time all these events seemed to fit into a universal pattern of communist expansion under centralised control from Moscow. With the advantage of hindsight we may question that this was so, but in the immediate postwar years there was less room for doubt and Britain saw the outbreak of violence in Malaya as forming part of this worldwide offensive.

The Malayan Communist Party (MCP) had been formed in 1930 from a branch of the Chinese Communist Party. When the Japanese invaded Malaya in December 1941 the MCP, following Mao Tse-tung's example, adopted an anti-Japanese policy. It was the only political grouping of any significance in Malaya at that time and, in consequence, took the lead in the peninsula and even received, in the last stages of the defence of Singapore, military assistance from the British Army. From this nucleus of trained men the MCP created the Malayan People's Anti-Japanese Army (MPAJA) which established a military organisation with regiments hiding in the jungle in every State.

The abrupt conclusion of the war in the Far East in August 1945 led to the collapse of the Japanese occupation of Malaya and in many areas the Japanese forces surrendered to units of the MPAJA. However, with the return of the British administration many members of the MPAJA accepted the government's call to disband and hand in their weapons.

Despite the somewhat chaotic situation which existed in the months following the Japanese surrender

Above: A British jungle patrol fords a river in Malaya while on a mission searching for terrorists. In order to destroy the bases of the MRLA, British security forces found that it was necessary to push deep into the jungle in order to engage an enemy that was extremely elusive. Overpage: After the surrender of the Japanese, the British found that the MPAJA was well established in Malaya. The 4th Regiment of guerrillas, armed with .30in M1 Carbines and Mk II Sten submachine guns, are shown on parade in 1945.

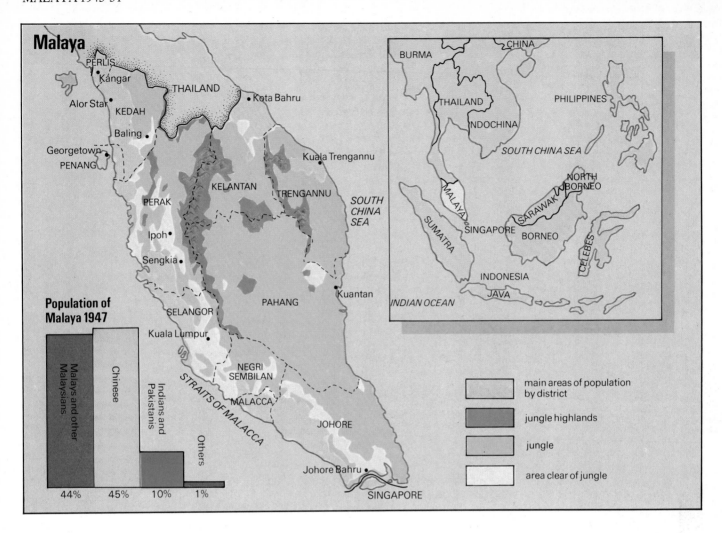

Malaya

PERLIS
Kangar
Alor Star KEDAH
THAILAND
Kota Bahru
Baling
Georgetown
PENANG
Kuala Trengannu
KELANTAN
PERAK TRENGANNU
SOUTH
CHINA
SEA
Ipoh
Sengkia
PAHANG
Kuantan
SELANGOR
Kuala Lumpur
NEGRI
SEMBILAN
MALACCA
JOHORE
STRAITS OF MALACCA
Johore Bahru
SINGAPORE

BURMA CHINA
THAILAND PHILIPPINES
NDOCHINA
SOUTH CHINA SEA
NORTH
BORNEO
SARAWAK
MALAYA
SUMATRA SINGAPORE BORNEO
CELEBES
INDONESIA
INDIAN OCEAN JAVA

Population of Malaya 1947

Malays and other Malaysians	Chinese	Indians and Pakistanis	Others
44%	45%	10%	1%

main areas of population by district

jungle highlands

jungle

area clear of jungle

the MCP chose not to attempt a military confrontation with the British at that stage. Instead, while retaining the nucleus of a military organisation, for the most part on paper, the party, under Secretary General Chin Peng, reverted to its pre-war policy of industrial disruption and sought to gain control of the trade union movement.

By the beginning of 1948 labour unrest had spread and with it came an increase of violence, with numerous incidents of intimidation and murder. It was in June 1948 that the MCP decided to initiate a military campaign with the long-term goal of driving out the British and establishing a communist republic in Malaya. The newly created force of the MCP, formed from men who had served during the war in the MPAJA, was known ultimately as the Malayan Races Liberation Army (MRLA). It was almost completely made up of Chinese, though there were always a few Malays and Indians involved. It was armed with

The structure of insurgency

regular units
of company
strength

DISTRICT
COMMITTEE

local
units

village
guerrilla
units

cells of
communist
sympathisers

terror and
sabotage
section

intelligence
section

propaganda
section

flow of supplies recruits & intelligence

flow of supplies recruits & intelligence

weapons hidden in 1945 which were supplemented by captures from the security forces.

The MRLA was generally organised into regiments, companies and platoons though the strengths and effectiveness of these units scarcely made a uniform pattern. Early on there was a tendency to operate in large groups of anything from 50 to 200 men who would all live in the same camp located within easy reach of the jungle edge. This was a necessity in order that the unit could obtain food and gain intelligence from isolated peasant communities 'squatting' illegally and remote from population centres and government supervision.

Following the example of Mao Tse-tung the MRLA at first sought to dominate one or two remote areas of the country. Isolated police posts were over-run and the local population was won over to the communists' side. It was soon realised, however, that conditions in the Federation of Malaya were rather different from those in China. The country was, in area, roughly the size of England and Wales and, although it was 80 per cent covered in dense jungle, communications were not too difficult for government officials, police or army. The security forces were able to counter insurgent activities with comparative ease so the attempt to 'liberate' selected areas was abandoned.

Instead the MRLA turned to less ambitious activities. Firstly they tried to weaken the resolve of the government and the morale of the security forces: police posts were attacked, police and army vehicles were ambushed on the roads and patrols into the jungle were also trapped in ambushes. Secondly they turned their attention to the European managers of rubber estates and tin mines. Through murder and ambush they hoped to intimidate these men and their families so that they would be forced to flee from the distant plantations they invariably inhabited. In this way the MRLA tried to slow down and eventually stop the production of tin and rubber, the lifeblood of the Malayan economy. Lastly they tried to win over the Chinese population by persuasion or intimidation. The Chinese 'squatters' were often easily persuaded by MRLA propaganda. They provided food and intelligence for the communists and a 'mass organisation', the Min Yuen, was formed so that the supply of food and money and the gathering of information was placed on a more organised footing. The Min Yuen also provided a steady flow of recruits for the armed and uniformed MRLA itself.

The more wealthy members of the Chinese community, the managers or owners of small estates, those employed in government service and particularly those working for the security forces, were

Top left: A British Army truck burns fiercely after being hit by grenades and smallarms fire in an ambush. Above left: Security forces break into an insurgent hideout. The British preferred to capture guerrillas alive so that they could provide information (above).

Ambush at Fraser's Hill

The funeral of Sir Henry Gurney.

The ambushes and small-scale attacks of the Malayan communist guerrillas were a constant source of danger to the security forces. Their most notorious exploit was the assassination of the British High Commissioner, Sir Henry Gurney, at Fraser's Hill in 1951.

The road to Fraser's Hill was an ideal place to site an ambush and yet, until October 1951, the communist Malayan Races Liberation Army (MRLA) had never attempted to mount a serious attack on the military and government vehicles which frequently used it. It was ideal in a variety of ways. In the first place, Fraser's Hill was a rest station to which many senior officers could escape from the high temperatures and heavy humidity of the plains, so there were many important targets on the road. The physical characteristics of the road itself also made it an attractive proposition for the terrorists. For the last 32km (20 miles) of its length it climbed steeply, winding its way through dense jungle country. The road twisted and turned as it clung to the hillsides and where the slopes were particularly steep it was cut into the hillside itself. Rocky cliffs up to 15m (50 feet) high rose from the roadside while, opposite, the ground dropped sharply away into deep ravines.

Documents captured later indicated that an ambush party was in position on 5 October 1951. The group comprised at least 38 men and they were well armed with two Bren guns, a Sten gun and rifles. The Bren guns were needed to bring down heavy fire onto the vehicles at the moment the ambush was sprung.

The position was sited on a sharp S-bend where steep cliffs rose sheer from the road. Individual and group positions were allocated carefully to give each other support and to allow fire to be concentrated on the selected killing zone. The party was spread out 180m (200 yards) along the roadside.

The ambush was ready from 1000 hours on 5 October and remained established until at least 1500 hours that day. A careful note was made by the commander of all vehicle movement in both directions along the road between those times. Several groups of vehicles would have made excellent targets in that they were small enough not to have been able to react against the attack and yet were likely to yield several weapons to the MRLA.

No more sightings were recorded on the 5th after 1500 hours.

and it seems probable that soon after that the 'bandit' force withdrew from the road to camp for the night. They were back next morning.

Just before 1300 hours on the 6th, High Commissioner Sir Henry Gurney, travelling in his official Rolls-Royce, approached the site. He had left King's House in Kuala Lumpur earlier that morning and was travelling with his wife and Private Secretary up to Fraser's Hill for the weekend. The High Commissioner always travelled with a minimum of escorting vehicles for protection and on this occasion, as a result of a breakdown, there were fewer than usual. In front of the Rolls was an open Landrover carrying five Malay policemen without any automatic weapons. The wireless vehicle, which should have been behind the Rolls, had broken down; as a result of this the police armoured car at the rear had dropped behind and was now desperately trying to catch up with the other vehicles. So it was that the ambush commander saw only a Landrover with lightly armed policemen and the official Rolls enter his killing zone.

He gave the order to open fire. In the first burst from the Bren guns the Landrover was brought to a halt with most of the policemen wounded. Within seconds, its tyres punctured and its body riddled with holes, the Rolls-Royce careered to the side of the road and came to a standstill. The chauffeur was wounded and slumped down at the wheel; Lady Gurney and the Private Secretary flung themselves to the floor of the car. The High Commissioner, unhurt at this stage, opened the door and made to cross the road, perhaps to seek cover. He took a few steps and fell dead at the roadside.

There was a brief lull in the shooting, as the weapon recovery groups scrambled down to the road. Then the armoured car arrived and engaged the terrorists with its twin machine guns. Instantly the ambush commander ordered a bugle to sound the signal to withdraw. Despite a massive follow-up by police and army units most of the ambushers escaped immediate retribution. They disappeared into the vast jungles of Pahang scarcely realising until later how important their action that day had been.

Major F. A. Godfrey

subjected to a campaign of terror in an attempt to prevent the government and the economy from functioning effectively. Murder, mutilation, torture, extortion and kidnap were the measures employed.

The sudden and widespread outbreak of violence caught the government of the Federation of Malaya off guard. It had neither the plans nor the resources to respond. In the first weeks after the declaration of a State of Emergency on 17 June 1948 there was much discussion on how to react and how to make the best use of the limited resources available. Within a few months a special constabulary was formed to protect the rubber estates, tin mines and vulnerable points; and the regular police force was expanded to maintain the government's presence in towns and villages. Once such protective arrangements were in hand the army, which was quickly reinforced, was released from static duties to go on to the offensive. Police recruitment allowed for the creation of what were known as 'jungle squads', which also went in search of MRLA units in the jungle.

As the situation developed the government acted to weaken the hold that the MRLA exerted over the scattered rural population. Of great psychological importance was the decision that the civil government should retain overall control of the security operations and that the army should be used, not just as the military commanders thought fit, but in a way agreed through civil, police and military consultation. Military domination of the government would have provided the MCP with a major propaganda weapon to be used to win over the more reluctant groups of rural Chinese to their side.

A further decision, aimed at depriving the MRLA of their essential contact with Chinese villagers, was implemented in 1949. In selected and particularly remote areas where the MRLA was known to be operating, whole 'squatter' settlements were dispersed. Their inhabitants were either repatriated to China, resettled with relations or in other villages under closer government supervision or simply left to fend for themselves away from their original homes.

To encourage the supply of information about the terrorists a system of monetary rewards was introduced; at the same time, terms under which a guerrilla could surrender were widely publicised and, under certain circumstances, included an element of financial inducement which proved very successful.

The MRLA rapidly became disillusioned at the prospect of spending years living uncomfortably and dangerously in the jungle. Hopes for an early success in their campaign seemed to be fading. The leadership had not achieved its aim of liberating areas of the country and establishing their authority and there was little, if any, support for their cause from communist countries outside Malaya. These failures aggravated the tensions which developed simply from living in the jungle where, at any time, a security force patrol might appear and inflict casualties.

For the government's part, the measures it introduced during the first years of the emergency were, by their very nature, only likely to achieve results in the long term and there were many agonising moments as the enemy appeared still to be capable of striking at will. The army was operating in the jungle on the basis of scant, frequently non-existent intelligence about the enemy. Further, it was expending much energy on very large scale operations, flooding areas of jungle with battalions and even brigades of soldiers, which quite frequently led to no kills or captures at all.

The truth was, however, that despite despondency on both sides the battle was far from being lost or won. The MRLA was still able to recruit to replace its losses; it could build up its armed strength through its attacks on the security forces and it grew more effective as its leadership gained in experience. The government's efforts were, in 1950, to receive a renewed impetus consequent upon the arrival in Malaya of a new director of operations, Lieutenant-General Sir Harold Briggs. He was to establish, in a very brief spell, the ground rules that would ultimately lead to success.　**Major F.A. Godfrey**

Below: Surrounded by belts of ammunition and sandbags, a soldier of a British Gurkha regiment mans a machine gun at a lonely jungle outpost.

Jungle patrols

Scouting, tracking and fighting in tropical forests

Successful patrolling in a country such as Malaya against an enemy like the Malayan Races Liberation Army (MRLA) made necessary the development of very sophisticated skills on the part of patrol commanders and men. While training in movement and navigation was of prime importance it seemed always to be the case that the great teacher was experience itself. As men became used to living and working in the jungle they developed what can only be described as a 'feel' for the best way to use this strange environment to their advantage.

A major problem was the limited range of visibility. Hilly primary jungle posed fewer difficulties in this respect, though even there the leading scout of a patrol of 10 men in single file would rarely, if ever, be within sight of the rear man. As most operations were carried out close to the edge of the jungle, patrols frequently found themselves in secondary jungle. This is the term given to an area of primary jungle which has at one time been cleared or partially cleared for cultivation and then allowed to revert to natural growth. In such conditions clear visibility could be reduced to 3 or 4m (10 to 12 feet), so thick was the undergrowth, and it was often necessary for the leading scout to cut a path for the patrol.

Visibility was also extremely poor in 'lalang', a tall coarse grass which grows when previously cultivated areas are left fallow. In parts of Malaya land which is left unused also becomes overgrown by a tough fern growing over 2m (6 feet) high. While negotiating such vegetation, a man, if he stumbled, would disappear from the view of the next only 1m (3 feet) away. Movement in such conditions was extremely slow and patrols would sometimes find their advance cut to a snail's pace, with progress being measured at 50 to 100m (45 to 90 yards) an hour.

The constantly changing speed of a patrol created problems with navigation. In the jungle it was not possible to make use of the normal aids to map-reading. Rarely was a patrol commander afforded a distant view; and even if, on a steep hillside, he caught a glimpse of a hazy skyline he could never be quite sure of relating the hilltop he could see to the map. He was normally reduced to marching with his compass in his hand to give him a feel for the general line of movement. He then relied on his experience to relate the shape of the feature on which the patrol was moving to the contours of the map.

A further problem was that of noise. To avoid giving the enemy warning of approach it was necessary, ideally, to reduce the noise of movement to a level that could be detected only up to the distance it was possible to see, although rarely was it possible to achieve this goal

Locating the enemy in the jungle was, of course, an easy matter if precise information existed as to his whereabouts. Yet, even after 1951, when information flowed more freely, many patrols were still sent

out to search for bandit camps without anything more than a general idea of their location. As patrol commanders built up experience they became skilled at converting what might seem an impossible, exhausting and time-consuming task into a carefully planned and meticulously executed fighting reconnaissance patrol.

It might be known that a bandit camp was located somewhere in an area of, say, six to eight map squares of jungle. The bandits would need to leave their camp and return to it, and although they would take great care to conceal their tracks they could not do so completely. It would be a waste of time searching the jungle edge to find a track used by the terrorists because the jungle would be entered at a different point by different men and on different occasions. However, the individual routes must converge at some point for the terrorists to gain access to their camp. If the jungle was particularly dense the indi-

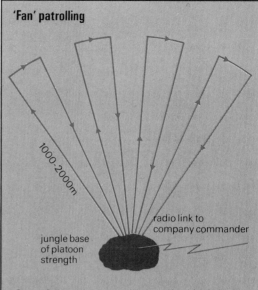

'Fan' patrolling

1000-2000m

jungle base of platoon strength

radio link to company commander

One of the most common methods of establishing enemy whereabouts was 'fan' patrolling. Having established a jungle base camp in the area to be searched, small detachments of three or four men, carrying only their weapons and ammunition, were despatched in radial formation on pre-set compass bearings. The area to be covered depended very much on the nature of the surrounding jungle and the fact that three hours was about the time limit to which the troops could operate effectively. On detecting an enemy encampment one or two members of the patrol returned to the platoon base and the platoon commander would move up to survey the target with all available men. Depending on the enemy's strength he would decide whether to attack or to call up for reinforcements.

Left: Armed with Belgian 7.62mm FN FAL rifles, Nigerian troops advance through rebel territory in Biafra. The density of the vegetation requires a gradual advance. Below: A unit of British soldiers and Gurkhas push through the jungle in search of guerrillas. With them they carry an assortment of arms; a 7.62mm SLR, a .303in Bren machine gun and various 9mm Owen submachine guns. Right: An illustration of just how dense jungle foliage can become: a British sergeant gives a corporal a helping hand to cross a fast flowing stream.

vidual tracks would come together sooner. If the army patrol cut into the jungle and then patrolled parallel to the jungle edge, but deep inside, it would in all probability eventually pick up the track running into the camp.

Another way of searching an area was systematically to follow all water courses, for the bandits needed to be within reasonable reach of drinking water. A terrorist camp might also be located by patrolling a ridge line a few metres below the actual ridge track. Bandits used ridge tracks for ease of movement and speed over long distances. When the time came for them to drop down to their camp, they would not all leave the track at the same place, for to do so would provide a clear trail for a patrol to follow. Once again, however, the individual foot tracks ultimately had to converge and often they would do so within a few metres of the top of the ridge.

All these methods of patrolling involved hours, days and weeks of painstaking effort, frequently without success. The jungle is a primitive and often frightening place, and yet thousands of young National Servicemen, having scarcely ever left their predominantly urban environment at any other time in their lives, adapted to it with remarkable ease. Most British battalions allowed just three weeks for acclimatisation and familiarisation for newly arrived drafts in Malaya. It was usually enough.

Major F. A. Godfrey

On the track of the terrorists

Arthur Hayward was a platoon commander in Malaya and was awarded the Military Cross after his tour of duty. Here he recalls an incident that occurred during the Emergency.

❝It was still dark as the vehicles moved off, almost noiselessly, back to camp. I made my way forward to position myself behind the leading scout and gave the signal to move. The rain was still falling heavily and we were already soaked through to the skin, but at least the drumming of the downpour on the thick foliage around us muffled the noise we made as we set out, slipping and sliding in the mud. With luck we would gain the jungle without detection. My aim was to get some 3km (2 miles) into the jungle by late afternoon. We could then set up a patrol base and start our systematic search for signs of the cultivated clearings which I'd been told the guerrillas had begun to establish as a safe source of food.

By three o'clock we were well into the jungle and making good progress when suddenly the leading scout held up his hand to halt the patrol. We stopped and crouched down in total silence. After a moment or two I made my way cautiously up to the leading scout. He nodded his head forward and, following his gaze, I saw that ahead of us the jungle appeared to thin out. I decided to go forward with the recce group to see what lay ahead. Before long I could see an open patch of ground. Nothing could be heard or seen which suggested the enemy was near and yet it was clear that the area was being prepared for cultivation. We had stumbled on what we were seeking but where were the guerrillas who should have been working there?

The clearing was roughly rectangular in shape and fell away from where we were, at the top corner, towards a stream at the lower edge. I decided to go forward into the open to get a better view. Almost immediately I noticed footprints in the soft soil, clearly made by the rubber soles of bandit boots. I moved a little further and realised that the scattered footmarks tended to come together and form a rough pathway which led out of the clearing at the far end.

Another step or two and, to my amazement, I saw water from a puddle trickling down into what was obviously a very recently made footprint. At least one man had been in the clearing until a few minutes before we arrived! I retraced my footsteps to where the recce group had covered my every move and crouched down to think.

The footprints had not been made by men running away – they were clear-cut and not blurred by slipping and sliding in haste. I decided that the guerrillas had in all probability gone off for the day and would return to work tomorrow. I therefore determined to set up a carefully planned ambush to catch them in the open when they returned.

My platoon was, as usual, divided into two sections and I decided to site No 2 Section (with my platoon sergeant) along the near side of the clearing where the jungle ran down to the stream. I would then deploy my own, No 1 Section, across the top of the clearing. I briefed my platoon sergeant on his positions and arcs of fire. We then withdrew some 180m (200 yards) from the clearing and ate.

Just after six o'clock, with one hour to dusk, we made our way back to the clearing. Having confirmed all was clear, my sergeant took his section down the side of the rectangle, deploying them in three groups with the Bren group in the centre. All three groups had a clear view across the open ground to where the path led into the jungle on the far side. I then moved cautiously along the high side of the clearing about 10m (30 feet) inside the jungle. I allocated the rifle

Below: A typical jungle clearing. It was in clearings such as these that MRLA units established operations bases and supply dumps. Right: Pushing through the dense foliage of the interior, a British officer armed with a .30in M1 Carbine leads a Gurkha unit on patrol. Note the tactical disposition of the unit as they advance in 'indian file', alternately watching left to right to guard against a possible ambush by guerrillas.

group their positions by moving forward to the edge of the open ground then moved on to where I judged was the halfway point of the area. Here I positioned my Bren group, to which I intended to return after siting the recce group at the far corner of the clearing.

With the recce group following me I moved slowly along on the same line until I judged we had reached the far end of the clearing. I soon realised that we had overshot the clearing and were in fact moving down through the jungle beyond the far edge. At that instant I saw in front of me, some 18m (20 yards) ahead, the clear shape of a hut roof. A moment later we heard the clink of a metallic object. The guerrillas were living just inside the jungle. Unbelievably, though they were so close, we had not disturbed them, even though I had deployed some 25 men into an ambush position, all within 45m (50 yards) of them.

We moved ahead, slithering under and crawling round broken palm fronds and dead wood and vegetation, fearful of making the slightest noise. As we advanced the outline of the hut became clearer. I could see two men sitting inside. One was cleaning his teeth, using an enamel mug, and the other was oiling his rifle. A Sten gun was lying across the knees of the former. A little closer and I discerned, just below the hut, a third man crouched on his haunches, fully dressed and equipped and nursing a Mark V rifle. He was positioned to look back along the track towards the clearing and was, obviously, the sentry.

I made a fast appreciation. The hut was only big enough to take the three but there might be others further on which we had not yet seen. It seemed likely, though, that only these men were associated with this clearing as all the digging tools were by the hut. I decided to attack. We crept further forward till we were within 10m (about 30 feet) of the hut. Still they had not sensed our presence. Slowly I raised myself to my feet, put my carbine to my shoulder and took aim at the sentry. I opened fire and the others instantly followed. There was a deafening roar as the jungle echoed back the firing of our weapons. Two of the guerrillas slumped down lifeless immediately but the sentry, my target, was thrown forward by the impact of the shots and started to crawl into the undergrowth. We lunged forward to make sure there were no others and my leading scout crashed into the undergrowth and returned to report that the sentry was also dead.

I called out to my sergeant to come across the clearing with his section, watching out for other terrorists on the way. I told him what had happened and despatched his section to carry out a quick sweep to check whether there were any other signs of life. I returned to my own section and ordered the section commander to take the rifle group and find a site to camp in for the night. I placed the Bren group on the edge of the clearing and with the recce group collected together the weapons, packs and equipment of the dead guerrillas. We also wrapped the bodies in poncho capes.

Soon afterwards No 2 Section returned, having seen nothing. Meanwhile my radio operator had got a message through to the company commander, who ordered me to return to the jungle edge the following morning. There we would be met by men from another platoon to help carry out the bodies, all of which had to be taken back for Special Branch to identify. 〞

Top: During Operation Unity, a British officer discusses with an Indian patrol leader the area to be covered. Above: A British patrol passing through this seemingly abandoned village has discovered a native without identification and takes him away for interrogation.

India breaks apart

The religious war over independence

The partition of the core of the British Empire – the subcontinent of India – between the two newly independent states of India and Pakistan in 1947 was one of the great political changes of the 20th century. The formal handover of power took place swiftly, and successfully. But it was accompanied by religious and racial violence that claimed hundreds of thousands of lives. Although the fighting was not sanctioned by either government, it was, in a sense, a spontaneous religious war, the expression of tensions that had been building up for decades.

Pressure for Indian independence from Britain, under the aegis of the Congress Party whose dominant figures by 1945 were M. K. (Mahatma) Gandhi and Jawaharlal Nehru, had been building up since the beginning of the century. Then, between the years 1937 and 1940, the Muslim League, under the leadership of Mohammed Ali Jinnah, began to demand a separate Islamic state, to protect Muslim interests against the Hindu majority.

Ever since the Islamic invasions of the 14th to 16th centuries and the establishment of the Mogul Empire there had been varying degrees of tension between Hindu and Muslim; and during the period from 1920 to 1940 there was simmering violence between the two communities, often touched off by petty causes. But Jinnah's call for a separate state was complicated by the fact that although there were Islamic majorities in some areas, the whole of the subcontinent contained Muslims.

For the British government, which by the end of World War II had basically accepted the principle of independence, the problems seemed insoluble. Negotiations dragged on, until finally, on 3 June 1947, the Viceroy, Mountbatten, proposed a plan that resulted in the creation of a fragmented state of Pakistan from east Bengal and the northwestern area, especially west Punjab, of the subcontinent. Both the Congress Party and the Muslim League accepted the proposals; and in July the Indian Independence Act was passed by the British Parliament. The situation in India was rapidly deteriorating and rather than wait until June 1948 (the date originally planned for British withdrawal), it was decided to bring independence forward to 15 August 1947.

Below left: The side of a house daubed with a message for the British. Below: As a dead Hindu's blood flows into the gutter, Muslim youths in Calcutta survey their handiwork. Below right: Gandhi, the symbol of Indian independence.

During the late summer and autumn there was spontaneous violence all over India against minorities – be they Hindu or Muslim – but the slaughter was at its most intense in the Punjab, because of the position of yet another religious group, the Sikhs.

The Sikhs populated the rich canal colonies of west Punjab, and the declaration that their lands would be turned over to a Muslim state was felt by them as a grave insult. While ostensibly originating from a religious order which sought to combine both Hinduism and Islam, the Sikhs, who had for many years held great sway in the Punjab, had an intense hatred for the Muslims against whom, in the past, they had fought many wars. They were bitterly opposed to a move which would place their richest lands under a Muslim government and considerably decrease their influence by dispersing them between two new states. Thus while the Partition Committee was attempting to divide the country and its assets and liabilities, bands of Sikhs were setting out from west Punjab on their way to the east while at the same time groups of Muslims were making their way out of India and into the new Pakistan or west Punjab. It was the meeting of these separate groups of transients that led to the disaster of autumn 1947.

At the beginning of August riots broke out all over the Punjab and as the date for partition approached, the disorders intensified. Most of the principal cities of the Punjab were in flames and in the countryside armed bands raped and massacred indiscriminately. Such was the confusion that even the Punjab Boundary Force (made up of both non-Muslim and Muslim troops), commanded by British senior officers, could not keep the peace. Its troops refused to fire on members of its own communities and it was finally disbanded leaving the Indian and Pakistani governments to provide their own security forces. But the local governments were completely overwhelmed by the emergency and were disorganised by the transfer of police and civil officers to the new states.

On both sides of the border minorities were desperately trying to reach safe areas but all along the roads they were butchered. Those who attempted to travel by train frequently failed to reach their destination; trains were derailed and the occupants slaughtered. Finally, horrified by the endless carnage, the governments of Pakistan and India established a Joint Military Evacuation Organisation at Lahore aimed at assisting the complete evacuation of both sides. Mixed guards were provided for refugee camps and armed escorts for the various convoys of both religions. Although it took some time to effect the complete exchange of populations, the system did eventually begin to work. It was estimated that during 1947 some 6,500,000 refugees entered Pakistan and that about 500,000 Muslims lost their lives. Conversely, some 5,500,000 Hindus and Sikhs left west Punjab but no figures were released as to the number killed. The division between Muslim and non-Muslim had been irrevocably established.

The effects of the partition were not, however, limited to the disputed boundaries of Pakistan. The Indian Empire had included not only the provinces of British India but also more than 500 states, each with an individual ruler. Prior to independence each of these rulers had recognised British paramountcy but this situation was nullified when British paramountcy ended in 1947 and the states, realising the unlikelihood of independent survival, set about acceding to either India or Pakistan – depending on the religious constitution of the state. This too was to prove a difficult process – especially in the case of the northern state of Kashmir.   **Simon Innes**

Sikh against Muslim

'The Sikh Jathas, armed mobs from 50 to 100 strong, assemble usually in the Gurdwaras, their places of worship, before making a series of raids. Many Jathas cross over from the Sikh states. The armament of a typical Jatha consists of one or two firearms, army and homemade grenades, spears, axes, and kirpans – the Sikh sabres, which are also religious emblems. The Muslims are usually only armed with staves. When threatened they assemble on their roofs and beat gongs and drums to summon help from neighbouring Muslim communities and prepare to throw stones at the attackers. The Sikhs attack scientifically. A first wave armed with firearms fires to bring the Muslims off their roofs. A second wave lobs grenades over the walls. In the ensuing confusion a third wave goes in with kirpans and spears, and the serious killing begins. A last wave consists of older men . . . who carry torches and specialise in arson. Mounted outriders with kirpans cut down those trying to flee.

'British officers have seen Jathas that have included women and even children with spears. Appalling atrocities have been committed; bodies have been mutilated; none has been spared – men, women, or children. In one village, out of 50 corpses 30 were those of women. One Viceroy's commissioned officer found four babies roasted to death over a fire.'

Report in The Times, *25 August 1947.*

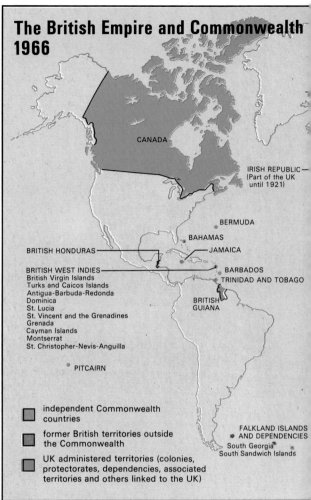

The British Empire and Commonwealth 1966

BRITISH WEST INDIES
British Virgin Islands
Turks and Caicos Islands
Antigua-Barbuda-Redonda
Dominica
St. Lucia
St. Vincent and the Grenadines
Grenada
Cayman Islands
Montserrat
St. Christopher-Nevis-Anguilla

CANADA

IRISH REPUBLIC —
(Part of the UK
until 1921)

BERMUDA

BAHAMAS

BRITISH HONDURAS

JAMAICA

BARBADOS

TRINIDAD AND TOBAGO

BRITISH
GUIANA

PITCAIRN

FALKLAND ISLANDS
AND DEPENDENCIES
South Georgia
South Sandwich Islands

☐ independent Commonwealth countries

☐ former British territories outside the Commonwealth

☐ UK administered territories (colonies, protectorates, dependencies, associated territories and others linked to the UK)

Withdrawal from Empire

Great Britain abandons her colonial role

In February 1947 a decision of momentous importance was announced by the British Labour government: Britain would be withdrawing from its Indian Empire. The date for withdrawal was set for June 1948 but, in the event, evacuation came sooner. The Indian Independence Bill was rushed through Parliament in July 1947, and at midnight on 14/15 August British rule over India officially ended. Two new states, India and Pakistan, came into existence. Two others, Ceylon and Burma, followed them into statehood early in 1948. The Raj, the jewel of empire, had passed into history.

In retrospect, the decision taken was realistic. Without the consent of the Indian people, continued British rule over India was hardly conceivable. The maintenance of British rule would have involved the purging of nationalist elements from the Indian administration and perhaps even the landing of further British troops. This the Labour government was not prepared to do. In any case, with an economy crippled by six years of world war, Britain simply could not afford to reassert colonial authority in India.

This decision could have led to a searching reappraisal of Britain's imperial role. With India gone

there was no longer any need to secure the routes to India. Moreover, as Clement Attlee's government itself acknowledged by its adherence to the Brussels Treaty in 1948 and to the North Atlantic Treaty in 1949, the principal threat to Britain's security was believed to come from the Soviet Union. In practice, however, the reorientation in British policy took 20 years to evolve. Adherence to Nato notwithstanding, Britain was unwilling or unable to disengage completely from the imperial role. India may have gone, but the empire lived on. There were colonies to prepare for independence. There were trade routes to safeguard. There were treaties to fulfil and allies to defend. Thus while the British Army of the Rhine trained to defend western Europe, British forces continued to operate outside Europe. As Britain slowly withdrew from empire, it fell to the armed forces to cover the withdrawal. The majority of Britain's operations and campaigns took place, indeed, in an imperial setting.

The withdrawal from India was followed by the evacuation of another imperial territory, Palestine, but the government was unable to disengage elsewhere. Many territories were simply not ready for

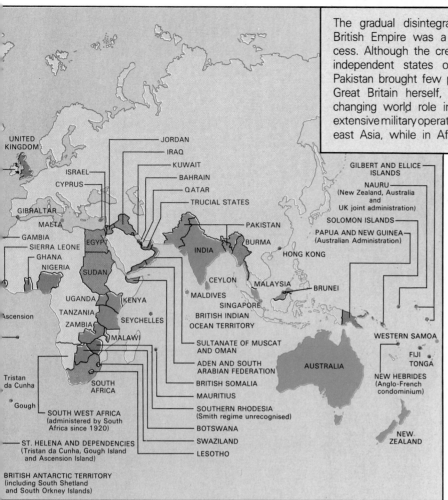

The gradual disintegration of the British Empire was a painful process. Although the creation of the independent states of India and Pakistan brought few problems for Great Britain herself, the nation's changing world role involved it in extensive military operations in southeast Asia, while in Africa and the Middle East there were a whole series of conflicts as British interests and treaty obligations clashed with the demands of local nationalists and radical politicians. The Americas presented different problems but ones which still required British armed intervention ranging from military presence to full-scale warfare.

to counter what was seen as a communist threat to that colony. The Conservative government stepped up the counter-insurgency campaign in Malaya and used force to check the Mau Mau revolt in Kenya after 1952. The emergency did not end officially until 1960, but the Mau Mau had been effectively defeated by mid-1956, when Britain was able to begin withdrawing its forces.

Another theatre of British operations was the Middle East, but here the outcome was less than satisfactory. In the Buraimi oasis affair, Britain acted with customary assurance, recapturing from Saudi Arabian forces an area of land belonging to Britain's Omani and Abu Dhabi allies. In other parts of the Middle East, however, Britain's record was a catalogue of disasters. In October 1954, after three years of Egyptian terrorism, Britain announced that she was to quit the Suez Canal base, a post she had earlier claimed was crucial. The Middle East base was to be moved to Cyprus which, Britain said, could never expect independence. Almost immediately, an armed campaign began which sought to oust the British and achieve union with Greece. It proved to be both bitter and divisive.

A more dramatic threat to Britain's position and prestige in the Middle East came in the form of Arab nationalism. This movement was epitomised in the person of Colonel Gamal Abdel Nasser, the Egyptian leader. Britain had initially attempted to appease Nasser, but when he nationalised the Suez Canal in July 1956 Britain switched to a policy of coercion. Indeed the Suez affair can be seen as an attempt by Anthony Eden's government to reassert British authority in an area traditionally dominated by Britain. The ostensible aim of the Anglo-French invasion was to secure the canal; the real aim, however, was to topple Nasser. As such, the venture was a failure. The military landings went well enough, but politically Suez amounted to nothing short of a debacle. A combination of world opinion and American pressure compelled the Eden government to desist. The consequences of the affair were profound. Suez demonstrated that Britain was no longer a great power, able to act independently of the United

Above left: The British flag is lowered as Kenya achieves independence. Below: Tempers flare after crowd trouble in Aden. Right: The disintegration of Empire: a Cypriot girl expresses her feelings.

independence. A British presence, and sometimes a military presence, remained necessary. In December 1947, for example, troops had to be sent to Aden to quell anti-Jewish rioting. In February and March 1948, naval units were sent to the Gold Coast (later called Ghana) because of riots there. At the same time, forces had to be sent to British Honduras (Belize) to deter an invasion by neighbouring Guatemala.

Even in territories now independent of Britain, the deployment of forces was still undertaken. In January 1949 a battalion of British troops was sent to Jordan, to deter an Israeli attack upon the port of Aqaba. The troops had been requested by Jordan's King Abdullah, and Britain, in view of its treaty commitments to Jordan, could hardly refuse the request. In Egypt, too, there was a continuing British presence in a nominally independent country. At the request of the Egyptian government, Britain had withdrawn its garrison from the Nile Delta in 1946-47, but only to transfer the troops to another part of Egypt, the Suez Canal zone. Despite the wishes of the Egyptian government and the original intentions of Attlee himself, British forces remained on Egyptian territory.

With the return of the Conservatives to power there was reason to believe that the disintegration of empire would be halted, or at least slowed down. However, the 13 years of Conservative rule from 1951 to 1964 saw a further fragmentation of the imperial estate, although in the early years Britain seemed resolved to put down any threat to her imperial position. In British Guiana (later Guyana), for example, force was used

ENGLISH: DO NOT PROVOKE OUR FEELINGS MORE. OUR PATIENCE WILL BE EXHAUSTED

Top: As the movement for independence grew, street protests in Aden were frequent. Above: A British UN officer is led away by a Greek-Cypriot irregular after being disarmed. The Cypriot carries a British .303in Lee Enfield rifle.

States. It also demonstrated that nationalist movements could not be countered easily by force.

Suez accelerated the withdrawal from empire and Harold Macmillan, who replaced Eden as prime minister in January 1957, was the man chiefly responsible for the new impetus the policy received. The 1957 Defence Review, with its emphasis on nuclear deterrence and the phasing out of a large conventional army based on conscription, seemed to point the way.

Immediate developments in the colonial field had little to do with this new policy of speedy withdrawal,

however. The two colonies that became independent in 1957, Malaya and Ghana, had long been earmarked for early independence. Accelerated withdrawal was seen in other cases though. After five years of counter-insurgency operations, Britain granted independence to Cyprus in 1960. Independence was also accelerated, voluntarily, elsewhere. In West and East Africa, in Central Africa and the West Indies, a rush into statehood occurred.

Yet British forces remained as active as ever, for the withdrawal had to be orderly. Moreover, there were still commitments to be honoured. In Malaya, British forces stayed on in strength until the state of emergency ended in 1960. Two years later they were putting down a rebellion in Brunei and in 1963 British forces were sent to help independent Malaysia resist Indonesian infiltration in Borneo.

The Borneo campaign was prosecuted to a successful conclusion. Indonesia called off its 'confrontation' in 1966 and British forces were able to begin to pull out. That campaign, however, was seen by the new Labour government as Britain's last major operation outside the ambit of Nato. The government planned to leave Aden by 1968 and relinquish its commitments east of Suez by the mid-1970s. With its traditional aversion to imperial adventure and its dislike of high defence spending, Labour resolved to abandon military commitments outside Nato as swiftly as possible, almost regardless of the local consequences. Aden was abandoned in November 1967, power being handed over to one of the nationalist groups against which British troops had fought.

In the following year, the retreat from empire was hastened further. Shaken by financial crisis, Harold Wilson announced in January 1968 that the withdrawal of British forces from east of Suez – that is, the Far East and the Persian Gulf – would be brought forward. All commitments east of Suez, except for a token presence in Hong Kong, would be ended by 1971. The effect of this decision was that, apart from a few residual responsibilities, Britain would cease to maintain bases or garrisons outside the Nato area. The legions had finally been recalled.   **Francis Toase**

Key Weapons
The
F-4 PHANTOM II
part 3

Phantom: A worldwide role

Besides being the United States' foremost combat aircraft during the 1960s and 1970s, the F-4 Phantom was exported in large numbers to America's allies, who were not slow in appreciating the qualities of this extraordinary aircraft. The West German Luftwaffe was an early purchaser, as was Great Britain who equipped both the RAF and the Royal Navy with a number of Phantoms. Other major buyers were Iran and Israel, while smaller orders were placed by Greece, Turkey, South Korea and Japan.

The first of Britain's services to take an interest in the Phantom was the Royal Navy, which decided to employ the aircraft in 1964. Developed as the F-4K this variant first flew in 1966 and deliveries to the Royal Navy were made in April 1968 when it was redesignated the Phantom FGR Mk 1. The Navy took 24 Phantoms while a further 28 were diverted to the RAF who subsequently bought a further 118 aircraft (the F-4M) designated as FGR Mk 2s. A particular feature of these Phantoms was the introduction of new engines, Rolls-Royce Spey 202/203 afterburning turbofans, capable of generating 9300kg (20,500lb) of thrust each; but despite the increased power of these engines actual performance deteriorated slightly although range was extended. Minor airframe modifications were made and avionic equipment uprated, including a revised nav/attack system, and in 1975 a

sophisticated analog-controlled radar warning system was introduced.

By the early 1970s the Phantom had become the mainstay of the RAF's fighter squadrons, providing increased bite to the UK's aerial defence force. Following the introduction of the Jaguar into squadron service in 1974 the Phantom FGR Mk 2s were progressively switched to air defence duties, thereby allowing the retirement of most of the RAF's ageing Lightning squadrons. Besides the five squadrons in Number 11 group a further two squadrons at RAF Wildenrath in Germany were equipped with Phantoms.

The availability of the heavily-armed long-range Phantom brought about a transformation in the fighting power of Britain's air defences; the aircraft was capable of carrying eight air-to-air missiles (Sparrow, Sidewinder and Sky Flash) and a substantial bomb load. Compared to the Lightning the Phantom has an improved air interception radar and fire-control system, offering a look down/shoot down capability which enables it to detect and attack low-level targets without the radar ground-return problems suffered by earlier systems.

In spite of the fact that Britain's Phantoms have not seen active service their value as combat aircraft was appreciated in 1982 when a number were sent to the

Previous page: Two RAF Phantom FGR Mk 2s carry out a patrol from their base at Wildenrath in Germany. Above: An FGR Mk 2 banks over to port to reveal bombs, Sparrow AAMs and a centreline reconnaissance pod.

Above: An FGR Mk 2 fires a stream of 68mm rockets from its Matra launcher. Against well-defined ground targets rocket attacks can be devastating.

Below: A Royal Navy FGR Mk 1 of No. 892 Squadron HMS *Ark Royal* is prepared for launch. One of the Phantom's rocket-launcher pods is visible under the port wing.

Falklands to protect the islands from any future hostile Argentinian intentions. Operating from an extended runway at Port Stanley, the Falkland Islands Phantoms act as a powerful deterrent to any possible aggressor.

A regular customer for American aircraft, it was only natural that the West German Luftwaffe should make an order for 88 Phantoms in 1968. Highly satisfied with the performance of the Phantom the Luftwaffe decided on a second batch of 175 aircraft to replace the controversial F-104 Starfighters in their interceptor and strike roles. Designated F-4F the German Phantoms are broadly similar to the F-4E variant (including wing slats) but the provision for a seventh fuselage fuel tank, tailplane slots and Sparrow air-to-air missile has been deleted. While assembled in America the J79-GE-17A engines are built in Germany by MTU. Optimised for an air-superiority role the Phantoms of the Luftwaffe have retained their

multi-role capability although the functions of strike aircraft and long-range interdiction will be largely assumed by the newer Tornado.

Of all the export Phantoms those in the service of the IAF (Israeli Air Force) have seen the most action by far. On 7 October 1968 the Americans agreed to supply Israel with 50 F-4E Phantoms. This was part of the biggest arms deal between the USA and Israel since America opened its arsenals to Israel – $285 million in all. The Phantom was the ideal combat aircraft for the IAF, capable of carrying over eight tons of variable ordnance (twice the load of the Skyhawk). One Phantom could carry a payload comparable to that of almost a squadron of the older French aircraft in IAF service. Its long combat range enabled it to hit targets as far away as Upper Egypt or Iraq – targets barely within range of the obsolete Vautour II twin-engined bombers. Furthermore, its multi-mission capacity suited it to aerial combat.

Above: A German Phantom flies above the McDonnell Douglas works at St Louis. Left: A slatted-wing F-4E of the Greek Air Force.

Left: One of the F-4Es loaned to the Royal Australian Air Force prior to the arrival of previously ordered F-111s.

Left: An F-4D of the Imperial Iranian Air Force comes to a halt with the aid of its parachute brake. Below: A Turkish F-4E, one of a batch of Phantoms that equip three squadrons of the Turkish Air Force.

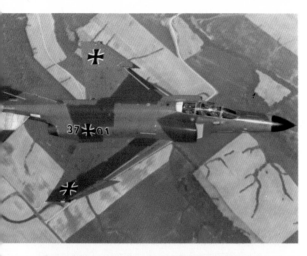

Left: An F-4F of JG 71 'Richtofen', the first Luftwaffe unit to be supplied with the Phantom. Right: A US-built F-4J, delivered to Japan in 1971.

Left: F-4Cs of the Spanish Air Force. Right: Phantoms of the Israeli Air Force, painted in a highly effective three-tone camouflage scheme.

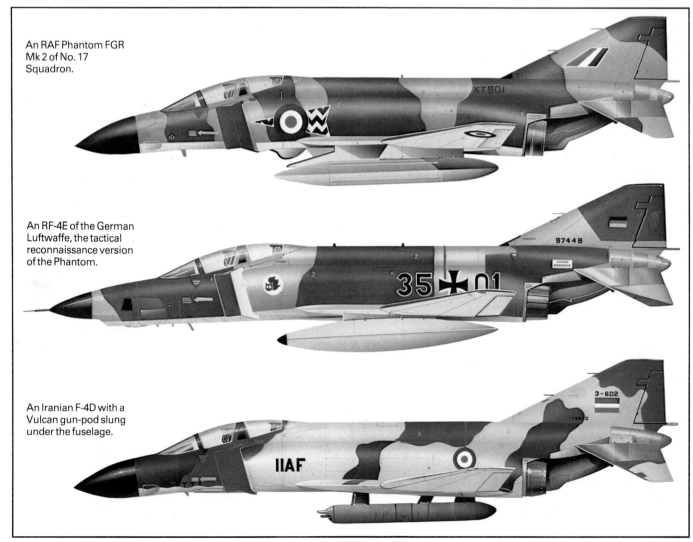

An RAF Phantom FGR Mk 2 of No. 17 Squadron.

An RF-4E of the German Luftwaffe, the tactical reconnaissance version of the Phantom.

An Iranian F-4D with a Vulcan gun-pod slung under the fuselage.

A further feature was its high precision bombing capability, thereby eliminating the effort-consuming top cover previously needed for these missions. The IAF insisted that the F-4E version include a 20mm M61-A1 rotary cannon internally mounted although at a later date the Israelis installed their own cannon. This armament suited the IAF tactics of close-range dog-fights, which had proved highly effective in the Middle East wars.

Altogether Israel has probably received 242 F-4E Phantoms as well as 12 RF-4E Phantoms for reconnaissance duties. Basic Israeli armament consists of a locally-built 30mm cannon, Harpoon anti-ship missiles, Shrike anti-radar missiles, Walleye TV-guided bombs and Maverick air-to-surface missiles.

The Israeli Phantoms saw their first sustained action during the Yom Kippur War in 1973 when they acted as both a fighter and battlefield strike weapon. The Arab MiGs were unable to offer serious resistance to the highly-trained crews of the Israeli Phantom squadrons and they soon became equal to the SAMs of the Arab air defence systems.

During the 1970s Israel began to develop its locally-built Kfis fighter and began to receive the F-15 from the USA. As a consequence, the heavier Phantom began to lose its air-superiority role in favour of being a powerful strike aircraft, thereby replacing the less effective A-4 Skyhawks. Nonetheless the Israeli Air Force will still expect and receive good service from the Phantom to the end of the century at least.

Above: A Phantom of the Israeli Air Force in its role of interceptor.

Above: Two Phantoms take part in a flypast following the Israeli victory in the Yom Kippur War. Bottom: An Israeli Phantom prepares to make a low-level strike during the fighting in 1973.

An Israeli F-4E with distinctive 'sharkmouth' markings.

187

Index

A